DATE DUE

Evolutionary Worlds
Without End

Evolutionary Worlds Without End

Henry Plotkin
Emeritus Professor of Psychology
University College London

OXFORD
UNIVERSITY PRESS

OXFORD

UNIVERSITY PRESS

Great Clarendon Street, Oxford OX2 6DP

Oxford University Press is a department of the University of Oxford.
It furthers the University's objective of excellence in research, scholarship,
and education by publishing worldwide in

Oxford New York

Auckland Cape Town Dar es Salaam Hong Kong Karachi
Kuala Lumpur Madrid Melbourne Mexico City Nairobi
New Delhi Shanghai Taipei Toronto

With offices in

Argentina Austria Brazil Chile Czech Republic France Greece
Guatemala Hungary Italy Japan Poland Portugal Singapore
South Korea Switzerland Thailand Turkey Ukraine Vietnam

Oxford is a registered trade mark of Oxford University Press
in the UK and in certain other countries

Published in the United States
by Oxford University Press Inc., New York

© Oxford University Press 2010

The moral rights of the authors have been asserted
Database right Oxford University Press (maker)

First published 2010

British Library Cataloguing in Publication Data
Data available

Library of Congress Cataloging in Publication Data
Data available

Typeset by Glyph International, Bangalore
Printed in Great Britain
on acid-free paper by the
The MPG Books Group

ISBN 978–0–19–954495–0

10 9 8 7 6 5 4 3 2 1

Oxford University Press makes no representation, express or implied, that the drug
dosages in this book are correct. Readers must therefore always check the product
information and clinical procedures with the most up-to-date published product
information and data sheets provided by the manufacturers and the most recent codes of
conduct and safety regulations. The authors and the publishers do not accept responsibility
or legal liability for any errors in the text or for the misuse or misapplication of material in
this work. Except where otherwise stated, drug dosages and recommendations are for the
non-pregnant adult who is not breastfeeding.

For Oliver Jack

Preface

Diversity and complexity are the hallmarks of living forms. Yet science aims for general causal explanations of its observations. How can these be reconciled? Is it possible for a science of life to conform to the requirement of a general theory? These are the questions that are explored in the following pages. I do so by first examining Ernest Rutherford's dictum as to what science is. In the later chapters I consider the possibility, usually within a loose historical framework, of a general theory being based upon selection processes – one cannot, after all, be an evolutionist and not be alert to the importance of history, especially if one is considering the possibility of an evolutionary account for changing human culture within the same explanatory notions as those generally accepted for the transformation of species. In the last two chapters complexity moves to centre-stage.

I wanted this book to be accessible to a wider public than just academic colleagues, and one important way to achieve this is to leave out the formal citation of sources. I modelled my approach on Robbins Burling's "The Talking Ape: How Language Evolved" (Oxford University Press, 2005) but configured the bibliography on a chapter by chapter and section by section structure. The reading list was never intended as comprehensive, but each section contains enough to give anyone wanting to pursue a particular topic a good start. I have tried to be fair in providing alternative points of view even when I don't agree with them. Thus, for example, do I provide in the last section of the final chapter a reference for a very recent analysis of reduced virulence in terms of it being an individual-level adaptation even though my own view is that it must be understood as a group-level adaptation.

As usual, my debt is to the work of all those who are named in the following pages. My thanks, too, to the staff of Oxford University Press; and especially to Carol Maxwell and Martin Baum.

October 2009

Contents

Chapter 1

The Rutherford dictum and its meaning for biology

Ernest Rutherford famously asserted that "all science is either physics or stamp collecting". Rutherford, needless to say, was a physicist; indeed, he was one of the outstanding physicists of the early 20th century whose work was seminal to the understanding of the structure of the atom. Was Rutherford correct? And if he was right, where does it leave the rest of us who like to think that we work within science but are not physicists? In one respect, Rutherford's dictum makes a clear point: philately does not tell us anything about the nature of the world. Collecting, whether it is stamps or data from observation or experimentation, and however rigorous that collecting is, is not enough to define a science. So what, if anything, has to be added to a strict empirical exercise to turn it into science? The obvious answer is theory and/or the formulation of general laws. Within the context of this book, which deals with biology and the social sciences embedded within it, is there theory in biology that has the scope of theory in physics, and are there laws of any generality? And can we structure whatever theory and or general laws there are in such a way that it includes both speciation and economics, for example, but also allows for clear distinctions to be made between them? In order to begin to answer these questions we need first to set aside our sorting of stamps and delve a little further into what exactly Rutherford might have meant.

Rutherford had worked in, and eventually directed, some of the most exacting experimental laboratories in the world, had been one of the co-discoverers both of the differences between alpha and beta particles as well as the phenomenon of radioactive half-life, and had been in charge of the experimental programme that led to the model of the atom as having a nucleus with positive charge surrounded, in atomic dimensions at very considerable distances away, by negatively charged electrons. This model of atoms as mostly empty space, entities that could never be directly observed because of their size and which are the fundamental building blocks of everything in the universe, was in complete contrast with the seeming solidity of the world with which we interact in our everyday lives. Quotidian experience had to be reconciled with powerful empirical scientific findings the theoretical interpretation of which told us that the world is otherwise. Together with Einstein's relativity theory and the soon to be born theory of quantum mechanics, physics presented the rest of the scientific community with an unparalleled example of empirical rigour, mathematical calculation and modelling, and awesome theory building. This, then, was the context within which Rutherford made his observation about physics and the rest of science, a context that may help us to understand what he might have meant.

Subsequent advances in physics led to the discovery of anti-matter, the theory of quarks, string theory, and super-string theory, the latter three being attempts at what is sometimes referred to as a theory of everything. And that, perhaps, was what Rutherford meant, even though he did not live to see these latter developments. Physics, because it deals with the most fundamental aspects of the universe, is the overarching science within which all other sciences must be contained; if it hasn't yet, in time it will lead to a theory of everything. All other sciences, therefore, must be explained ultimately by physics. Another way of phrasing this is that all other sciences must be reduced to physics.

Rutherford's dictum in the context of reductionism

Reductionism and the possibility of reducing sciences from one to another have a long history in the philosophy of science. There are, in fact, several identifiably different forms of reduction. The most basic form, which would seem to support Rutherford's dictum if it was reductionism that he was referring to, is usually labelled as ontological reductionism. Most often referred to as materialism or physicalism, this was a point of contention within science, especially the biological sciences, in the 19th century. But for at least a century, the materialist position has been almost universal amongst scientists. Ontological reduction refers to the view that all things are physical things, material entities, and nothing else. Living creatures, including their minds if such they have, are nothing but physico-chemical processes and mechanisms. There are no ineffable or immeasurable properties of life or mind; no *élan vital* or life force beyond the confines of complex chemical organization, no immortal soul or mind that stands outside of physical and chemical law as constituted by the millions of nerve cells and the many billions of connections between these cells within the brain. The same argument holds for culture, as will be argued in a later chapter of this book. No matter how strange and complex human culture is, and it is certainly the most complex phenomenon on earth, it is the product of interacting individual minds, minds which are themselves complex physico-chemical entities. In this sense, then, Rutherford was right;

geologists, botanists, and sociologists may observe, categorize and sort, even experiment, but in the end, all they are dealing with are aggregates of atoms, the stuff of physics.

The obvious response is that this is correct but it is a trivial truth because it misses one of the objectives of science, which is to understand the world by offering some form of explanation. The philosopher Karl Popper wrote that theory is an essential part of any science, and that "theories are nets cast to catch what we call 'the world': to rationalize, to explain, and to master it. We endeavour to make the mesh ever finer and finer". An "ever finer mesh" is indeed a nod towards the ultimate goal of a theory of everything, but Popper's key point is that theory must provide explanation. For Harré, also a philosopher of science, "theories are the crown of science, for in them our understanding of the world is expressed. The function of theories is to explain".

Setting aside for the moment what it means to say that a theory x explains a phenomenon p, it requires no thought at all to see that while all of biology encompasses the physical world of living organisms with material structure and organization and nothing else, it is a world in which explanation of the phenomena it deals with have little or no overlap with the world of the physical sciences. Elliott Sober, another philosopher of science, notes that explanations in biology and those in physics have little in common: that planets have elliptical orbits has an explanatory basis quite different from that which tells us how and why species are transformed in time or what intelligence is and how it leads to learning in some species of animals. The advent of molecular biology in the last five decades has narrowed the gap a little; as will be seen later in this chapter, our understanding of development, for example, has been significantly advanced by growing knowledge of molecular interactions within cells. And, of course, the ideal is for explanations in biology to be consistent with those of physics. In practice, however, as Sober notes, this is an ideal that at present cannot be met. We have no idea at all, for example, how to explain ecological succession in the same terms as physics understands the scattering of light by the atmosphere of our planet. It is even debateable whether we can explain all, or even many, **biological** phenomena within some single theoretical framework, which is what this book aims to examine.

So while Rutherford might not have meant to be derogatory to the rest of the sciences outside of physics and might simply have been extolling the virtues of the physicalist stance within all of the sciences, his was a declaration of little conceptual force and was merely a statement of what, for the last 100 years, has been the obvious. The way biologists or social scientists think of the phenomena they study are mostly quite different from the thinking of physicists, but they never have explanatory recourse beyond the chemical and physical constituents of the creatures that they study. Or perhaps he was saying something quite different. Perhaps he was asserting that complex phenomena, which is what the biological and social are by definition, should always be studied at the most fundamental level of that system that is possible. This is what is known as methodological reductionism. Consider the phenomenon of memory and how early memory may significantly alter later thought and behaviour, as in well documented cases of childhood abuse. Memory, of course, is rooted in the connectivity of nerve cell networks, that is to say, in the patterns of the transmission of action potentials (nerve impulses) and their synaptic transmission. Action potentials and their transmission between neurons are increasingly understood in physico-chemical terms. Memory, as a subjective psychological state, however, is explained within a complex cognitive framework without necessary reference to events at a cellular or sub-cellular level; and the effects of early experience upon the development of specific personality traits and their force in determining behaviour in adults is yet another level of explanation, even if, at present, a very poorly understood one.

Methodological reductionism says that quite apart from the necessities imposed by budgetary restrictions in the sciences and the limitations of human resources, it is at the cellular and sub-cellular levels that the science of personality formation should be restricted because this is close to molecular understanding, and the molecular is within conceptual touching distance of the atomic and hence to chemistry and physics. At bottom, personality is a product of cellular and sub-cellular events, and that is the level at which the science should be conducted. If that is what Rutherford meant, then the study of memory at a cognitive level and its effects on personality is mere stamp collecting and a scientific waste of time and resources.

It should take little thought from both scientist and non-scientist to realise that this is a ridiculous stance. It condemns our understanding and treatment of childhood abuse to some indeterminate future time when the functioning of the brain in its entirety is understood within the compass of chemistry and physics, and the brain and its relationship to mental states has been completely worked out. It asserts that understanding the relationship between early experience and personality formation has little or no practical, therapeutic value, which is manifest nonsense. Above all, there is no compelling conceptual argument of any form as to why the study of complex phenomena should be directed only to their most fundamental level. A neurochemistry of individual choice that casts out notions of peoples' needs and wants would be an absurd form of economic science. If Rutherford's statement was an assertion of the necessity of methodological reduction in the practice of science, then it was an absurd and pompous error. It might be noted with regard to the specific example of memory and childhood abuse that in recent decades eliminative materialism has been advanced as an argument that there are no mental states; that mental states are inaccessible, solipsistic, and not within the province of science. Eliminative materialism, however, applies only to mental states and is an entirely different argument from a supposed generality of reductive materialism; it is also one which has only the tiniest of followings amongst philosophers of science.

But while it may be neither desirable nor practical only to study empirically the most fundamental level of a complex system, another form of reductionism, explanatory reductionism, avows that the best, the most encompassing and complete scientific **understanding** of complex phenomena comes only with an understanding of such phenomena expressed in terms of their most fundamental level, whatever that level is. This, perhaps, comes closest to what Rutherford might have meant, but his reference to stamp collecting is not appropriate to what most scientists who are not physicists are doing, for at least two closely connected reasons.

The first has to do with what biologists and social scientists consider to be their normal manner of functioning as scientists; the second concerns the complexity of the structures with which they are dealing. With regard to this second point, everyone who works with living forms, be they the workings of organelles within the cell, the interactions between populations of different species, or cultural change in humans should know that what they are studying are complex structures made up of multiple levels of organization. If they do not know this then Rutherford is absolutely right – they really are merely collectors of stamps. But most biologists and social scientists do know this and understand that their theories and explanations must take such structural complexity into account.

That leads back to the first point of the previous paragraph. Along with the near universal tacit understanding of complexity of structure, most biologists are concerned with understanding mechanisms the functioning of which drive primary processes such as evolution, ontogenesis, and cognition, with the implicit realization that in trying to establish causal mechanisms they are actively seeking such mechanisms at the most fundamental level possible. In other words, most scientists do act on explanatory reductionism. It is a normal part of their work as scientists. However, for many scientists the structural complexity is such that what for them is the most fundamental level of explanation lies quite high up within the complex structure. It is simply not known at present, for example, how to get from a cultural belief to a neural network. More importantly, and it is difficult to overstate the importance of this point, in many cases, the causal complexity, **of necessity**, rules out explanatory reduction because the causal framework itself **requires** multiple levels of causal mechanism. A cultural belief is part-caused by cognitive states whose very existence is a result of a shift of causal force from ones that are wholly genetic and epigenetic, to the functioning of neural networks and to changes within the contents of those networks through experience and learning within the lifetime of an individual. This is not a stubborn refusal to follow explanatory reductionism, of which social scientists are sometimes accused. It is a necessary consequence of the presence of additional levels of causation. For all these reasons it is debateable as to whether the notion of a fundamental level has any validity at all when biological and social phenomena are the object of science.

Thus we are faced with a seeming contradiction. The conceptual impulse of most scientists is, when possible, to conform to explanatory reductionism. This is perhaps a measure of a wider view of physics as the ideal science, of which Rutherford's dictum was simply one manifestation – what is sometimes labelled as "physics envy", though "physics admiration" may be the more apt phrase. But the very nature of the phenomena studied by the biological and social sciences usually stands as an impassable obstacle to that impulse. Another way of putting this is simply that the notion of an ideal science is wholly wrong. Rutherford's dictum, in this sense, makes no sense at all.

It is interesting to note that in his defence of reductionism, specifically within evolutionary biology and specifically explanatory reductionism, G.C. Williams, one of the great 20th century advocates of reductionism in biology, claimed as recently as the 1980s that changes in gene frequencies as "the essence" of evolution is much to be preferred to any consideration of "emergent properties" at different levels of complexity. In the light of recent developments in evolutionary theory, particularly the contributions of epigenetic conceptions, niche construction and the consideration of adaptations like immune system function and cognitive states that alter continuously across the life span of individual organisms, this now sounds like a hopelessly outdated view. It sounds antiquated precisely because the pejorative reference to "emergent properties" is now judged by many to miss the point about complex causation within complex systems.

There is another form of reductionism, theory reduction, but this is unlikely to be what Rutherford was referring to. The subject of much investigation by philosophers of science, theory reduction concerns the possibility of establishing relations between theories so that one can be subsumed, and replaced by, another such as Kepler's laws of planetary motion falling within Newtonian mechanics and the laws of gravitation. This may work in certain areas of physics and chemistry, but it has never done so in biology. One of the best known failures of theory reduction concerned Mendelian genetics and molecular genetics, as David Hull's magisterial review showed. Moreover, philosophers interested in the possibility of theory reduction have been much concerned with the procedures that must be used and the structures of the theories involved in the reduction. Formal theory structures, however, are rare in biology, and non-existent in the social sciences. Whatever one's views on the virtues or otherwise of theory reduction, these are procedures without relevance to any form of biology.

All things considered, then, apart from the obvious case of physicalism, it is unlikely that Rutherford's dictum can be understood and applied to the biological and social sciences within the framework of any form of reductionism. What else, then, might he have meant? What does physics do that other sciences, for our purposes biology and the social sciences, cannot do and places them on a par with stamp collecting? One possibility lies in the precision of physics, in its ability to predict and observe events with astonishing accuracy, from the smallest of entities to the largest that can be imagined; the notions of the uncertainty principle and wave-particle duality of quantum mechanics do not contradict this precision because they originated in the ability of physics to operate at the extremes of exactness. Another possibility touched on earlier, is how physics provides a vision of the world and the universe that is simply unavailable either to other sciences or to ordinary experience. Insofar as physics can take us to conceptual worlds in a way that no other science is able to do, then it is different from other sciences. In this alone Rutherford may have been correct in claiming a difference. Astronomy, however, whilst it leans closely on physics, is quite different in many significant ways, yet no one would seriously describe astronomers as merely stamp collectors.

There is another possible difference, which also hinges on reductionism, specifically explanatory reductionism but of a strictly within-science kind rather than between sciences. What is meant by this is that within physics – and this would extend to chemistry as well since chemistry is determined by atomic structure and the charges of sub-atomic particles – all things might be reduced to the level of physic's principle theories of relativity and quantum mechanics (or its more recent versions in quark or string form), whereas in the rest of science there are no such overarching theories that offer that possibility of complete within-discipline reduction. In short, there are no general theories in the rest of the sciences, and specifically none within biology. This may be what Rutherford meant; that insofar as there are other empirical sciences that do collect data, even if not quite as some collect stamps, the lack of general theory within that science means they are sciences that are not on the same footing as physics.

Laws, theories, and explanation

Philosophy, as the systematic investigation of every aspect of human existence and what it means to be human, is the oldest and richest form of scholarship that we have. Unsurprisingly, it has, for over two and a half thousand years, been riven by differences of view and opinion. This applies as much to the philosophy of science as it does to any other part of philosophy. Neither now nor in the past has there been a general consensus amongst philosophers of science as to how science should be conducted beyond the universal agreement that stamp collecting is fundamental. Data about the world must be gathered. The differences arise from what we do with that data. Thus far, only theory has been considered as the possible basis for Rutherford's dictum. However, for some philosophers, and some scientists too, what empiricism should drive is not theory building but the establishment of general laws. Two examples from very unlike sciences demonstrate just how differently science can be approached.

The first is the most famous science of all, that of Isaac Newton. Newton's observations led him in his *Principia Mathematica* to promulgate two sets of laws. The laws of motion, and the law of gravitation which stated that every particle of matter attracts every other particle of matter, the force of attraction varying directly with the products of the mass of the particles and inversely with the square of the distance between them. Whilst now superseded by the theory of relativity, Newton's laws remain sufficiently accurate for the prediction of planetary motions and the trajectories of spacecraft, and the important point is that they are accurate wherever the spacecraft are in the universe. Scientific laws should have generality wherever and whenever they are applied. In the case of gravity and motion, universal generality is possible because, as Newton stated in his *Principia*, the ultimate conditions of the universal system of time, space and motion exist everywhere and at all times. The power of Newton's laws to predict and control the motion of bodies has never been questioned. But what has been doubted are his assumptions of the universality of the ultimate conditions, and hence whether his laws really explain motion and gravity rather than just encapsulate these forces within the mathematical statements of those laws.

The second example is behaviourism, a school of thought that arose within psychology in the early part of the 20th century and which for half a century exerted very considerable influence, especially amongst American psychologists, until the rise of cognitivism in the 1960s. In some ways, running these two examples together is absurd because Newton's science was the product of a scientific mind of genius and the power of his laws are unquestioned, whereas behaviourism as a movement established no psychological laws of any significance and was one of the singular conceptual failures of modern science. Yet there is a common thread to Newton's science and behaviourism. Newton rejected speculative notions and hypotheses when it came to gravity and motion and insisted on the adherence to observation and experimentation.

In the same way, behaviourism not only rejected introspection as the predominant methodology of a science of mind, but essentially rejected the notion of mind and its accompanying states such as consciousness: "Psychology as the behaviourist views it is a purely objective experimental branch of natural science. Its theoretical goal is the prediction and control of behaviour", wrote its founder, John Broadus Watson, in 1913. Only that which can be observed was considered to constitute a science of psychology. The unobservable was rejected, and that included not only the mind, but genes, nervous systems, evolution, and any other possible causes of behaviour that could not be directly seen and measured. Behaviourism sought only predictive laws and drove explanation from psychology and left it a theoretically impoverished science.

Behaviourism was an unmitigated disaster for psychology and its slow death came not a moment too soon – it is impossible to imagine sciences like genetics or physics based solely on what the human eye can detect and which rejected explanatory recourse to theoretical entities like units of inheritance or electrons. But in one important respect Newton and Watson shared a similar philosophy of science, and this relates to the issue of what is termed the opposition between instrumentalism and realism.

Newton's laws did not explain gravity. Instead they provided a mathematical device by which Newton could move from his restricted observations of events here on earth to a set of generalizations about motion and attraction between objects anywhere in the universe. Explanation was judged to be epistemologically risky and ontologically inferior when compared to the rigour of mathematical prediction based on observation. Newton wrote "I do not make hypotheses; for whatever is not deduced from the phenomena is to be called an hypothesis; and hypotheses, whether metaphysical or physical, whether of occult qualities or mechanical, have no place in experimental philosophy". Known now as instrumentalism, the Newtonian approach is one of the principal divides amongst philosophers of science. During the positivist era of the 20th century instrumentalism was much in favour; it then declined in strength, especially amongst philosophers of biology, and was later revived to some extent in physics by the truly perplexing views of quantum mechanical theory.

Behaviourism was an extreme manifestation of instrumentalism without any of the advantages that Newton's laws gave to science. Eschewing any form of theoretical account, lacking the universal systems that were fundamental to Newton's laws, and without any of the predictive mathematical framework, behaviourism led to minimal prospects of behavioural control, predicted little outside of the learned behaviours of a very restricted group of animals, and explained nothing. The power of instrumentalism, then, is proportional to the strength of its inductive base. The many laws of physics, which cover not only motion and gravity, but the behaviour of gases, the effects of temperature, the forces of leverage, and many others, are testament to that strength. There is nothing like that strength of induction specifically within psychology, nor is there any within biology or the social sciences at large.

However strong that inductive base is, and physical laws are held literally to be universal, the criticism of instrumentalism is that it fails to explain. Newton did not tell us what gravity is. Instrumentalist science does not explain the world. Scientific realism, on the other hand, aims to do just that by making truth claims about the world – saying what is out there, and how it works. Twentieth century physics was less concerned with the law-like properties of sub-atomic particles and more with what they actually are. If string theory can explain gravity by way of a graviton, a sub-atomic particle, then, the realists say, this is better science than a mathematical law.

As with so many dichotomies, modern science is actually an endless, unresolved mix of both instrumentalism and theoretical realism. We need laws which describe the regularities of the universe, but we also need to understand the sources of those laws. And this, most likely, is what Rutherford's dictum **really** means, even if he would never have used these phrases. Physics can deliver both instrumentalism and realism, whereas other sciences can't. Indeed, in the case of biology and the social sciences, there has been discussion as to whether general laws can exist at all.

The philosopher J.J.C. Smart argued that for a statement in science to be a law it must have unrestricted universality. Newton's first law of motion, that every body continues in its state of rest or of uniform motion in a straight line unless it is compelled to change that state by forces impressed upon it, applies everywhere and at any time. But unrestricted universality does not apply to any statement that we can make about living forms, social or otherwise. Biology restricts whatever generalizations it makes to life here on earth, and even then these earth-restricted generalizations are limited. It was long thought, for example, that energy from the sun and oxygen are essential to all life; now it is known that, for a small number of living forms that are capable of chemosynthesis, this is not the case. As Smart points out, in biology "all" really means "almost all", as in "all animals that suckle their young do not lay eggs" has now been changed to "nearly all" because the platypus and the echidna lay eggs and do suckle their young. Closer to the heart of this book, it was long thought that tool use and the sharing of knowledge are uniquely human traits. However, studies of recent decades have shown that this is not correct, both being present in a number of species of birds and other primates and perhaps some other species of mammal as well. The numbers may be very small in the context of the estimates of tens of millions of extant species that do not use tools or share knowledge, but just what kind of law is it that states that *most* living forms do not use tools or have cultures? The answer, clearly, is that this is not a law at all but just a weak generalization.

Even those generalizations that do seem to be strong, like Fisher's sex ratio and the Hardy-Weinberg law, are mathematical truths, a consequence of the mathematical terms they contain, as Sober puts it, and hence might be deemed to be rather high-class forms of tautology. There are, of course, chemical generalizations, like the structure of genes or the role of enzymes in the cellular function of our planet's living forms, but there is no reason to suppose that life in other parts of the universe is the same as that on earth. And anyway, as others have pointed out, claims to biological laws based on physico-chemical properties is essentially a reductionist exercise to chemical and physical laws.

There are two responses to the assertion that biology does not have the universal laws that makes physics the kind of rigorous science that it is. The one is to question whether any laws are truly general. Do Newton's laws of motion and gravity hold in a black hole, and did they hold immediately after the big bang? The second is to concede the superiority of physics within the instrumentalist view of what science is about but to question whether instrumentalist science really delivers understanding. Biology may not have laws, but it does have a history of theoretical realism, and theory is what gives science an explanatory base that compliments its empirical foundations.

As might be expected, philosophers are not in agreement as to what constitutes a theory. According to Ernest Nagel, a theory must have three components: the first is a "logical skeleton of the explanatory system" that implicitly defines the basic notions of the system; the second is a set of rules by which empirical content is assigned to the abstract explanatory system; and the third is an interpretative model by which the abstract system can be interpreted within a familiar conceptual scheme. The central conceptual aim of theory for Nagel is *explanation*. Popper's is a very similar scheme but is more explicit in providing for explanation as being causal in form, a causal explanation comprising a statement of initial conditions as applied to a general law. For example, in providing a causal explanation for why a thread breaks under specific circumstances the universal law states that when a thread is loaded with a weight that exceeds its tensile strength the thread breaks; the singular statement of initial conditions is the actual weight loaded onto a thread of specific tensile strength. The combination of the two statements allows for a specific prediction as to whether the thread does or does not break depending upon the weight exceeding or not exceeding the tensile strength of the thread. The initial conditions describe the cause of the event and the prediction the effect, the application of a theory thus supplying a cause-effect explanatory framework. Whatever is now thought of these positivist nomological-deductive theoretical frameworks, which is not much in recent times, is beside the point, the point being that they nicely encapsulate the causal explanatory "purpose" of theories.

However, Popper went on to say that in physics the use of the expression "causal explanation" is restricted as a rule to the special case in which the universal laws have the form of laws of "action by contact", or "more precisely, of *action at a vanishing distance*, expressed by differential equations". Thus he is cautious in his use of the cause-effect explanatory framework. Bertrand Russell, by contrast and long before positivism, was openly contemptuous of the notion of cause: "The law of causality, I believe, like much that passes muster among philosophers, is a relic of a bygone age, surviving like the monarchy, only because it is erroneously supposed to do no harm". Russell gives a number of reasons for dismissing the notion of cause, most of which concern the difficulties of separating causes from effects for which he substitutes an overarching scheme of functional relations. The latter, however, fails to give an explanation; they bring us back to the instrumentalist view. Theoretical realism demands explanation which instrumentalism cannot give. "To explain a phenomenon" wrote Harré, "to explain some pattern of happenings, we must be able to describe the causal mechanism which is responsible for it". Harré acknowledges this as an "ideal", but it is an ideal that must be pursued because, as Harré and Madden argue, causal propositions have a conceptual necessity which is irreducible either to logical necessity or to psychological illusion; it tells us, or tries to tell us, how the world actually is. That is why theory is "the crown" of science.

Biology may have few, if any, general laws, but it is awash with explanations couched within causal mechanisms that drive certain processes. From gene transcription to animal migration, from the transport of oxygen between organ systems to problem solving in humans, all have known, or in principle knowable, explanations framed within causal terms. The question that is asked in this and subsequent chapters is whether there is any commonality in the explanations that can be construed as general theory in biology. Do biology and the social sciences have any general theory that approximates to the breadth of theory in physics? The correctness or otherwise of Rutherford's dictum depends in large part on the answer to this question. Furthermore, any answer depends upon the making of a very important distinction.

Process and mechanism

The most fundamental feature of evolutionary theories is that they deal with change in living forms. For Lamarck, his understanding that species are transformed in time was the basis of the first theory of evolutionary change, even if the form his theory took was of a constant *scala naturae* with all species being present at all times somewhere on the planet. That, however, was a rather quirky feature of his *Philosophie Zoologique*, the essential point of which was that individual species change in time as a result of a dynamic interaction that occurs between each member of a species and its environment, which is in constant flux. Darwin's theory had a causal structure entirely different from Lamarck's, but its central thesis was the same: if there is a single constant characteristic of life it is, paradoxically, change, and that is what a theory of evolution must explain. Even Gould, a rather different 20th century evolutionary theorist whose work drew attention to stasis as well as transformation, considered that if it were possible to "wind the tape of life back" hundreds of millions of years and then let evolutionary events unfold again, the pervasiveness of change and the way it is brought about means that it is extremely unlikely that we would end up in the same state of the diversity of living forms as now exists.

This pervasiveness of change drives a fundamental distinction that must be made between process and mechanism, because it is upon this distinction that the possibility of a general theory in biology rests. The Oxford English Dictionary gives a number of definitions for "process", including "a fact of going on", a "series of events", a "continuous operation", and a "natural series of changes". The last of these is closest to the meaning and usage of this book. For our purposes a process is a sequence of events occurring in time, with either a relatively fixed or variable outcome, but which results in change in some form. Evolution is a process. As Dennett rightly pointed out in *Darwin's Dangerous Idea*, Darwin's theory was mostly based upon an abstract set of ideas framed in terms of a process of variation, selection, and inheritance. He could see the phenotypic variation and hypothesized a link between observed variants and the world in which they did or did not thrive, and so his notions of the process of evolution were based upon concrete evidence. But he had absolutely no ideas as to the mechanisms by which the process occurred. Dennett has a fine phrase for considering a process without regard to its mechanisms which he terms "substrate neutrality". When a substrate neutral process can be broken down into a fixed sequence of sub-processes, the repetitive cycle of which leads to some end-state, such a substrate neutral process is an algorithm. Amongst the most common forms of algorithm are arithmetical procedures, and it matters not, as Dennett notes, whether the algorithm is run with a pen on paper, long hand, or by way of mental arithmetic with the sub-processes embodied in a sequence of neural network states, or by a calculator such as a computer; the sequence of operations comprising the process and end state are the same. "The power of the procedure is due to its **logical** structure, not the causal powers of the materials used in the instantiation, just as long as those causal powers permit the prescribed steps to be followed exactly" as Dennett put it.

Some of the best papers on theoretical biology of the 20th century resulted from a series of symposia held near Lake Como in the late 1960s and early 1970s, organized and edited by C.H.Waddington. In two chapters published as part of that collection, the physicist David Bohm avowed "all is process ... there is no *thing* in the universe. Things, objects, entities, are abstractions of what is relatively constant from a process of movement and transformation". He went on to argue that nothing is permanent. "Change is what is eternal". Bohm's was a theory of everything and he regretted that "biology and psychology are moving closer" to mechanism. It was a compelling vision. However, his principal conceptual engine was quantum theory and his arguments ran into all of the problems of reducing the biological and social sciences to physics outlined earlier in this chapter. In eschewing entitivitiness, Bohm left out the greater part of almost all of biology's disciplines, most of which are bound up in the mechanisms that instantiate processes. The social sciences are the exception having long resisted the drive to mechanism which generally has been derided as a form of crude simplification and unwarranted reductionism. This is an issue that will be returned to in several later chapters.

Evolution, of course, is not the only process in biology. Growth and development are processes. So too are learning and thought. All, though, are embodied in mechanisms that are different from one another. Mechanisms are structures of mutually adapted parts. But unlike processes, they are moulded entities that have substance. In principal, mechanisms are things that can be seen, touched, and eaten. Enzymes are things, as are neurons and the chemicals that transport oxygen around the body. All can, if one's hands were small enough, be touched. But you can't eat a process, though you surely can eat the causal structures that run that process and those things that are its end-product. Development is a process instantiated in complex interactions within and between cells. The chemicals entering into these interactions are entities; so too are the organisms, the phenotypes, that are the result of development. But different mechanisms rest on different entities. Even when the same function is being served, such as the absorption and transport of oxygen, different organ structures and different respiratory pigments are carrying out these functions in different kinds of organisms.

Just as laws in biology are weak generalizations, so too are any claimed generality of mechanism. This does not mean that mechanisms are not an essential part of biology, and that includes the social sciences. It simply means they are not the stuff of general theory. If there is any general theory in biology, it must rest on process.

Have there been any general theories proposed for biology?

The answer to the question is a guarded yes; there have been general theories put forward within biology. These have not, however, usually been pressed for true generality. The two most obvious of these have been replicator theory as put forward by Dawkins and others and extended to culture in the form of memetics; the other was the evolutionary epistemology, perhaps better known now as selection theory, of Campbell, Popper, and Hull, amongst others. With the exception of the 2001 paper by Hull and his co-authors, however, neither replicator nor selection theory has been tested for true generality. Since they will be examined at some length in later chapters, what will be considered here are two other examples of theory writing, one recent and the other some decades old, whose authors explicitly intended a generality of application and from which lessons about the generality of theory can be learned. The first is Leo Buss' strangely neglected *The Evolution of Individuality* published in 1987; the other, which appeared almost 20 years later, is Jablonka and Lamb's *Evolution in Four Dimensions*.

Buss' case is not that the theory of evolution as framed by 19th century biologists, principally but not solely by Darwin, and then incorporated into the synthetic theory of evolution which married the Darwinian concept of selection with the developing science of genetics, was wrong. Far from it. It was mostly correct. But it was also seriously incomplete because it was a theory centred upon the individual organism, and usually that organism was a multicellular adult animal. This was perfectly understandable because these were the organisms most 19th century naturalists were working with and thinking about. The error was compounded by the increasing acceptance of Weismann's absolute separation of germ cells from somatic cells in **all** organisms. This error itself was reinforced by the neglect of developmental biology by evolutionists, and the fruit fly being so widely adopted as the organism upon which so much 20th century research into genetics was based.

Buss, whose criticism of Weismann is offset by equal admiration for his foresight in other matters, was not arguing for the reintroduction of some form of unreconstructed Lamarckian notion of the inheritance of acquired characters into evolutionary theory. But what he does conclusively show is that, contrary to Weismann, the conception of a relative, and even an absolute, separation of germ cells from somatic cells is far less common across all major phyla of organisms than conventional evolutionary theory allows for – if it allows for it at all. Buss recognizes three modes of development: somatic embryogenesis where a distinct germ line is lacking, epigenesis (a word he uses with somewhat different meaning to contemporary usage) where there is a clearly differentiated germ line but which appears only after the major primordia of the organ system of the adult have become established, and preformation where the germ line is terminally differentiated in earliest ontogeny. Only the last of these conforms to Weismann's conception of absolute differentiation between germ and somatic lines, and is almost completely absent in all taxa other than the *Animalia*. Even amongst the animal taxa the separation is relatively rare, though such separation is present amongst the *Arthropoda* (to which the fruit fly belongs, of course) and the *Chordata*. It is not appropriate to present the detailed evidence which Buss provides in his monograph. But his point is simple and very strongly made: virtually all the major theorists who contributed to the synthetic theory of evolution worked with or thought about organisms with preformistic (according to Buss' definition of preformism) development, whereas what a truly general theory of evolution must include is knowledge about development in all organisms. This is what he attempts to provide, and in doing so he expounds an expanded theory which is based upon the notion of multiple levels of selection.

The central point in Buss' thesis is stated right at the beginning of his monograph: the history of life, he stated, is the history of the elaboration of new self-replicating entities, what he calls the units of selection, by the self-replicating entities **contained within them**. Thus he immediately envisages an extension of evolutionary theory within a hierarchical perspective. Furthermore, he argued, with the emergence of each new level in the hierarchy, what he referred to as each transition at which a new class of self-replicating entities arises, the rules for the operation of selection changes. Thus does he see the potential for a synergism, positive or negative, between the units of selection at different levels, and hence for the possibility of conflicts to arise between levels. (As with so many accounts in biology, the words "higher" and "lower" are used with confusing effects. More or less fundamental will be substituted here and in later chapters, but such usage itself has serious limitations because in historical terms there is only one fundamental level, and that is the process of evolution in its classical meaning, that of Lamarck, Darwin, and others concerned with the transformation of species. All subsequent levels are indeterminate in terms of whether they are more or less fundamental than other levels.)

For Buss the history of life is the history of the primacy of differing units of selection. He focusses specifically on the transition from the eukaryotic cell, one unit of selection in the history of life, to the multicellular organism, another unit of selection. However, he does so within a potentially much wider framework that encompasses the evolution of multiple units of selection, from self-replicating molecules, through complexes of such molecules, the evolution of prokaryotes, eukaryotes with their membrane-bounded nuclei, and on to multicellular organisms. In each and every case, the history of life is the history of the elaboration of new self-replicating units which incorporate older units of selection within them, each new unit of selection having its own characteristics, and, very importantly, expressing a synergism between previous units of selection and that most recently evolved.

Buss' monograph is an early and powerful exposition of the "evo-devo" movement: heritability, he wrote, is controlled by development and that means that understanding patterns of developmental determination are just as important as knowing about the molecular mechanisms of transmission. But insofar as he is also a selection theorist through and through, he is very much a Darwinian evolutionist, though one who takes an explicitly hierarchical stance – more of which in a later chapter. In one respect, though, Buss fails to expand upon the generality of his thesis; he does not consider in any detail the possibility of including within his scheme the phenomena of cognition and culture. In his summary of the final chapter of the book, he notes that just as transitions in the units of selection preceded the transition that established the multicellular individual as a unit of selection, so must new units of selection have emerged in the hundreds of millions of years that have followed. He makes fleeting reference to the "association of individuals into kin groups and the association of neuronal activities into ideas capable of replication and variation", but does not pursue the matter beyond fleeting reference to language as a mechanism for the transmission of ideas. He must have thought such matters of cognition and culture beyond his competence to be pursued in any depth, which is entirely reasonable. However, he clearly saw even greater generality to the notion of an expanded selection theory, and in this regard should be judged one of the most important evolutionary theorists of recent times.

Some years later, Maynard Smith and Szathmary presented a not dissimilar scheme, incorporating eight major transitions in the evolution of life, but based on a very different notion of increases in complexity deriving from the way information is stored and transmitted. These transitions were the transformation of replicating molecules into populations of compartmentalized molecules; the linkage of replicators into chromosomes; the transformation of RNA as gene and enzyme into DNA and proteins; change from prokaryotes to eukaryotes; the evolution of sexual from asexual reproduction; the change from protists to multicellular fungi, plants and animals; the evolution of colonies and non-reproductive castes from solitary individuals; and finally, and most recently, the evolution of human societies with language from non-linguistic primate societies. There is a close similarity between this scheme of evolutionary transitions and Buss' levels of selection based on evolving units of selection, though it lacks the explicitly selectionist basis of Buss' theory.

Though just as ambitious as Buss in scope, Jablonka and Lamb offer what is in one respect an almost entirely different approach, and yet in another, something rather similar because of their emphasis on epigenesis. Insofar as the aim of this chapter is to consider biology in the context of Rutherford's dictum, the old physicist would have delighted in Jablonka and Lamb's book as hard evidence for his assertion that all science outside of physics is stamp collecting. This is because whilst Buss sought for generality within an expanded selectionist viewpoint, in essence a process theory, Jablonka and Lamb are mainly concerned with the mechanisms of two of their four "dimensions", namely the genetic and epigenetic, and then, because of a current lack of precise knowledge about mechanism in their other two dimensions, behavioural inheritance and symbolic inheritance, revert to a rather confused and incomplete process account.

As noted earlier in this chapter, mechanism in biology never provides true generality. Half way through their book, Jablonka and Lamb provide an interim summary of their account of evolution in four dimensions in the form of two large tables couched in terms of more abstract accounts of this mix of mechanisms and processes; the overriding impression given by these tables is one of difference between the dimensions. The reason for this is simple. In their 2007 response to a simultaneously published set of critical reviews of the book, Jablonka and Lamb begin their reply by stating that in their view evolutionary theory is currently undergoing a radical reorganization, and what their book does is consider this reorganization from the specific perspective of heredity. What distinguishes their four dimensions of evolution are different combinations of features of four inheritance systems. Their work is awash with the acceptance of selection operating within each dimension, but because their principal concern is with inheritance of specific forms of information, what becomes the dominant theme, at least to this reader, is one of differences based on an abstract categorization of whether the information is modular or holistic, whether there are dedicated copying systems, and the direction of transmission (vertical or horizontal) amongst other features. Whether information is constructed through direct planning, or whether it can change the selective environment, two additional ways of comparing their four inheritance systems in more abstract terms, results in "yes", "no", "probably" and "sometimes" answers. The net result is an account that looks much more like stamp collecting than a general theory, even though it is clear that their laudable aim is to provide a form of unified account across an unusually wide swathe of the biological and social sciences.

Jablonka and Lamb's first dimension of evolution is that which centres on genetics as the form of heredity acting between individual organisms. Their emphasis is on the need to move away from the oversimplified notion of "the gene" that was fostered by the formal models of the modern synthesis, and later taken up by replicator and selfish gene theory, and identified in bio-chemical terms with the sequence of DNA that codes for a specific product. For Jablonka and Lamb, the conceptual enemy are the simplistic assumptions that are made about the gene as a sequence of DNA and that variations in that sequence are what cause changes in the product and hence in the phenotype. Coding sequences, they argue, are only a small part of DNA, and DNA is just one part of the cellular network that determines the end product, be it a single protein or an entire phenotype. The very fact of DNA as the means of trans-mitting information relies on a plethora of mechanisms that protect and repair it and ensure accurate copying. They do question whether variation is entirely random but also do concede that such regulated change as is known to exist is itself the product of evolution as conventionally understood. As Haig points out in his review of the book, the foundational models of evolution are a good deal older than the discovery of the double helix and the subsequent flood of molecular detail as to how such information is generated and maintained. Consequently, it is unsurprising that such models are neutral as to the molecu-lar details of heritable change; in short, their criticism of what they consider to be simplistic evolutionary theory is misplaced and wrong.

The epigenetic inheritance system is their second dimension of inheritance. The term "epigenetics" was first advanced by the developmental evolutionist C.H.Waddington with reference to the complex causal interactions between genes and between genes and the environment. Waddington was a highly original evolutionist who insisted that not only development, but what he called the exploitive system, were as causally potent in evolution as those that he labelled the natural selective and genetic systems. The exploitive system concerned the ways environments are "chosen" and "modified" by at least some organisms (Waddington was inclined to confine this system to animals). Waddington's exploitive system was a pioneering idea, the general notion of which will be present throughout much of what follows. However, his concep-tion of an epigenetic system was equally far-sighted and anticipated many of the ideas of what is now called evo-devo. Waddington, though, was at pains always to stress that his ideas were consistently cast within what he described as a conventional Darwinian scheme and he would not ever have anything to do with the so-called Lamarckian conception of the inheritance of acquired characters (the next chapter explains the "so-called"). The same cannot be said of Jablonka and Lamb, who use the word epigenetics in a different and much more recent sense to refer to systems of cellular heredity which are not based on DNA sequences, specifically it refers to the transmission of information from parent to descendent cells. This is one of the central problems of biology. In any multicellular organism, all the cells that have a nucleus contain identical genetic information in the form of identical DNA sequences. Yet skin cells give rise only to other skin cells, and liver cells only to liver cells, even though all these cells contain the same DNA sequences. How this occurs is by way of a number of epigenetic mechanisms, some of which are increasingly well understood.

The complex macromolecular details of these epigenetic inheritance systems, which include DNA methylation and RNA interference, are given with admiral clarity by Jablonka and Lamb. What is unclear, however, is how widespread many of these mechanisms are in different forms of organisms, and precisely how, if at all, they relate to evolutionary change. The heart of any theory of evolution in the classical sense, what Haig calls the foundational models, constitutes species transformation in which adaptation is often, though perhaps not always, the main driving force. Jablonka and Lamb use the devise of a devil's advocate who at the end of each chapter asks searching questions of their arguments. At the end of the chapter on epigenetic inheritance systems, their devil's advocate asks "has anyone ever found any heritable epigenetic variation that is adaptive – that gives a selective advantage to those inheriting it?" "No" answer the authors, "there is no direct evidence". In a similar manner, West-Eberhard, no enemy of the notion that a complete theory of evolution needs to incorporate developmental phenomena, concludes in her review of the book that the examples Jablonka and Lamb give of epigenetic inheritance systems are too few to be convincing as to the general role that cross-generational epigenetic inheritance has for evolution in the foundational sense of species transformation. West-Eberhard extends the point to the third and fourth inheritance systems, behavioural and symbolic inheritance, which she considers to be comparatively rare amongst organisms and hence to be of limited evolutionary importance. In this regard, though, West-Eberhard may be too harsh in her judgement. The issue for Jablonka and Lamb is less that these inheritance systems are of universal importance for the evolution of all species. How could this be when Jablonka and Lamb include a symbolic inheritance system which with certainty is restricted to a very few species of animal, and perhaps only one, viz. *Homo sapiens*? What they are exploring is whether there are indeed four dimensions of evolution and what their units of inheritance are. In this they are correct.

The third of their evolutionary dimensions is the aggregate of behavioural inheritance systems in which learning becomes the agent of evolutionary change. All such inheritance systems create cultures which they define as a system of socially transmitted patterns of behaviour, preferences, and products of animal activities that characterize a group of social animals. This is an unusually wide definition of culture including as it does various species of rodents and lagomorphs, individuals of which acquire dietary preferences by way of their nursing mothers, as well numerous species of birds and mammals in which some of the behaviour of these animals is affected by filial and sexual imprinting. Such "passive" social learning is one form of behavioural inheritance system. Another inheritance system is found in animals which acquire behaviours **individually** but as a result of their attention being drawn by the behaviour of other con-specifics to specific features of their environments, sometimes labelled as social facilitation though there is considerable argument about terminology in this small corner of animal behavioural science. The well known example of such social learning was the opening of milk-bottle tops which spread through populations of birds in the United Kingdom over a period of just a few years in the last century. The third behavioural inheritance system involves imitative learning, the best known examples of which include the learning of song in songbirds and some species of cetaceans, as well as specific motor behaviours like potato-washing in monkeys, and gestures and tool use in apes.

Jablonka and Lamb are in no doubt that all such instances of social mediated learning that occurs by way of interactions with other animals, specifically through the learned behaviours of other animals, is "not essentially different" from other types of evolution. In every case, through selective retention or elimination, learning may lead to change, and hence such change is evolutionary in nature. They are aware that constraints operate in learning, be it socially mediated or not; the receiving animal is "not just a vessel into which information is poured" but is able to select information appropriate to its needs. This is important because it points to the way this inheritance system is connected to the first (genetic) and second (epigenetic) inheritance systems (more of which in later chapters of this book). They also assert that social learning, the learning that lies at the centre of all forms of behavioural inheritance systems, is not fundamentally different from all other forms of learning. That is, the neural basis of such learning is not in any way significantly different from learning that occurs in which what is learned is not connected in any way with the behaviour of other animals. The point is important.

Yet what Jablonka and Lamb fail to do is make a connection with what evolutionary epistemology – selection theory applied to learning –regards as its central claim: this is that all forms of learning occur by way of the evolutionary processes of variation and selective retention. It is an odd omission, because earlier in their book they cite the way the immune system functions as an instance by which DNA in lymphocytes is altered to provide variation in lymphocyte structure in order to combat antigens. Such immune system function has often been referred to as an instance of clonal selection, of within-organism evolution, comparable to the way in which learning might occur within neural networks. If immune system function is an instance of within-organism variation and inheritance, an epigenetic inheritance system, then behavioural inheritance systems, as forms of learning no different from other non-social forms of learning, might also be instances of within organism variation and selective retention. In other words, it is not just the behavioural system that evolves, but the neural networks that are the basis of such learning; and by extension then of Jablonka and Lamb's own argument that social learning is no different from other forms of learning, all learning is a form of evolution. Chapter 4 will examine this argument more closely.

The symbolic inheritance system is their fourth evolutionary dimension which they consider to operate exclusively within our own species. The unit of information that is transmitted is not behaviour, as in song or tool use, nor the consequences of behaviour, as in a specific dietary preference, but instead is the astonishingly flexible system of symbols, grounded in language, upon which human culture is built. As they note, the power of symbols, entities that "stand for" every aspect of human experience, allows not only for an understanding of the past and the planning of a future, or multiple possible futures, but for the construction of social worlds of virtually endless variety. The fifth chapter of this book will concern itself with some of these issues.

There is nothing within the biological and social sciences that is excluded from the compass of Jablonka and Lamb's four evolutionary dimensions. They also chart interesting and important connections between these dimensions. In these ways they come close to real generality. However, to repeat the earlier point, in focussing on inheritance, and specifically on the mechanisms of inheritance, they lose the possibility of creating a general theory. In this respect, Buss is much closer to what Rutherford would have approved of as a science on a par with physics.

Explicit in both the Buss and the Jablonka and Lamb accounts is the assumption that evolution, the transformation of organic systems in time (whether it be of species as in its original formulation, or of individual organisms, or of components of individual organisms) is what any general theory in biology must be built on. In the last few decades a significant addition to evolutionary biology has been postulated which must take place alongside variation, selection and transmission as one of the essential elements of evolution as a process. This is what John Odling-Smee and his collaborators call niche construction.

In a seminal paper of 1969, Waddington argued that there are two essential components for evolution to occur. One is some form of stable memory; the other is a kind of "operator" that acts as an effective means of testing, and in consequence, altering and updating that memory. The latter component, a less passive entity than Dawkins' vehicle, Hull later referred to as an interactor. The operator/interactor is an active causal agent in the evolutionary process.

In a similar vein, Lewontin, who had long been critical of neoDarwinism's assignment of a relatively passive role for the phenotype (the classical form of the vehicle or interactor), advocated a more constructivist approach by evolutionists. In a 1983 paper, Lewontin considered two differential equations which captured for him the quintessence of the neoDarwinism of the 1970s and 1980s: one represented the change of the evolving organism in time as a function of the current state of that organism and its environment, and the other representing environmental change as a function of environmental events. The error of neoDarwinism, argued Lewontin, was to hold these equations as separate, and thus did not take into account the role of the organism in determining changes in the environment.

Influenced by Waddington's notion of an active operator as well as by Lewontin's view that the two equations should be coupled and hence that the history of change in both organism and environment are inseparable, Odling-Smee and his collaborators advanced the conception of niche construction as a significant causal element in the process of evolution. Niche construction refers to the multiplicity of ways that organisms have of altering their environments, either passively as in the chemical changes to the environment induced by photosynthesis, or actively as in the building of burrow systems by some species of lagomorphs, or the construction of nests by many species of insects and birds. Niche construction has two consequences: one is that constructed niches may often form an ecological inheritance stable across multiple generations and so constitutes an additional inheritance system, and the other is that in altering the environment and passing these changes on to their offspring, many organisms play a causal role in altering the selection pressures that act on them and their offspring.

In their monograph, Odling-Smee et al. present a powerful argument for the importance and pervasiveness of niche construction and ecological inheritance. All living forms are instances of negative entropy which exist contrary to the second law of thermodynamics, that entropy always increases. In order to maintain their state, organisms must extract and exchange energy from their environment, mostly, though not always, in the form of extraction. This most fundamental feature of life surely imposes niche construction on any fundamental biological theory. But it is not "just" the consequences of photosynthesis or leaf fall that is encompassed by the conception of niche construction. The changes in atmosphere consequent upon the evolution of cyanobacteria, alterations in soil caused by the burrowing activity of earthworms, and the development of literate human societies are all instances of the same process, namely the effects of living forms on the world in which they exist. Niche construction is, according to Odling-Smee, a truly general aspect of change across the biological and social sciences.

The reaction to Odling-Smee's work has been mixed. Some have shrugged their shoulders, pointed to Darwin's own work on earthworms, and declared that this is nothing new. Some have been openly critical, arguing as has Dawkins, that it introduces a form of circular causation which is suspect. Others have judged niche construction and ecological inheritance to be a significant theoretical advance that provides a basis for causal complexity entirely appropriate to the science of life in all of its forms, and one which gives us the possibility of a truly general conception that unites evolutionary theory as proposed in its "foundational models" to use Haig's phrase, with intelligent behaviour as the product of cognitive mechanisms, and the most complex forms of human culture and cultural change.

In their monograph, Odling-Smee and his co-workers provide a table that runs a "comparison of the two selective processes in evolution, natural selection and niche construction". This will be referred to repeatedly in subsequent chapters because the addition of niche construction to the foundational models of evolution may just have brought us closer to the kind of science that Rutherford would have approved of. First, though, a little history is necessary, and it is to this that we turn in the next chapter.

Chapter 2

Plus ça change

Heraclitus, the best known of the early Ionian philosophers, thinking and writing around 500 B.C., expounded upon the doctrine of universal flux. Everything changes, he declared, nothing stays the same. Little remains of the writings of philosophers prior to Plato, and it is to him and his pupil Aristotle that we owe any knowledge at all of what was thought before their own work was recorded in relatively voluminous quantity. In his history of western philosophy Bertrand Russell quotes Plato as stating that Heraclitus taught that "nothing ever is, everything is becoming", which doctrine Aristotle described as "nothing steadfastly is". The notion of universal flux was expressed in Plato's metaphor that "you cannot step twice into the same river; for fresh waters are ever flowing in upon you".

A few decades later, Parmenides of Elea in the south of Italy, was propounding the opposite doctrine: nothing changes, everything remains the same. Only fragments of Parmenides' poem *On Nature* remain, the sweeping title of which is an indication of the breadth of his vision: "How, then, can what *is* be going to be in the future? Or how could it come into being? If it came into being, it is not; nor is it if it is going to be in the future. Thus is *becoming* extinguished and *passing away* not to be heard of" (the italics are in Russell's quotation). It is impossible from such fragments to understand exactly what Parmenides believed. Anthony Kenny interprets it as some form of singularity of Being. "Being is everlastingly the same, and time is unreal because past, present, and future are all one".

Heraclitus and Parmenides present extreme views, neither of which accords with normal human experience, but in presenting completely contradictory positions these earliest of known philosophers show us how different can be the stances adopted on this most fundamental aspect of human experience. Night follows day, and always has done throughout human history. Yet we all have knowledge of change, in ourselves, in others, and in the physical world about us. Some things change, and some do not. Commentators like Russell suggest that in the need to reconcile change and constancy lies the origins of religious belief – an unchanging omnipotent Being and an eternal life after death are a near universal human response to obvious uncertainties of life and the certainty of that ultimate form of change, death. The alternative to religion, of course, lies in science as the means of resolving what is constant with what changes. Night has not always followed day, at least not on this planet for there was a time when the earth did not exist and we know that there will come a time in the far distant future when it will again no longer exist. Science itself is a search for explanations of change that are themselves without change, and in that sense places a greater value on constancy than is given by ordinary experience. And as already mentioned, before science there were the philosophers who differed so radically amongst themselves on this most fundamental aspect of existence. There is a strong case to be made that these opposite states of change and constancy, flux and sameness, are at the root of all thought and ideas.

One interpretation of Parmenides' concerns is that they were as much epistemological as ontological. He was arguing, perhaps, that if we are to be able to know anything of the world, and to communicate that knowledge, then there has to be some constancy in the world outside of ourselves, the knowers. One cannot have knowledge of a world that is constantly changing. This duality of ontological and epistemological concern, of just what constancy there is in the world, and how we can know it, is a consistent philosophical theme that runs over two thousand years that extends at least to Kant in the 18th century, and continues to be a live issue in the cognitive sciences of the present day.

One exception to the linkage between ontological assumptions and epistemology is to be found in the thinking of the Sophists, perhaps the first explicit philosophers of knowledge, which took the form of an ancient relativism without regard to any ontological concerns as to what comprises the world outside of the knower. For Protagoras "man is the measure of all things", which contemporary philosophers like Kenny have taken to mean that what any person knows is a consequence of the needs and nature of each individual, and what actually is in the world, whether constant or changing, is irrelevant. However, a radical relativism, whether of the Sophists of the ancient world or the postmodernists of the present day, is a solipsistic evasion of this most fundamental of all philosophical issues: what is in the world (ontology) and can we know it (epistemology). Thus we have two dichotomies which do not map neatly onto each other: there is flux and constancy, and there are matters of ontology and what we can know of what exists, epistemology. Clearly change and constancy fit directly onto ontology, but epistemology is a much less clear-cut issue. Since these are matters that cover much of the history of thought, what follows is the tiniest of samples of how change and constancy have been dealt with, both ontologically and epistemologically.

Before evolutionary theory

Stonehenge, the astronomically related features of which date back to around 2000 B.C., bears witness to an ancient understanding that the winter and summer solstices are unchanging landmarks within the constantly altering cycle of the seasons. Recorded explanations of any kind for these coupled features of ordinary experience, of change and constancy, religious beliefs apart, appear almost two millennia later with ancient Greek philosophy. The atomists, notably Democritus around 420 B.C., provided a strikingly modern conception of how the world is. They believed that everything is, and always has been, made up of tiny indivisible particles that exist within otherwise empty space – a conception that Ernest Rutherford would largely have approved of – these atoms being infinite in number and existing in infinitely varied forms each of which have specific properties that account for the differences in the objects that we experience. Greek philosophers invented science as the attempt at systematic inquiry into the nature of the world and the application of mathematics to aid in that understanding, but it is one in particular, Aristotle, who is usually considered to have been the first practising scientist. Born in Stagira in 384 B.C., he eventually succeeded Plato as head of the Academy in Athens, from which city he was subsequently driven because of his connection with Alexander the Great. He died in 322, having developed a system of formal logic, a complex notion of causes, and made extensive observations of, and wrote a number of tracts, on biology especially, though he also wrote on physics and psychology.

Aristotle's early work was strongly influenced by his mentor, Plato. He wrote on politics, ethics, and rhetoric, amongst other topics. Yet even in his early work he observed that the best form of philosophy came from observing nature. After the death of Plato he left Athens for a long period, settling initially in the northwest coast of what is now Turkey, and it was there that he began to do what would now be considered as empirical science. He observed, dissected, sketched and classified a wide variety of organisms, sometimes drawing conclusions from his observations that G.E.R. Lloyd noted were often only confirmed many centuries later. His writings cite the work of many predecessors, but in the clarity, breadth and precision of his observations Aristotle must surely be judged the first working scientist with some remarkably modern views. In *On the Generation of Animals* he wrote as follows: "… we must trust observation rather than theory, and trust theories only if their results conform with the observed phenomena". Thus it was that for Aristotle what is out there in the world, what exists, must come to be known through the exercise of our sensory apparatus, a view that simply extends scientific practice to careful observation and anticipates the British empiricists by almost 2000 years. In this regard, he came to a view different from Plato, for whom our ability to know the world rested on certain eternal verities, on constancies in the world. On the other hand, Aristotle's detailed observations extending over significant periods of time must have left him with strong sense of at least a degree of constancy in what is in the world, which may account for his relatively mild judgement on Heraclitus when compared to Plato. But it was only a "degree" of constancy. Aristotle was well aware of the seeming contradiction of constancy and change in the world. The stuff of Aristotle's science were what Jonathan Barnes terms "middle-sized material objects", usually living things visible to the naked eye, which come into existence, grow and die. So for Aristotle, as he wrote in his *Physics*, "nature is a principle of motion and change". He considered that all material entities are "composites" in two senses: a mouse consists of organized tissues of different kinds, and in that way is a composite of different matters, as is a temple or a chariot. However, the mouse has a form which makes it different from a sparrow even though they may share many different matters. Matter and form are in themselves also the composites of all things, and when a mouse, or any thing, changes, as it does when it develops or dies, decays or erodes, it changes in terms both of matter and form. Thus did Aristotle acknowledge change in the world, but thought it could be understood within a universal framework of composites – a constant explanation of change, which again has a very modern ring.

Plato's views were quite different, perhaps for the very reason that he did no science. His writings were extraordinarily broad in scope including metaphysics, politics, and ethics, and his thoughts on knowledge were the foundations of the rationalist school of epistemology which has been built upon in the last few decades in cognitive science, referred to as the new rationalism by the philosopher of mind Jerry Fodor. How much Plato's views on knowledge were derived from earlier philosophers, apart from Socrates, is uncertain, though clearly he held Heraclitus in some contempt and his starting position was very similar to that expressed a few decades earlier by Democritus. The latter had considered knowledge to come to us in two forms. One of these derived from our senses and the other by way of thought and reasoning. The senses, however, are unreliable, thought Democritus; true knowledge is arrived at by thought.

Plato understood well enough that some things change, but for him constancy, epistemologically, was what ruled supreme. Knowledge lies in the apprehension of certain unchanging features of the world, what he referred to as ideas or forms. Precisely what the ideas or forms are is not easy to understand. In one of his dialogues he has Socrates pose the question as to whether the person who knows "knows something or nothing", and answers that of course it must be something, and hence that the forms certainly exist but they are special because they exist within an eternal realm. This is what gives them substance and reality. Nor are they to be thought of merely as an invention of the mind but instead are things that exist independently outside of any knower; knowledge is a state of mind relating to the forms, these being the essence common to everything falling under one concept, which makes any entity what it is. The form of beauty encompasses all things that are beautiful, as does the form of equality embrace all instances of equal things. Thus the forms are not mere propositions about what exists, such as all people have language or what a prime number is, but are things that exist in the eternal realm.

It is not easy to understand precisely what a form was for Plato. More simple was what it meant for one to have knowledge of the forms. The modern classical philosopher R.M. Hare describes Platonic knowledge as a "vision of the eternal" which comes to us through thought, not, emphatically not, through our senses. Sensory experience merely provides instances of these eternal truths, but in a manner that is not to be trusted. Our senses are corrupt and unreliable and at variance with one another. We cannot see sounds or feel tastes, and colours change with light levels. Knowledge, in contrast, is a product of thought, and thinking our way to knowledge is a form of reminiscence, or remembering what has always been in our minds because all knowledge is innate, present in our minds since birth and even before birth. Modern evolutionary theory asserts that many of the features of all organisms are part-caused by the history of selection pressures acting upon the traits of their antecedents, and there is no reason to exclude knowledge from this account: evolution, genetics and development provide a modern explanation for the knowledge of reincarnated souls that Plato believed in.

In the 4th century A.D. Augustine married Platonic forms with his Christian belief that knowledge is given to us by God, a view not dissimilar to that of Descartes over a thousand years later. Like Plato, Descartes in the 17th century placed little trust in conscious experience coming to us through our senses. It was in what he considered to be the unique human capacity for thought that God conveyed to us knowledge, this being certain universal truths contained within mathematical reasoning. Born a few decades after Descartes, Spinoza provided a bridge between rationalism and the soon-to-be-born school of empiricist philosophers. Spinoza suggested that what we know could be best understood within a scheme of four levels, a framework that chimes well with current cognitive science. Sensation and perception constitute his first two levels; "essences", abstract qualities, including mathematical relationships, derive from the third and fourth levels.

Common to all rationalist epistemologies, from Democritus to Spinoza, and on to the new rationalists of today, is the belief that true knowledge connects to what is constant in the universe. If we can know anything, it will in some way relate to what is constant. However, what is constant, eternal truth, has more than a touch of mysticism about it, especially to someone of a pragmatic frame of mind, who was a friend of Newton and Boyle, the most famous scientists of the day, and who asked "what is the *use* of poetry?" Such a one was John Locke, a contemporary of Spinoza, but with a very different view about knowledge. Maurice Cranston's essay portrays Locke as a man with some exceedingly strange notions, and whose epistemology was based less on some notion opposite to the rationalists that knowledge must be centred upon the need to keep pace with change, than upon his wanting to get away from "imagination, from the vague glamour of medieval things, from unthinking adherence to tradition … away from all private, visionary insights and down to the publicly verifiable, measurable, plain, demonstrable facts". As perhaps the first philosopher of science since Aristotle, Locke in his *Essay Concerning Human Understanding* begins with a criticism of the conception of innate knowledge. He argued that this is a wholly wrong view that derives from our being unable to remember, or understand how, each one of us comes to theoretical "ideas" about identity, quantity, and substance. "Ideas" are a product of our minds and experience of the world, and simple ideas, such as black and white, sweet and sour, develop before the more abstract principles such as identity and equality: "The senses at first let in particular ideas, and furnish the yet empty cabinet". We are born knowing nothing and what knowledge we acquire comes to us in the first instance through our sensory surfaces.

As noted earlier in this chapter, Aristotle as the first practising scientist was also the first empiricist philosopher. It was Locke, though, who began the modern empiricist philosophy which extends through to the present and which continues strong in contemporary psychology. David Hume was perhaps the most celebrated of Locke's conceptual descendents. Indeed there is a case to be made that Hume was the first modern psychologist since he thought that the application of the Newtonian scientific method to the human mind would yield a mental mechanics analogous to physical mechanics, with comparably powerful results in understanding. For Hume, whatever knowledge is, and to what extent it can or cannot be trusted, it begins at the sensory surfaces. But it was within his notion of a science of mind that the issue of change versus constancy arises for Hume, and which comes, ironically, to form the basis of a profound epistemological pessimism which comes not from the traditional rationalist distrust of sensory information, but from Hume's scepticism about induction coupled with his doubting that any significance can ever be attached to the concept of cause-effect relations. This is what makes Hume so hard to understand. On the one hand there is his admiration for science in general and Newton in particular, especially, according to A.J. Ayer, his veneration of Newton's famous avowal that his method was the generation of experimental evidence and not the fashioning of hypotheses (see Chapter 1); and on the other, his doubts as to the epistemological potency of inductive reasoning and the great weakness of conceptions of cause and effect relations, the root cause of all Humean doubts being a largely unspoken assumption that change is universal and hence all knowledge is limited at best, and always uncertain.

Hume's scepticism finds early voice in the first volume of his *Treatise on Human Nature*, in the introduction to which he asserts that "It is evident, that all the sciences have a relation, greater or less, to human nature; and that, however wide any of them may seem to run from it, they still return back by one passage or another". In other words, however magisterial may seem to be the power of science, and in the 21st century this includes the gradual eradication of diseases deadly in Hume's time, the interfacing of the minds of humans and other primates with computers, and the almost certain sending of people to other planets in the not too distant future, a power that must depend upon science being a closer approximation to the truth of what the world is than has ever been the case before, nonetheless, Hume was telling us, science is the product of the human mind, and the mind is a fragile and not-to-be-trusted thing. Well, perhaps that is the case for any one mind, but science is the product of many minds within a historical progression – a kind of collective form of knowledge, more of which in the next chapter.

For Hume the uncertainty of knowledge was the result of two main and related problems. The first concerned induction. Induction is a form of ampliative inference by which a conclusion relating to all members of a class is drawn from direct observation of only some of them: one observes, for example, that spiders spin silken webs and have done so, as far as can be ascertained, since observations began, and so we make the inductive inference that that the spinning of silken webs has always been one of the activities of spiders and always will be so. What Hume taught us is that such reasoning is hazardous. Knowledge from the past or present cannot guarantee that such knowledge will be true in the future: "that instances of which we have had no experience, must resemble those, of which we have had experience, and that the course of nature continues always uniformly the same … is derived from nothing but custom". What Hume was saying, albeit in a very indirect way, is that custom is a weak thing, and that change is universal and no constancy can ever be guaranteed as lasting and permanent – nothing is permanent. Spiders have not always spun webs, and indeed some do not do so in the present. Night has not always followed day, nor will it in the future.

Philosophers now consider induction to take many different forms but the basic Humean problem has continued to plague philosophers down to the present time. One instance, of significance to this book and which will be returned to in a later chapter, is the work of Karl Popper, in which he declared in 1971 that "I think I have solved a major philosophical problem; the problem of induction".

The second and closely connected difficulty raised by Hume was even more shocking. This was the issue of cause-effect relations. In Part 3 of the first volume of his *Treatise* concerned with "Knowledge and Probability" Hume builds upon the same scepticism as to whether we can ever be certain that "those instances of which we have had no experience resemble those of which we have had experience" and applies it to the "constant conjunction" in terms of contiguity and succession by which we come to the judgement that any two objects or events are related in terms of cause and effect. However, "not only our reason fails us in the discovery of the *ultimate connection* of causes and effects, but even after experience has informed us of their *constant conjunction*, it is impossible for us to satisfy ourselves by our reason, why we should extend that experience beyond those particular instances which have fallen under our observation. We suppose, but are never able to prove, that there must be a resemblance betwixt those objects, of which we have had experience, and those which lie beyond the reach of our discovery" (the italics are in the original text). Thus did Hume argue that while there is a real psychological need to attribute a cause-effect structure to the world that we experience, there is no necessary reality behind this propensity of human reasoning. We cannot ever really know that one event is an effect caused by another event. The notion of cause-effect relations is merely a habit of thought rather than a form of true knowledge about the nature of the world, just as is reasoning by induction. Psychological compulsion, he argued, does not necessarily reflect how the world is.

In a recent review of universal Darwinism, Richard Nelson notes that a contemporary, and indeed a close friend, of Hume, Adam Smith, also contributed to the growing literature on constancy and change. In his famous work, *An Inquiry into the Nature and Causes of the Wealth of Nations* first published in 1776, Smith provided not only what was perhaps the first major account of economics within an analytical framework that warrants its description as social science, but did so within a context of a systematic history of human cultures. If any single word describes Smith it is that of a historian, his having also written on the history of languages, physics, astronomy, and the arts. In his *Wealth of Nations* Smith married the concept of change intrinsic to all of history to the notion of a general principle driving that one particular form of change, and one that is ever constant under changing conditions, namely, the division of labour, is and always has been, the principal ingredient of economic growth that drives historical change in human cultures.

In casting doubt upon our ability to know about cause-effect relations, Hume "believed himself shut up in a solipsistic world, and ignorant of everything except his own mental states", as Russell wrote, which reduces empiricism to no form of knowledge at all, a danger for empiricist epistemology of which Locke had been cognizant. Thus did Hume's version of empiricism convey a deep pessimism about the possibility of humans ever having certain knowledge, and there is a strong case made by historians of philosophy like Russell, that all subsequent epistemological writings are attempts to rescue our understanding of knowledge from Hume's critique. Immanuel Kant, considered by many to be the greatest philosopher since Plato, wrote that he had been aroused from his own "dogmatic slumber" by Hume's pessimism. Arguably the most difficult of all philosophers to understand, Kant's views are of little relevance to the main theme of this book and can be dealt with very briefly. Kant argued that there is a world of the noumena, things-in-themselves, outside of ourselves, which we come to know *a posteriori* through a conjunction of our senses, as well as through certain innate features of our minds, the *a priori* intuitions (relating to space and time) and categories (concerned with quantity, relation, modality, and quality). Thus it is that we are able to have knowledge that transcends our sensory experience, but that knowledge, based as it is on the *a prioris* which do not relate in any meaningful way to the properties of the world outside of the knower, does not necessarily match with the noumena. It is worth noting that modern Kantians, like the ethologist Konrad Lorenz, rejected the idea that the *a prioris*, in effect what we now term our cognitive apparatus, should not be connected fairly directly with the nature of the world because they evolved precisely to do so. More important to this book, Kant entertained the idea that time has no beginning or end and was one of a number of 18th century European thinkers who seriously considered the possibility that our planet is ancient, at least tens of millions of years old. This is a figure vastly different from biblical accounts of the age of the earth, and one which came to be very important in paving the way for the eventual understanding that it is life itself that represents the greatest example that we have for perpetual change.

PreDarwinian theories of species change

As Ernst Mayr documented, biology as an independent scientific discipline began in the 18th century with increasingly detailed descriptions of more and more species leading to increasing appreciation of the extraordinary diversity of living forms. Carl Linnaeus, the founder of taxonomy, constructed hierarchies of relationships amongst animal and plant species that provided an eventual factual and conceptual basis for the ideas of common origins and subsequent diversifications. However, it was Pierre de Maupertuis, argues Mayr, who played a key role in establishing the foundations of evolutionary

theory by introducing Newtonian thought to French scientists and philosophers, but at the same time rejecting the notion that biology could be explained
solely by physics. Maupertius advanced the view that living forms change constantly by some kind of unexplained mutational force by which he anticipated
Lamarck's theory of evolution, but his really significant role was the influence
he played in the intellectual development of George-Louis Leclerc Buffon.
Buffon was the most accomplished biologist of his time, his multi-volumed
Histoire Naturelle being the widest read and most influential natural science
writings of the 18th century. Buffon presented no theory, but the 1766 volume
contained the following, for its day, extraordinary statement: "If it were admitted that the ass is of the family of the horse, and different from the horse only
because it has varied from the original form, one could equally well say that the
ape is of the family of man, that he is a degenerate man, that man and ape have
a common origin; that, in fact, all the families, among plants as well as animals,
have come from a single stock, and that all animals are descended from a single
animal". One cannot get closer to a statement that all living forms are transformed in time, that is, that they evolve, and are the result of descent from
pre-existing organisms, perhaps just one. Yet in the same paragraph, as quoted
by Mayr, he declared that "we are assured by the authority of revelation that all
animals have participated equally in the grace of direct Creation and that the
first pair of every species issued fully formed from the hands of the creator". So
great seems the contradiction between a near outright statement of evolution
on the one hand, and a retreat into biblical tradition on the origins of life on
the other, that one is tempted to think that Buffon was succumbing to the
same social forces that led Darwin almost a century later to declare that speaking publicly or publishing material in support of his theory felt like confessing
to murder. Mayr, however, avows that Buffon, in fact, did then advance arguments as to why the transformation of species could not be a correct view, not
least being the lack of observed and recorded instance of such transformation
and the lack of evidence of intermediate forms.

Nonetheless, as Mayr notes, whilst Buffon may have rejected evolutionary
explanations for himself, he was crucial in the history of biological theory in
bringing them to the attention of others, notably Charles Bonnet in France and
Erasmus Darwin in England. Of particular importance was the direct role he
played in advancing the career, and likely influencing the thoughts, of one Jean
Baptiste de Lamarck. After a period of military service, Lamarck, with the considerable assistance of Buffon, began his work as a botanist, and later as a specialist in invertebrate animals. It was around 1800 that he became a convinced
evolutionist and subsequently advanced the first theory of evolution.

History is never simple, and a brief account such as is being presented here
cannot do justice to the development of an idea, the transformation of species

in time, that was so at odds with the prevailing religious doctrine of the countries, notably France and England, in which it first appeared and where it was nurtured to the point that it became the central theorem of biology. That clash between a scientific theory of origins and the concept of Divine creation is still with us, especially in the United States. In the late 18th and early 19th centuries it was in France that the conflict was greatest because in that period French biological science was the most active and important in the world. In addition to Buffon, Bonnet, and Lamarck, Georges Cuvier was another leading French anatomist whose pioneering studies of comparative form and the fossil evidence from the Paris basin established the new science of palaeontology.

As mentioned earlier, science in the 18th century, including the new discipline of geology, was increasingly challenging biblical accounts as to the age of the earth. In 1795 the Scottish geologist James Hutton proposed the doctrine of uniformitarianism, which held that the processes of geological change are constant, yet another instance of the opposition and marriage of the opposite notions of flux and constancy; the world does indeed change all the time, but always for the same reasons. For Hutton this meant that the causes of change are always the same: "no vestige of a beginning, no prospect of an end" was how he put it. Moreover, hand in hand with the increasing awareness of diversity in the living world grew an understanding of patterns within the fossil record. The older a fossil is, according to the geological understanding of the time, the less it resembles modern living forms; more recently fossilized forms are more similar to those alive today. There did, then, seem to be some continuity in changing forms across geological time; and contrary to Buffon's claims, intermediate forms could be discerned in the fossil record. Even more startling was the pattern of increasing diversity with time. If the earth and its living forms had indeed been created very quickly, in a matter of days according to the literal biblical account, then if extinction does occur, and few could deny the fossil record on extinction, then the diversity of living forms should have decreased with time, not increased.

Now Cuvier, much the most influential French biologist after the death of Buffon, pioneer of the scientific study of fossils and how they relate to the comparative anatomy of living forms, was a militant anti-evolutionist. He explained the fossil record by expounding a kind of "catastrophism"; extinctions, he argued, were the result of periodic global floods, after which new forms of life appeared. This was an argument so empty of content, and so at odds with the soundness of his work as a comparative anatomist, that it must surely be concluded that Cuvier's anti-evolutionism arose from a source different from his own considerable gift of reasoning. An ambitious man, Cuvier eventually rose to positions of considerable political power, including serving in the cabinet of King Louis XVIII and becoming minister of the interior under

Louis Phillippe. These appointments came after the main body of his scientific work was completed, but there may have been a link between an anti-evolutionist stance as a scientist and political ambition in a time when evolution was an idea deeply abhorrent to all Christian faiths.

Lamarck was a very different kind of man. Whilst born into a family of lowly aristocrats, he had lived a life of abject poverty, developed an interest in Mediterranean flora, and then came to Buffon's notice and appointed a tutor and companion to his son. By all accounts Lamarck was the most humble of men, yet his study of the fossils of molluscs led him to a belief in evolution and the formulation of the first explanatory theory of the transformation of species. Self-effacing he might have been, but he was not lacking in courage, and unlike Darwin 50 years later, who excluded almost all reference to humans in the *Origin of Species*, in his *Philosophie Zoologique* Lamarck explicitly references the evolution of humans by way of a bipedal gait, opposable thumbs, the shift in centre of gravity resulting from an upright posture, dietary and hence jaw and teeth alteration, and an intense sociality which resulted in signalling of some kind and the eventual appearance of language and its subsequent diversification. It was a remarkably modern construction of the evolution of our species. What complicates the story is that Lamarck himself did not seem to believe that extinctions occur.

Lamarck's evolutionism comes in two parts. The first is the notion of a directionality in the change of living things, a *scala naturae*, which goes back as far as Aristotle and which was present also in the writings of more recent philosophers like Leibniz. Life, thought Lamarck, begins with the spontaneous generation of the most simple forms, those with "only the rudiments of organization" which very slowly and gradually are transformed into organisms of ever increasing complexity. However, contrary to the fossil evidence, Lamarck entertained the strange idea that no species ever become extinct and that if we only knew where to look, these supposedly extinct forms remain present somewhere on earth, and since the *scala naturae* is a constantly renewing force, even if some do become extinct it is not permanent because they will evolve again as part of the great chain of being which is constantly renewing itself.

Much more important is the second part of his thoughts which provided the first causal explanation of how evolution occurs. The 7th chapter of his *Philosophie* has a title which captures the explanatory heart of the theory: "Of the influence of the environment on the activities and habits of animals, and the influence of the activities and habits of these living bodies in modifying their organization and structure". How this occurs was captured by Lamarck in two "laws". The first, the law of use and disuse, states that after individual development has ceased, the frequent or continuous use of an organ will develop and enlarge that organ and "give it a power proportional to the length of time it has been so used", whereas the disuse of an organ "weakens and deteriorates it" to the point where it finally disappears.

The second, the law of the inheritance of acquired characters, states that changes wrought by the actions of the first law "are preserved by reproduction to the new individuals which arise" provided that the modifications acquired by use and disuse are "common to both sexes". As has been repeatedly pointed out by commentators, the inheritance of acquired characters is an element of folk biology that is thousands of years old, and it continues to exert an influence to the present day – witness Jablonka and Lamb's work as described in the previous chapter. Whatever the merits of casting epigenetic and cultural inheritance systems within a Lamarckian framework in the present, of epigenetics and culture Lamarck knew nothing, and the form in which he and his few followers used it was effectively destroyed by Weismann some 70 years later. As a theory of the transformation of species as evolution was understood to mean in the 18th and 19th centuries, Lamarck's explanatory framework was simply wrong, even though Darwin himself, after the publication of the first edition of his *Origin*, considered both laws as being possible useful expansions to the notion of species change caused by natural selection.

There is, though, another aspect to Lamarck's theory that is central to the development of general theory in biology. As Mayr notes, Lamarck's real contribution was to bring change, constant flux in both the environments of living organisms and in the organisms themselves, to centre stage. The influence of Lamarck on Darwin in these broadest terms is difficult to gauge, but there is no argument as to the centrality of flux to any theory of evolution. What is of real interest to any modern evolutionist is not use/disuse and the inheritance of acquired characters, but the causal chain of events that Lamarck thought initiated the operation of these two "laws". The causal chain that Lamarck considered is change in the environment effecting changes in the needs of an organism, and those changes in need leading to alterations in the organism. He was quite explicit in rejecting the idea that the environment works directly to modify the organism; it is changes in need that mediate the modification in structure and function, and if the organism in question is an animal, then for Lamarck the most important changes brought about by alterations in need are changes in behaviour. There are a few places in the *Philosophie* where Lamarck depicts behaviour as itself being the engine of change – changes of "abode, climate, habits, or manner of life" – which is an idea close to the notion that something within the organism itself may be the initial origin of environmental changes bringing about altered needs and hence further changes both within the organism and its environment. Here is a hint of a two-way causal interaction between changes in both environment and organism, an idea not far from that of

Waddington's operator or Hull's interactor, and the Odling-Smee concept of niche construction (see Chapter 1).

Lamarck's great successor as a proponent of evolution as a theory of flux in the living world was, of course, Charles Darwin. Before Darwin, however, came the enigmatic, and in some circles, very influential figure of Herbert Spencer. Never a scientist, the confusion and ambiguity surrounding Spencer's writings and ideas is immediately obvious in his being described, having coined the phrase "survival of the fittest", as the leading proponent of all times of "Social Darwinism", when he was, in fact, a "Social Lamarckian" who paid scant regard to Darwin's work. Darwin himself was contradictory in his response to Spencer's ideas. In his autobiography Darwin wrote of his never having profited from the writings of Spencer, whose deductive approach to all things was wholly opposed to Darwin's empirical frame of mind, and whose conclusions seemed to Darwin not to be "of any strictly scientific use". Yet in the last edition of *The Origin of Species* published in 1872, Darwin altered one of the most famous passages of his great work to read as follows: "In the future I see open fields for far more important researches. Psychology will be securely based on the foundations already well laid by Mr. Herbert Spencer, that of the necessary acquirement of each mental power and capacity by gradation". It has been noted by others that Darwin's interests lay close to psychology and but for his fascination with a wider natural science, Darwin might have been one of the first great empirical psychologists. He must have known that Spencer's psychology was, like all his other writings, pure speculative deduction and could not have been the foundation of a science of mind anymore than his other writings were the basis for any other form of science. Yet in that later edition of the *Origin* he could not have praised anyone more highly with the change to his original text. Such contradictory judgements carry through to the present time. Most historians of science hold Spencer in contempt, yet some important scholars consider his ideas and writings to have been of real significance.

It should be noted that in contrast to the generosity of Darwin, as well as the significant approval of the likes of John Stuart Mill and T.H. Huxley, Spencer's treatment of the works of others that he incorporated into his own ideas can best be described as insouciant, at worst as a kind of negligence bordering on intellectual theft. This is especially the case with regard to Lamarck, whose theory of evolution Spencer first came upon in the early 1840s, long before almost anyone had ever heard of Darwin's ideas. Lamarckian theory was absolutely central to Spencer's writings, yet in his two volume autobiography Lamarck was given three very casual references and in his *Principles of Psychology*, the first edition of which was published in 1855, Lamarck's name does not appear at all.

Yet it must be said that in making connections that none had made before, Spencer was important, even if virtually everything that he wrote proved to be wrong. In the 1970s, the psychologist Donald T. Campbell coined the phrase evolutionary epistemology to describe ideas that place the science (not the philosophy) of knowledge within a naturalistic, specifically an evolutionary, framework. As part of the development of a truly synthetic philosophy that linked all living forms and functions, including the human mind and human societies, Spencer was undoubtedly the first evolutionary epistemologist and evolutionary psychologist, if only in "theory". He did this by considering that all transformations of living things, be it of species, of individuals during development, of the growth of individual knowledge, or of the changes that can occur in human societies, are all the result of the same three fundamental processes, the combined effects of which provide an account for all forms of change in all organisms. If ever there was an attempt at a grand overarching theory in biology, it was Spencer's.

The first of these processes was the Lamarckian conception of a constant dynamic interaction between an organism, or a group of organisms, with a constantly changing environment such that all living forms maintain a state of equilibrium with the world in which they live. This notion of a state of equilibrium between changing environments and alterations in living forms is a constant feature in all of Spencer's writings. The second process builds upon the conception of the *scala naturae* in which organisms gradually change from simple to more complex forms, evolution for Spencer being "definable as a change from an incoherent homogeneity to a coherent heterogeneity". Evolution, he believed, comprised change along a dimension of complexity based upon an increasing division of labour between the entities, the organ systems, of any single living form or between organisms within social groups (more than a hint of Adam Smith). The third process was Lamarck's so-called second law, the inheritance of acquired characters.

The result of the operation of all three processes was constant progressive change in all living things. However tenuous and empirically unfounded his vision, it was, nonetheless, a vision grander than any before him. All organic transformation comprised "adaptation as a uniform principle of bodily life" involving an ever increasing "adjustment of internal relations to external relations", such change accounting not only for transformation of simple into complex organisms, of insectivore mammals into, for example, primates, and of apes into humans; it also applied to the transformation of "primitive human societies" into the most complex of human cultural systems. Thus is it perfectly justified to consider Spencer also to have been the first sociologist, albeit one with a strong naturalistic bent. The range of his thinking led some of his contemporaries to consider him the Newton of the biological world.

Whatever final judgement is made of Lamarck and Spencer, it is unquestionable that Lamarck was the first truly evolutionary theorist in that he provided a causal account of the transformation of species in time, an account based upon an empirical understanding of the living world. The central features of his theory were wrong, but it was based upon a correct interpretation of the fossil record that species are indeed transformed in time, and it was cast within a specific causal framework that was intended to explain such change. Spencer was different because he was no scientist and built wholly upon deductive speculation and often grotesque analogies. He is probably best described as a naturalistic philosopher on the grandest scale. But whereas Lamarck was essential to the development of general theory in biology, Spencer certainly was not, even if he did provide us with an example of the scope of such a general theory.

Darwin and his immediate successors

Charles Darwin's *Naturalist's Voyage*, an account of the years he spent when he was a young man as the official naturalist aboard the Beagle, was dedicated to Charles Lyell "with greatest pleasure, as an acknowledgement that the chief part of whatever scientific merit this journal and other works of the author may possess, has been derived from studying the well-known and admirable PRINCIPLES OF GEOLOGY". It is interesting that it was through reading the same work that Spencer first came across the ideas of Lamarck. Lyell advanced Hutton's uniformitarianism to a new generation of geologists and naturalists, yet he was himself fanatically opposed to the concept of species transformation. Darwin's paternal grandfather, in contrast, had been a celebrated evolutionist, and as a student in Edinburgh Darwin had been introduced to the ideas of Lamarck by one of his mentors, Robert Grant, who was later to become an influential evolutionist in his own right lecturing at University College London. Such were the conflicting influences working on the young naturalist as he sailed around the world observing, collecting specimens, and recording his thoughts. Writing about extinctions in his journal of that voyage, he noted: "We do not steadily bear in mind, how profoundly ignorant we are of the conditions of existence of every animal; nor do we always remember, that some check is constantly preventing the too rapid increase of every organized being left in a state of nature. The supply of food, on an average, remains constant; yet the tendency in every animal to increase by propagation is geometrical". Later in the same journal, commenting upon the extraordinary natural history of the Galapagos islands, Darwin wrote: "Most of the organic productions are aboriginal creations, found nowhere else; there is even a difference between the inhabitants of the different islands; yet all show a marked relationship with those of America, though separated from that continent by an open space of ocean, between 500 and 600 miles in width". Thus, with the advantages of hindsight, do we see the young naturalist groping towards one of the greatest scientific advances of all times, as he simultaneously retreats from biblical accounts of the creation of life on Earth.

Stopping off at Cape Town as the Beagle headed back to England, Darwin made a point of meeting one of his intellectual heroes, John Herschell, the astronomer, who had openly referred to the appearance of new species in place of those that are extinct as the "mystery of mysteries". On his return to England, as Desmond and Moore document in their detailed biography of Darwin, the young Charles entered into an intellectual climate in ferment with regard to what, if anything, conservative religious views could explain, and the ever increasing influence of the voices of dissenters in terms both of how best to live a life and how to understand the world in which that life is lived. It was within this London world of shifting views about profound issues that Darwin began to review the ideas that had begun increasingly to occupy his thoughts during the later stages of the Beagle voyage.

As Gavin de Beer, the editor of the Darwin and Huxley autobiographies notes, it is wise to be cautious in accepting what Darwin himself wrote when he was in his late 60s, some 30 years after the events that he describes. It is clear from his Beagle notes as well as his writings in his unpublished notebooks that by the time Darwin returned to England he was, at the least, toying with the idea of evolution as a unifying concept for biology; the transformation of species giving rise to new forms answered so many of the questions then being raised by naturalists and palaeobiologists, and accorded so well with his own observations and musings. By all accounts, within a year or two of returning to England he had become a convinced evolutionist. The general conception of the importance of understanding almost everything in terms of change was all about him. As Desmond and Moore document, Herschell ran parallel cases for the gradual development of languages and rocks, implying that even if the processes causing change might be different, gradual change is itself universal; in medicine people were increasingly seeing nature as being in a constant "process of change". The big question was how to explain change in any one of its forms, particularly the appearance of new species; and could such explanation apply to different forms of change, such as the alterations of languages in time. Darwin recorded his memories as follows:

> "I worked on true Baconian principles, and without any theory collected facts on a whole-sale scale. More especially with respect to domesticated productions, by printed enquiries, by conversation with skilful breeders and gardeners, and by extensive reading. … I soon perceived that Selection (sic) was the key-stone of man's success in making useful races of animals and plants. But how selection could be applied

to organisms living in a state of nature remained for some time a mystery to me. In October 1838, that is fifteen months after I had begun my systematic enquiry, I happened to read for amusement 'Malthus on Population', and being well prepared to appreciate the struggle for existence which everywhere goes on from long-continued observation of the habits of animals and plants, it at once struck me that under these circumstances favourable variations would tend to be preserved and unfavourable ones to be destroyed. The result of this would be the formation of new species".

However accurate his recollection, it is famously the case that he did not publish his ideas for some 20 years, and did so then only when he learned that another English naturalist, A.R. Wallace, had independently discovered the principle of natural selection. His reluctance to make known his theory, along with the general spirit of the times already alluded to, meant that others had entertained similar ideas without the influence of Darwin's considerations. For example, in a letter of 1860 published in the *Gardeners' Chronicle and Agricultural Gazette* Darwin freely acknowledged that a certain "Mr. Matthews had anticipated by many years the explanation which I have offered of the origin of species, under the name of natural selection", though he did go on to suggest that none would be surprised that neither he nor other naturalists had known of the views of Mr. Matthew considering that they appeared in the appendix to a work on "Naval Timber and Arboriculture". Matthews and Wallace may not have been the only ones independently to arrive at the same theoretical position as Darwin; after all, when Darwin's friend and champion, T.H. Huxley, first learned of Darwin's theory years before it was published, he is said to have pondered aloud why others had not had the same idea since it seemed to be so obvious.

However obvious, and however delayed in public appearance, Darwin's theory as expressed in his first book, *The Origin of Species*, the first edition of which was published in 1859, provided theoretical detail and supportive observations that made it the founding work of the modern theory of evolution. The following paragraphs provide an extreme truncation of that profoundly important work.

Like so many naturalists, Darwin was astonished by "those exquisite adaptations of one part of the organization to another part, and to the conditions of life, and of one organic being to another being". The big question was how to explain "that perfection of structure and coadaptation which justly excites our admiration", and in the first edition of *Origin* he employed a number of "facts", some derived from his own observations, and some from the work of others, in order to provide that understanding. The first of these, which he had pondered on board the Beagle as noted above, was the potential for very rapid increase in the populations of most species of organisms. The second, seemingly in contradiction to the potential for population growth, was the apparent constancy in population size, despite the long-term march to extinction shown by the fossil record. The third fact was that required resources, he thought, were always limited. It was the combination of these three "observations" that led him to read such significance into the Malthusian comparison between the increase in "geometrical ratio" of unchecked population growth on the one hand, and increases in subsistence which occur "only in arithmetical ratio", on the other.

One chapter of the *Origin* is entitled the "laws of variation". Darwin's own acute observations, as well as those of increasing numbers of 18th and 19th century naturalists, led to a belief in the uniqueness of each individual organism of any species, and such individual variation is often passed on to offspring. What was later to become known as the heritability of variants was especially attested to by the plant and animal breeders with whom Darwin consulted. Darwin's genius lay in his knitting these observations and facts, the empirical evidence on which he laid such stock, together to lead to two inferences that lay at the heart of his theory.

The first of these, the central causal feature of his theory of evolution, was the principle of natural selection. Darwin proposed that every living form is an organized collective of variable traits which together determine the extent to which that organism is able to survive and reproduce in a particular environment – what was in the 20th century to be termed its "fitness". Many of these variable traits will be inherited by offspring, and hence the relative fitness of offspring will be determined, at least in part, by that of its parents. Over time, those members of a breeding population with traits that favour survival and/or reproduction will increase in number; those with less favourable traits will decline in number and eventually disappear. The net outcome is a gradual change in the predominant traits of the individuals making up the descendent population. The second inference followed in a simple manner from the first: over sufficiently long periods of time, the changes in the heritable traits of a population will be sufficient for a population to have altered such that its previous form is extinct and its present form comprises a new species.

It is not hard to appreciate Huxley's puzzlement as to why it had taken so long for biologists to arrive at what was a plausible explanation for evolution, an explanation entirely different from that of Lamarck. The latter had considered evolution to be a constant procession of perfected living forms, such perfection being directly imposed by the conditions of the world mediated by the altering needs and behaviour of the organism. In effect, the environment instructs life to acquire perfect forms. Darwin's theory was wholly different. Darwin's principle of selection implied that living forms are never perfect, but being composites of variable attributes, the sources of which variation neither

Darwin nor his contemporaries ever understood, they have varying degrees of success at survival and reproduction: those best suited to the current circumstances of the world are **selected** by those environmental conditions, they are not **instructed**. Lamarck's theory was based on the notion of instruction. Darwin's was a theory at the centre of which was the notion of selection.

Darwin was not a dogmatist, and through successive editions of the *Origin*, and in other books and writings, he pondered upon the possibilities of other causal explanations for speciation apart from natural selection. Both use and disuse and a form of inheritance of acquired characters, Lamarck's two principal laws, were considered. So too, in his writings on earthworms, was the possibility that the actions of organisms altering the environment, niche construction though he did not use that phrase, might also have a causal force in evolution. He also, in his book, *The Descent of Man*, explicitly extended his evolutionary thinking to our own species, and most particularly to many aspects of the human mind, especially human thought and intelligence. In one respect, though, he never wavered, and certainly never altered his own mind. Natural selection was a key causal component of evolution: after all, the full tile of his first and most famous book was *The Origin of Species by Means of Natural Selection*, which title was maintained through all six editions of the book.

The importance of the difference between a theory of evolution based on selection as opposed to instruction cannot be overstated. An instructional theory implies infinitely malleable organic structures that respond directly to the changing circumstances of the world. A selectional theory is one in which the causes of variation are at least partially decoupled from circumstances external to the organism, and hence the changes in form and function are always constrained by the mechanisms that generate variation. Darwin had no idea as to what the mechanisms are that generate variation, and so this aspect of his theory did not dominate his thinking. However, the importance of selectional processes operating within an historical framework certainly did not escape him – Darwin, as Stephen Jay Gould once commented, taught us that history matters – and this bears upon another aspect of "Darwin's causal pluralism", to borrow Stephen Asma's apt phrase. This concerns the distinction made between what came to be known as evolutionary functionalists and strucuralists. Most neoDarwinists in the 20th century emphasized the teleological aspect of Darwin's theory. That is, in placing the emphasis on the way in which the history of selection provides a functional account of evolution and the present form of adaptations in any organism, Darwin solved the problem of teleology, as Mayr put it, by placing selection by the environment of variation within the organism as the central engine of evolutionary change. However, quite apart from his awareness of what is now termed niche construction which is a significant causal addition to a selection-based theory, there is also no doubting that Darwin was deeply aware of the causal consequences of historical constraints on evolutionary change, a major concern of some later evolutionary theorists like Gould. As the historian Robert Richards points out, Darwin was at pains to make this clear in many passages in the *Origin* and other works, as, for example, the following shows: "If we suppose that the ancient progenitor, the archetype as it may be called, of all mammals, had its limbs constructed on the existing general pattern, for whatever purpose they served, we can at once perceive the plain signification of the homologous construction of the limbs throughout the whole class". Darwin was as much a structuralist as a functionalist. The significance that he points to is that history always places constraints on what can occur in the future. The constraints may seldom, if ever, be absolute, but they are a universal of any historical process of change. As will be argued in Chapter 4, such constraints are an important part of accounting for changes in knowledge within a selectionist framework. As Richards notes, "The term 'evolution' is pregnant with its history", and Darwin continues to be "the patron saint of evolutionary biology" both now and in the future.

Darwin's immediate successors did little to advance the theory of evolution as formulated by Darwin. As mentioned above, Darwin had considerable interest in matters of psychology and George Romanes, who is often described as Darwin's intellectual heir, had a particular fascination with issues of human and non-human minds. That could be the only reason why Darwin held him in such high regard. Romanes' science, such as it was, was based entirely on the anecdotes about animal behaviour that he assiduously and indiscriminately collected. A great admirer of Spencer, he believed in a Lamarckian progressivism of all animal minds towards human intelligence. If Romanes had any role at all it was to steer Conway Lloyd Morgan towards a strict empiricism with regard to animal behaviour, and a massively pared down theoretical approach to how any learner, human or animal, gains knowledge. But with regard to theory, Morgan contributed nothing to Darwin's ideas.

Most historians of biology argue that little more was added to Darwinian theory until the appearance of the modern synthesis more than 30 years after Darwin's death. The theory of evolution did have a strong following in Germany, with August Weismann leading the way to a decisive, if now considered by some an incorrect (see Chapter 1) rejection of Lamarck (and Darwin's flirtation with the inheritance of acquired characters) by advancing a theoretical account of the mechanisms of inheritance that firmly separated germ line and somatic inheritance; and the likes of Ernst Haeckel and Karl Ernst van Baer arguing for and against different structuralist approaches to evolution. The birth of the new science of genetics, if anything, initially weakened the following of Darwin's theory of natural selection.

In one respect, though, potentially significant advances were made in Darwin's theory both before and not long after the great man's death not in terms of any details of the main planks of the theory, variation, and selection, but with regard to the possible application of the theory to forms of change other than the transformation of species. We have already seen how Spencer attempted to broaden Lamarck's theory of species transformation by applying it to changes within individuals and within societies and cultures. Something not dissimilar began to occur soon after the publication of the *Origin* with attempts to broaden the explanatory scope of selection theory.

In his review of the history of ideas concerning preformation and epigenesis as applied to the nervous system and behaviour, Ronald Oppenheim documents how T.H. Huxley in an 1869 review of a book by Haeckel, drew a parallel between the Darwinian theory of change being the result of selection between organisms and that which might be driving change within organisms:

> It is a probable hypothesis that what the world is to organisms in general, each organism is to the molecules of which it is composed. Multitudes of these, having diverse tendencies, are competing with one another for opportunity to exist and multiply; and the organism as a whole, is as much the product of the molecules which are victorious as the Fauna and Flora of a country is the product of the victorious in it.

Huxley was not alone in his speculation. According to Oppenheim, the writer and commentator G.H. Lewis made a similar suggestion in a book he wrote on the physical basis of mind which was published just a few years after Huxley's review. Darwin himself, however, wrote in a letter to Huxley that "I am very glad that you have been bold enough to give your ideas about Natural Selection amongst the molecules, though I cannot quite follow you". Exactly what Darwin meant, especially with the ambivalent "quite", is unclear. It is also somewhat at odds with Darwin's own writings about a form of change other than that which occurs to species of organisms.

As noted above, Herschell had speculated on whether change as observed in geology and languages over time might not share some characteristics with species transformation long before Darwin had first made public his theory. Herschell had not been alone. As Darwin himself recorded in his 1871 book *The Descent of Man*, Lyell himself had drawn similar parallels. In the third chapter of his 1871 book, entitled "Comparison of the mental powers of man and the lower animals" Darwin wrote as follows:

> The formation of different languages and of distinct species, and the proofs that both have been developed through a gradual process, are curiously parallel. But we can trace the formation of many words further back than that of species, for we can perceive how they actually arose from the imitation of various sounds. We find in distinct languages striking homologies due to community of descent, and analogies due to a similar process of formation. The manner in which certain letters or sounds change

when others change is very like correlated growth. We have in both cases the redupli-
cation of parts, the effects of long-continued use, and so forth. The frequent presence
of rudiments, both in languages and in species, is still more remarkable. … Languages
like organic beings, can be classed in groups, under groups; and they can be classed
either naturally according to descent, or artificially by other characters. Dominant
languages and dialects spread widely, and lead to the gradual extinction of other
tongues … We see variability in every tongue, and new words are continually cropping
up; but as there is a limit to the powers of memory, single words, like whole languages,
gradually become extinct. As Max Muller has well remarked: 'A struggle for life is
constantly going on amongst the words and grammatical forms in each language. The
better, the shorter, the easier forms are constantly gaining the upper hand, and they
owe their success to their own inherent virtue.' To these more important causes of the
survival of certain words, mere novelty and fashion may be added; for there is in the
mind of man a strong love for slight changes in all things. *The survival or preservation
of certain favoured words in the struggle for existence is natural selection"* (Italics not in
the original)

Anyone familiar with Darwin's writings can see at once that he is drawing a
strong parallel between his theory of the transformation of species with how
languages are changed in time. He was, in effect, exploring the idea of expanding his theory from its narrow confines as an explanation of species change to
language change. That he should have seen the possibilities of his theory of
selection as having wider application than he had originally conceived of it is,
given his extraordinary intellect, not strange. What is odd is that he must have
been writing this passage around the time that he saw Huxley's review of the
Haeckel book and wrote his curiously guarded rejection of his friend's even
wider application of selection theory to developmental change generally.

Darwin and Huxley were not alone in toying with the idea that selection
theory might have wider application. More than a decade after Huxley's review,
the experimental embryologist Wilhelm Roux published a book with the title
Der Kampf der Theile im Organismus (*The Struggle of the Parts of the Organism*).
What Roux attempted to do in his book was to draw parallels between the
Darwinian notion of competitive interactions between organisms, inter-
organism selection, and intra-organism selection between cells and tissues
resulting in functional adaptations during individual development. Another,
even more striking, move to apply Darwinian selection theory to a seemingly
quite different form of change came about the same time from the philosopher
William James.

A graduate in medicine from Harvard University, James became one of the
most significant philosophers advancing the cause of the new science of psychology in the United States. And it is difficult to overstate the influence of the
writings of Herbert Spencer in the United States of the 1860s and 1870s on
thinking in the infant social sciences, especially on economics and psychology.
Thus it was that James began his intellectual life as a follower of Spencer.

But as we have seen, Spencer's philosophical system was based on Lamarckian evolutionary theory, and Lamarckian theory was instructional, not selectionist. The organism was the passive responder to environmental events. In his magisterial account of the effect of evolutionary theory on theories of mind and behaviour, the historian Robert Richards shows how the switch in James from a Spencerian to a Darwinian viewpoint was closely bound up with the resolution of a psychological crisis in the young philosopher's life. The problem for James was that Spencer's view was dominated by the subservience of the organism to the environment. He quotes as follows from James' papers: "My quarrel with Spencer is not that he makes *nothing* of the glaring and patent fact of subjective interests which cooperate with the environment in moulding intelligence. These interests form a true spontaneity and justify the refusal of a priori schools to admit that mind was pure, passive receptivity".

Appalled by the passive determinism of Spencer's analysis, James turned to the Darwinian model where selection of variants are at least partly initially independent of the selection pressures of the environment, thus implying a degree of autonomy and intra-organism determination of evolutionary change. This, to repeat the point yet again, is the central difference between the Lamarckian/Spencerian theory and that of Darwin: Darwin causally decoupled variation from selection. If the Darwinian view is then applied to some aspect of the internal workings of the mind, especially that relating to creative thought, then we have a theory that gives due causal regard to some aspect of the internal workings of that mind rather than its passive response to the world in which that mind exists. This is exactly what James did in an 1880 paper entitled "Great Men, Great Thoughts, and the Environment". James wrote as follows:

> "Now I affirm that the relation of the visible environment to the great man is in the main exactly what it is to the 'variation' in the Darwinian philosophy. It chiefly adopts or rejects, preserves or destroys, in short, *selects*. And whenever it adopts and preserves the great man, it becomes modified by his influence in an entirely original and peculiar way. He acts as a ferment, and changes its constitution, just as the advent of a new zoological species changes the faunal and floral equilibrium of the region in which it appears". (italics in the original)

The "great man" is the creative thinker, and what James was doing was internalizing Darwinian theory by explicitly applying the theory to the way thinking, creative thinking, changes:

> "And I can easily show that throughout the whole extent of those mental departments which are highest, which are most characteristically human, Spencer's law is violated at every step; and that, as a matter of fact, the new conceptions, emotions, and active tendencies which evolve are originally *produced* in the shape of random images, fancies, accidental outbirths of spontaneous variation in the functional activity of the excessively unstable human brain, which the outer environment simply confirms or

refutes, preserves or destroys, – *selects*, in short, just as it selects morphological and social variations due to molecular accidents of an analogous sort".

Just a year later, Huxley returned to his own earlier thoughts on the extension of Darwinian theory to account for within organism change, this time, like William James, specifically to thought: "The struggle for existence holds as much in the intellectual as in the physical world. A theory is a species of thinking, and its right to exist is coextensive with its power of resisting extinction by its rivals". Thus, in the writings of both James and Huxley, was born what later would be called evolutionary epistemology, the notion that individuals acquire knowledge by way of internalized processes of variation and selection.

James was explicit in his rejection of within-organism evolutionary processes as being causal in the production of learning in the "lower strata" of the mind, that is, in "the entire strata of habit and association by contiguity". It fell to the psychologist James Mark Baldwin in the 1890s to extend Darwinian selection theory to associative learning: "The individual's learning processes are by a method of 'trial and error' which illustrates 'natural' in the form of 'functional selection'" wrote Baldwin, for whom the only acceptable form of psychology was one built wholly upon a theoretical basis compatible with, if not directly derived from, Darwinian evolutionary thinking. Baldwin was the first evolutionary psychologist, the first developmental psychologist to describe cognitive development as a series of stages of knowledge gain each different from that of adult cognition, the first memeticist, and the psychologist who coined the phrase "organic selection". In one of his final works on psychology he wrote:

> "The problem of 'educability', of 'profiting by experience', has been attacked throughout the entire range of organic forms, with striking harmony of results, summed up by the phrase 'trail and error'. From the infusoria's limited modification of behaviour to the child's extended education, it is found that all learning is by a process of strenuous, excessive, and varied discharges. Through such discharges adjustive modifications occur. ... It takes place in a manner to which the Darwinian conception of selection is strictly applicable."

More than anyone else, Baldwin was responsible for placing psychology firmly within the biological sciences. In analysing associative learning within the causal framework of Darwinian selection theory, he extended the scope of Darwin's ideas to what is one of the oldest and most widespread forms of learning.

Thus it is that the differences voiced by Heraclitus and Parmenides in ancient Greece about flux and constancy were, at the start of the 20th century, reconciled by the notion that while change is universal and present in a number of different forms in living systems, it might be possible to analyse and understand change, however it manifests itself, within a single, constant explanatory framework. Some one hundred years later, in 2007, in a brief essay considering the contrast between physics and biology in the importance ascribed to the search for all-encompassing laws and theories, Evelyn Fox Keller too considered the possibility of natural selection as being the only candidate for such a role within biology. Here, then, is the possibility of a general theory in biology which stands in contradiction to Rutherford's assertion that those of us who are not physicists are mere collectors of stamps.

Chapter 3

The expansion of selection theory

Two hundred years after the birth of Darwin, and one hundred and fifty years since the first publication of his *Origin of Species*, it is almost impossible to overstate the importance of the work of this self-effacing and rather reclusive man. In providing an explanation of the transformation of species, and of the common origin of all forms of life on our planet, Darwin gave us both the most powerful argument in the history of thought for an ontological materialism, sometimes referred to as materialism or physicalism, that denies the special creation either of the world we live in or of ourselves, as well as the basis for understanding most of what we now take as commonplace phenomena and forms of study in the biological sciences. In a recent paper celebrating Darwin's enduring legacy, the evolutionist Kevin Padian listed ten ideas or areas of study in which Darwin's work remains fundamental. These include the concept of a single "tree of life", which he first tentatively sketched whilst on the Beagle voyage, the basis for schemes of genealogical classification, the geographical distribution of species, the material basis for adaptations, the coevolution of species' characteristics, what he termed "the economy of nature" which we now know as the science of ecology, and, above all, the notion of natural selection, which was the first scientific explanation of change. Darwin's theory of evolution was, in fact, the first scientific theory for which the notion of flux was central, and predated by decades the astrophysical concept of change in the form of the big bang, the subsequent expansion of the universe, and the appearance of the chemical elements. Contrary to Rutherford's dictum, here was an important instance of biology showing the way for physicists.

Whilst meticulous in his empiricism, one of Darwin's problems, as he saw it, was that evolution occurs so slowly that direct observation of species' change could not occur. The detractors of the notion of evolution, of course, took this to be good reason to dismiss the idea altogether. However, in the early part of the 21st century, we now know that the criticism of the inadequacy of indirect evidence no longer has any potency in the light of what has, in the last 30 or so years, been directly recorded. This is not an appropriate place for an exhaustive review of species change of the kind that Darwin set out to explain. What follows, therefore, is a brief account of some of the more recent findings that would likely have astonished Darwin himself both because of the briefness in time over which such change can occur, and the directness of the observations.

An example that might have delighted Darwin the most comes from recent studies of what in his Beagle journal he described as "a most singular group of finches" which were first described (and drawn) by him when the expedition visited the Galapagos islands. (It should be noted that the Beagle journal was published in May of 1839, some two and a half years after Darwin's return to England, and after he had had much time to consider what he had observed and arrived at the theory of evolution by natural selection. It is possible that at least some of the journal contents were edited, written, and drawn, with the hindsight of someone who had devised the theory after the voyage was completed.) Some fourteen species of finch occupy specific niches on the different islands, the most prominent features of their differences lying in the sizes and shapes of their beaks, such differences relating to the foods they eat. Peter and Rosemary Grant have studied Darwin's finches for over thirty years and recorded their findings in both the technical literature and in a recent accessible book. The Grants have recorded changes in beak size and form across single generations, occupying a time span of just one or two years, as a function of marked shifts in climate from year to year; and over a thirty year period they have documented repeated character displacement as a result of interspecific competition when new competitor species arrived on different islands, and hybridization (not usually thought to be important in animal evolution) arising from chance occurrences, such as the sudden death of a parent, amongst other microevolutionary changes, all being predicted by the appropriate population genetic models. The striking point of the Grants' work is the rapidity of such phenotypic changes when compared to Darwin's estimates of the many thousands of years needed for such effects to occur.

About the same time as the Grants began their work in the Galapagos, John Endler started to record the power of selection to drive microevolutionary change amongst populations of small fish called guppies. He first set up experimental streams in his laboratory, some populated just with guppies, and others with the guppies and other species that are guppy-eaters. He knew that guppies can change colour in order to blend with the background and so be less conspicuous to predators. Endler showed significant microevolutionary changes in body colours under the predatory versus non-predatory selection conditions in about ten guppy generations, covering a period of less than a year. He then extended his observations to natural populations in the wild, which he relocated to areas of high and low predation pressures, and was able to confirm his laboratory findings showing phenotypic changes in free-living populations within the same rapid time span.

In 1997 a report in *Nature* detailed changes in the morphology, especially in limb structure, in populations of *Anolis* lizards introduced onto previously lizard-free Bahamian islands from a nearby island. Within about ten years, clear morphological changes evolved, which showed strong relationships to the predominant forms of vegetation on each of the islands. Similarly rapid microevolutionary change has been reported for egg size in fish, and seed structure and size in plants on Canadian Pacific islands, the latter instance being an especially interesting demonstration of what had previously been a theoretical notion called the Founder effect – the phenomenon whereby new colonies of a species may quickly diverge away from the parent population as a result of the founding organisms being atypical examples of the parent population. A very recent study, using appropriately modern molecular chemical methodology of sequencing microchondrial DNA showed how selection pressures will even override theoretically expected gene flow in allopatric and sympatric populations of snakes which mimic the phenotypes of dangerous species.

One possible response by creationists to such evolution observed directly is that it is only microevolutionary change that has been recorded – changes, albeit rapid changes, within a species. But that is not the same thing as macroevolution observed – that is, actual speciation. Conventional Darwinian theory, or neoDarwinism, considers microevolution to be inextricably linked to macroevolution, though there is not universal agreement about this. Hence even some evolutionists, those who do not believe microevolution is causally related to speciation, may not be convinced by evidence of species transformation based only on microevolutionary change. Such scepticism can now be countered by observed speciation in ring species.

Ernst Mayr, in the 1940s, declared that ring species are the "perfect demonstration of speciation". Ring species are formed when geographical dispersal drives divergence between neighbouring populations of an originally single species, such divergence increasing with increasing dispersal away from the original parent population to the point where the original species has branched into two separate species which, were they to meet, would not interbreed. Such speciation could only be observed if the divergent, descendent, populations do meet, and this would only happen if the successive geographical dispersion takes the form of an encircling of some physical barrier – hence the phrase ring species. In effect, the migrating populations fan out around some obstacle, and the descendent populations then meet when the ring is closed on the side opposite to that of the original divergence.

Until just a few years ago, actual observations of ring species have always been incomplete – the ring has never been a perfect one. That is no longer the case, as shown by the work of Darren Irwin and his colleagues. Two species of warbler song birds exist in central Siberia. They do not interbreed, and have a number of morphological differences, the most striking being in their song structures. Playback experiments show conclusively that the members of these different Siberian species do not recognize or respond to the song of the other species. However, sampling the behaviour of neighbouring populations of each species as they encircle the high-altitude desert of the Tibetan plateau, where no warblers live, adjacent populations of warblers gradually diverge away from the two separate northern species and become, south of the Tibetan plateau, a single species with the same song structure. The behavioural divergence is supported by molecular evidence, based on both mitochondrial and nuclear DNA, of structural divergence in the ring.

These are extraordinary findings, combining as they do significant phenotypic changes and accompanying alterations at a molecular genetic level. In the context of deep geological time, the Himalayas and the Tibetan plateau are relatively recently formed, and hence provided Irwin and his colleagues with an ideal opportunity to study a complete case of ring speciation in birds that could not survive at high altitudes, but which could, and did, gradually disperse around the obstacle presented by the plateau. Here is as close an account as one can get of speciation being observed.

The rise of genetics and the near death of Darwinism

Darwin, of course, had no idea as to the mechanisms by which inheritance occurs. Less than twenty years after his death the work of Mendel became known and the new science of genetics was born. One immediate result was the near death of Darwin's notion of natural selection as the most important causal force in speciation. Part of the problem lay in the conceptual chaos that acceptance of the notion of evolutionary change resulted in – replacing a conceptualization of fixed creation with one of constant shifting and change created a host of further questions and uncertainties. For example, are there any consistencies in the pattern of organic change in time, people asked – usually this took the form of asking whether there is any form of progressivism in the changes dictated by evolutionary forces? How does such change relate to the more easily discerned changes that occur in development, this being an especially pressing question given, as noted in the previous chapter, the prominence in 19th century biology of the study of embryology. Then there was the question of the rate of evolution. Did it occur gradually, as Darwin repeatedly insisted, or in rapid bursts. Even T.H. Huxley, Darwin's loyal supporter, suggested in his famous review of Darwin's *Origin* that Darwin was in error with his repeated use of the aphorism "*natura non facit saltum*" whereas "nature does make jumps now and then, and a recognition of the fact is of no small importance" wrote Huxley. And, of course, the biggest question of all: how does this apply to our own species, not just in terms of our origins, but as regards to those aspects of ourselves that we like to think make us unique, namely our mental powers and our culture.

As noted in the previous chapter, Spencer had anticipated many of these questions by adopting Lamarck's incorrect theory of evolution and applying it on a conceptually massive scale: a form of universal Lamarckianism, but one presented to a world which in the main rejected the notion of evolution. Darwin's work, by contrast, especially his *Origin,* changed everything. Evolution, at least amongst biologists, came increasingly to be accepted. The evidence for species change, albeit it indirect, was overwhelming. But that acceptance led to a host of questions including those set out in the previous paragraph, and the failure to find easy and agreed answers resulted in a curious conceptual mixture which rejected the seemingly intangible aspect of Darwin's theory, natural selection, and a concentration for a time on that aspect of his theory that could indeed be seen, variation. The discovery of Mendel's work resulted in a corresponding shift in emphasis for understanding evolution towards what was then believed to be the sole cause of variation and how it is transmitted, namely the genes. "Variation, whatever may be its cause is the essential phenomenon of evolution. Variation, in fact, is evolution" wrote William Bateson, one of the earliest of English geneticists.

Contrary to the implications of Rutherford's dictum, there is a strong case to be made that genetics was the most successful science of the 20th century. The work of an obscure Moravian monk, Gregor Mendel, during a brief period in the 1850s and 1860s, when discovered some decades later, served as an exemplar as to how the new science of genetics was to be conducted. Mendel had carried out carefully controlled experiments and subjected his results to a quantitative analysis which revealed surprising regularities (too surprising according to some commentators) both in terms of the generation of variation and its inheritance. Subsequent discoveries included the concentration of Mendel's "factors", what came to be known as the genes, on chromosomes, the way in which gene expression can be altered by mutation, the characteristics of cell division in somatic cells and gametes, gene linkage and cross-over, and the dependence of gene expression on the presence of other genes. The most legendary of all advances came in the 1950s with the identification of DNA as the molecular basis of inheritance and the subsequent unravelling of knowledge as to how DNA finds expression in proteins. We now live on a world in which genomics, proteomics and systems biology have come to dominate the sciences that are key to many aspects of human existence, including food production, the fight against diseases, human reproduction and the maintenance of species diversity.

Essential as inheritance is to the process of evolution, as argued in Chapter 1, any account of inheritance framed within mechanism will be awash with differences depending upon which inheritance system is being considered. Genetics itself has been the extraordinarily successful scientific unravelling of the mechanisms of the genes and their translation into specific phenotypic structures. It might have been, and remains, wonderful science. But it cannot give rise to a general biological theory. That requires a process that is substrate neutral, and for which change is absolutely central. Variation is also crucial, but so too is the force that drives changes in variation. Such a process had been discovered by Darwin and then ignored or forgotten in the early boom years of genetics. It was the modern synthesis that restored Darwin's concept of natural selection as central to an understanding of how evolution works, and hence to the restoration of the possibility of general theory in biology.

The modern synthesis arose out of the work of three legendary theorists, R.A. Fisher, J.B.S. Haldane, and Sewell Wright, who in the 1920s and early 1930s, formulated a synthesis between genetics, specifically the genetics of populations of organisms, and Darwin's resurrected concept of natural selection which, acting upon variant individuals of breeding populations, drives changes in the frequencies of genes within populations in time to result in changes in the predominant forms of the individuals making up the breeding population. The synthesis of selection and genetics, expressed by formal mathematical models, thus envisaged evolution as occurring in a two-step process: the generation of variant phenotypes based on genetic mechanisms rich in the capacity to generate variation, and the selection of those variations that result in the greatest levels of fitness usually measured in terms of reproductive success. In the following decades the modern synthesis was advanced by the work of Mayr, Dobzhansky, Simpson, and Julian Huxley amongst others as the explanatory power of the new synthetic theory of evolution was applied to real populations of organisms, their diversification and interactions, and their changing distributions in space and time. The triumph of the modern synthesis was that it achieved a marriage of laboratory science on the one hand with the work of naturalists in the field on the other.

Post-synthesis advances

The centenary of the publication of Darwin's *Origin of Species* was marked by a number of symposia and published works, as was the centenary of Darwin's death in 1882. There was a marked contrast in the mood of these two sets of events. A student of evolutionary biology in the 1950s worked within a self-confident and conceptually united science. Less than a quarter of a century later evolutionary theory had become a fractious and sometimes quite hostile set of different schools of thought. With the advantages of hindsight, some of these can be dismissed as having had almost no impact or importance. Notions of constructivism or structuralism, non-equilibrium thermodynamic theory, and in more recent years complexity theory, have given us very little, all being attempts to cast evolution within physico-chemical terms that have added nothing to the explanatory scope and strength of the theory of evolution. Only complexity and self-organization theory with their emphasis on the notion of evolvability, the potential for the order which characterizes life to emerge from a world of positive entropy, may have something to offer as a "meta-engineering" notion, to borrow Daniel Dennett's phrase, in helping us understand the basic principles of design that characterize all living things. It should be added that most of those floating such ideas were and are convinced Darwinians in the sense that they did not deny Darwin's central notion of the causes of species change.

Virtually all other critics of the modern synthesis stood on the more substantial conceptual grounds that the synthesis, often referred to as neoDarwinism, is incomplete; that there is more, perhaps much more, to evolution than changing gene frequencies in breeding populations driven by natural selection. One such grouping arose from the spectacular growth of knowledge of molecular biology from the mid-1950s onwards. The "beads on a string" conception of genetics had to give way to a much more complicated set of ideas of reactive complexes of molecules smeared across chromosomes that are in constant dynamic interaction with other genes and families of gene types, as well as with the products of genes within the cell. Such molecular complexity gave rise to the idea of evolutionary causes other than selection by the environment acting on phenotypes. Neutral theories postulated the occurrence of random changes in the chemistry of genes that might not initially be sifted and sorted by natural selection because they might not find immediate expression in the phenotype. Sheltered from immediate selection by the environment, such autonomously generated molecular changes might accumulate and become molecular drivers of evolutionary change that occur independently of natural selection. Such neutral theories, and their more active drive theories of the 1980s, were not intrinsically anti-Darwinian, but argued for the incompleteness of neoDarwinism. Complex intracellular events, they argued, are also causal agents in evolution.

Claims of incompleteness also came from at least three other quarters. Ever since Waddington's arguments of half a century ago that there is more to evolution than genetics and selection, developmentalists in particular have pushed the claims for the importance of ontogeny for a full account of evolutionary change. Recent decades have seen "evo-devo" grow to be an accepted addition to evolutionary biology, as exemplified by the work of Jablonka and Lamb discussed in the first chapter of this book. As noted in Chapter 1, Waddington also included what he termed the "exploitive system" alongside the natural selection system, the genetic system and the epigenetic system, for a complete account of evolution. Waddington clearly felt himself unqualified to write much about the exploitive system, describing it in very general terms as "the set of processes by which animals choose and often modify one particular habitat out of the range of environmental possibilities open to them". Ernst Mayr made a similarly broad claim: "A shift into a new niche or adaptive zone is, almost without exception, initiated by a change in behaviour. The other adaptations to the new niche, particularly the structural ones, are acquired secondarily. With habitat and food selection – behavioural phenomena – playing a major role in the shift into new adaptive zones, the importance of behaviour in initiating new evolutionary events is self-evident".

What, however, initiates the change in behaviour? One obvious candidate, of course, is natural selection of genetic modifications that results in changes in central nervous system function and hence alterations in behaviour. In this case, behaviour as an especially dynamic phenotypic trait, enters into the processes of evolution in an entirely conventional way. Another means by which behaviour may become significant in evolutionary terms is by way of cognition, itself a product of evolution (see next chapter), but as a process or set of processes that has a degree of causal autonomy from the principal evolutionary programme, and hence which operates at a level removed from the evolution of species. The idea of cognition entering as a causal process in evolution goes back at least to James Mark Baldwin.

In a rather curious coincidence of timing, the notion that phenotypic plasticity might enter into the evolutionary process was virtually simultaneously put forward by the explicitly Lamarckian palaeontologist Henry Fairfield Osborn and the Darwinians Conway Lloyd Morgan and Baldwin in the years 1895–1896. It was Baldwin, however, who persisted with the claim of phenotypic plasticity, especially learning, as a "new factor in evolution" which 50 years later, long after Baldwin's death, was to become known as the Baldwin effect. What Baldwin suggested was that populations of organisms each of which has the capacity to adapt to specific environmental conditions by means of individual phenotypic plasticity might be able to survive and reproduce in circumstances that would not be favourable to individuals lacking such plasticity until, in the fullness of time, genotypic change in the population would replace such adaptive plasticity by hard-wired, genotypic, adaptations that accommodated the fitness demands of the environment that had previously been supplied by individual plasticity.

The "new factor" was entirely Darwinian in nature, though it superficially resembles a Lamarckian inheritance of acquired character. More importantly, the possibility that Baldwin's "new factor" might sometimes have been a cause in the evolutionary process has never been denied by any evolutionist of significance. What has been questioned is why, if a population of organisms is capable of adapting to environmental demands by way of individual plasticity, cognitively based or otherwise, should there be any selective pressure for changes at a genetic levels to take on the same adaptive role. The Baldwin effect might be theoretically possible, but is causally redundant.

This does not, though, rule out the more general argument that individual plasticity, specifically that residing in different forms of cognition, as being a causal force in evolution. There is tentative empirical data that supports this idea. In the 1980s, A.C. Wilson and his colleagues published a series of studies which showed that both in birds and fish, especially the cichlid fish of Lake Victoria which demonstrate "explosive evolution", there is a positive correlation between brain size and rates of evolution. More recently, Reader and Laland have shown in a meta-analysis of some 1000 journal publications that there is a positive correlation in primates between relative brain size and novel cognitive capacity, including innovative behaviours (behaviours never recorded before in a species), tool use and social learning. These are very indirect indications of a causal relationship between cognitive processes and evolution, but they do in very general terms support the ideas from Baldwin through to Mayr that behaviour in general, especially novel cognitively driven behaviours, may play a causal role in evolution.

More important developments in the theory of evolution, centring upon claims for the incompleteness of the modern synthesis, have arisen around the issue of levels of evolution and levels of selection. Two very different claims for theoretical advances have arisen. The first has its source in Darwin's own work. In one of the chapters of his *Origin of Species*, Darwin had considered the problems that his theory of evolution had to deal with, one of which lay in the existence of sterile castes in some species of insect. Why, he wondered, were there insects that displayed wonderful behavioural and morphological adaptations, "and yet, from being sterile ... they cannot propagate their kind"? In attempting an answer, Darwin had strayed from one of the central conceptions of his theory, which is that it is the individual organism that displays variation, that it is the individual that survives or does not, and it is the individual that reproduces or fails to do so. In the case of sterile insect castes, however, he, probably unwittingly, shifted focus from the individual to the group: "... if such insects had been social, and it had been profitable to the community that a number should have been annually born capable of work, but incapable of procreation, I can see no especial difficulty in this having been affected through natural selection". What Darwin had done was switch from the general tenor of his work in which the individual is the unit of selection, to use a 20th century evolutionary phrase, to what in the 1960s and 1970s would be called a group selection argument; the adaptations of sterile castes had evolved because they are good for the group, "profitable to the community", not the individual. It was simply not part of the consciousness of 19th century biology to see this as an important conceptual shift. But a century later, the issue became central to the theory of evolution, especially as the synthesis has been grounded in Darwin's more usual assumption that it is the individual that is the unit of selection.

Despite this prevalent assumption, there had been some lapses into explicit group selectionist claims. The ethologist Konrad Lorenz, for example, had made frequent reference to "the good of the species", though always ambiguously because it was never clear whether he was adopting a true group selectionist position, or merely asserting that if individuals survive then that is to the good of the species to which they belong. The Scottish biologist V.C. Wynne-Edwards, however, in the early 1960s offered an explicit group selectionist account, and one which proved popular amongst biologists, when providing an explanation for the many behaviours of animals that appeared to reduce the fitness of individuals displaying the behaviour, to the advantage of others; what came to be referred to as altruistic behaviours and their selection "for the good of the group". It was around this time that biologists, or at least some of them, were becoming aware of general systems theory, of the need to understand the relationships of complex entities, "problems of organized complexity at all levels" in the words of van Bertalanffy; sexually reproducing social multicellular organisms have genes inside cells which make up organs and organ systems, which comprise an individual organism that is a part of a social group which interacts with other social groups of the same or different species depending upon the wider ecological characteristics of that organism. In the face of such complexity, what should be the focus of theoretical attention? Specifically, what are the units of variation and selection, and what are evolving?

For many biologists, the seminal work with regard to these questions was done in the 1960s by W.D. Hamilton in an exercise of groundbreaking mathematical modelling, and then expanded into wider theoretical terms by G.C. Williams. What Hamilton showed was the Darwinian notion of the centrality of the individual organism, his lapse into group selectionist thinking with regard to sterile insect castes notwithstanding, needed to be bolstered by taking genetic relationships into account. Altruistic behaviours, which lay at the heart of this thinking, is displayed, in the overwhelming majority of cases, between animals that are closely genetically related. When one animal behaves in a manner that potentially reduces its fitness, by threatening its survival, for example by attempting to distract a predator with a warning display, the beneficiaries of this behaviour are usually close genetic kin. Thus to individual selection was added the notion of kin selection, and individual fitness was subsumed under the wider notion of inclusive fitness. What really matters is not the survival of the individual, but the survival of genes: the survival of genes is very strongly determined by the fitness of each individual, as in the original Darwinian conception, but is significantly supplemented by the survival of close genetic relatives. At the heart of the complex mathematical modelling was a relatively simple notion that came to be known as Hamilton's rule. Every altruistic behaviour has, in principle, measurable costs for the altruist and benefits for the recipient. A behaviour will evolve if the cost of the behaviour to the donor is outweighed by the benefits to the recipient, those benefits being weighted by the degree of genetic relatedness between donor and recipient.

In his very influential book published shortly after Hamilton's papers, G.C. Williams presented a broader account of what became known, after the title of a popular review of such thinking by Richard Dawkins, as selfish gene theory. Williams drew a clear distinction between an adapted group or population and a group or population of adapted organisms; the former is always vulnerable to invasion and take-over by selfish mutant individuals whose adaptations increase individual fitness without regard to the well-being of the group as a whole. Thus while a Wynne-Edwards type of explanation of co-operative and altruistic behaviour might hold in a few instances, in the fullness of geological time group selection must inevitably succumb to individual selection, and at the heart of individual selection is not survival of the individual but survival of the genes of that individual. No matter how complex biological systems might be, in developmental, social, ecological or any other terms, "the real goal" of such complexity, wrote Williams, is "the continuity of the dependent germ plasm". As Dawkins was later to express it, "all adaptations are for the preservation of DNA; DNA itself just *is*"; or as E.O. Wilson put it, "the organism is only DNA's way of making more DNA".

Selfish gene theory did not deny in any way that selection might operate on any of many organizational levels, including the whole organism; nor did it deny the essential role of processes such as development. What it did assert is that genes are what are being selected. Parenthetically, it might be noted that the application of selfish gene theory to humans, in what Ullica Segerstråle rather understatingly called the sociobiology debate, led to one of the most bitter disputes of 20th century science.

Dawkins and Williams later developed an ontologically less odd form of the notion of genes as the primary unit of selection for neoDarwinism in the form of replicator theory. A replicator, of which genes are the principal example, are able to copy themselves with a high degree of accuracy. Gametes are never replicas of their parent cells, neither are cells resulting from mitotic division, nor are the offspring of sexually reproducing organisms replicas of their parents. The structure of DNA, however, is such as to allow genes to make accurate copies of themselves, and this is what they do; and if different replicators overlap in terms of utilizing conditions that favour replication, they will compete with one another. There is no intentional agency implied; replicators copy themselves because of their chemical composition, and will compete with other replicators in order to do so. Some replicators are directly exposed to the conditions of selection; others, as a result of the competitive circumstances, evolve a protective cloak, the phenotype, itself not a replicator, but able to assist the replicators contained within themselves. Dawkins referred to the phenotype as the vehicle for replicators. Others, notably David Hull, disliked the connotation of passivity in the word vehicle, and preferred interactor, a word much closer in meaning to Waddington's operator as his description in the 1950s of the relationship between phenotypes and the genes that they carry; the words interactor or operator offer a vision of the phenotype as having a causal force in its own right, which assertion is inherent in theories that assert that development, cognition and culture are active causes in the overall process of evolution. In the rest of this book, the word interactor will be used when referring to the phenotype in the context of replicator theory.

Another (powerful according to some) theory appeared in the 1970s which shared the general criticism of neoDarwinism as excluding causal forces outside of selection and population genetics. This was the punctuated equilibrium theory of Eldredge and Gould. More than any other theoretical development, punctuated equilibrium theory came closer than anything else to a radical departure from neoDarwnism. In advocating stasis, at least for some species, over long periods of time, followed by rapid transitions to new species, the Eldredge and Gould theory departed from the Darwinian conception of universal gradualness; and differed significantly in divorcing microevolution from macroevolution. However, as Gould wrote in his very fine 1982 review of what punctuated equilibrium theory sought to achieve, it "is larger than the independence of macroevolution. It is not just macroevolution vs. microevolution, but the question of whether evolutionary theory itself must be reformulated as a hierarchical structure with several levels – of which macroevolution is but one – bound together by extensive feedback, to be sure, but each with a legitimate independence … Genes, bodies, demes, species, and clades are all legitimate individuals in some situations … and our linguistic habit of equating individuals with bodies is a convention only. Each type of individual can be a unit of selection in its own right. Natural selection operating on bodies will not encompass all of evolution. Genes are units of selection in the hypothesis of selfish DNA …; demes are units in Sewall Wright's shifting balance theory … Species represent one level among many; evolutionary theory needs this expansion."

Often portrayed by his critics as an enemy of neoDarwinism, Gould, in fact, was an advocate of an expanded form of evolutionary theory in the form of a universal Darwinism on a scale at least as large as that offered by Campbell (see next chapter), Dawkins, Dennett and others. The difference between Gould and many of his opponents was that he offered hierarchy as an explicit theoretical structure to account for what Herbert Simon called the architecture of complexity. This is an issue that will occupy much of the succeeding chapters of this book, especially the last. Suffice it to say here that one of the most important post-synthesis developments was the realization that Darwin's evolutionary theory needed to be expanded not merely by way of genetic considerations but through the application of the process of selection to multiple levels in order to achieve a real synthesis of von Bertalanffy's "problem of organized complexity at all levels".

Odling-Smee and his colleagues' conception of niche construction and ecological inheritance has consistently taken complexity into account by applying the theory at least three levels, in terms of population-genetic processes (such as the effects of the evolution of web spinning on the evolution of specific anatomical features such as limb structures), information acquiring ontogenetic structures (for instance the use of tools by woodpecker finches changing selection pressures on beak structure), and cultural processes (for example the effects of dairy farming on the evolution of lactose tolerance in humans). Explicit in many of the diagrams illustrating their ideas, and implicit in their writings is a loose adherence to some form of hierarchical thinking. Thus does niche construction theory encompass more than a single important theoretical contribution to the modern synthesis.

Whilst an entire chapter of this book will be taken up with this issue, for completeness here it must be noted that culture in general, and human culture specifically, is also a candidate for inclusion in the argument that the modern synthesis was a causally incomplete account of evolution.

In his paper on Universal Darwinism given at the Cambridge University conference marking the centenary of Darwin's death, Richard Dawkins conceded the possibility of selection operating on multiple levels, but noted that "Darwinian Law", in the form of the explanation of adaptive complexity by way of the process. or processes, of selection, is likely to hold wherever in the universe life exists. Here, then, is a truly universal Darwinism. If he is correct, then selection is a theoretical notion to rival anything that Rutherford's physics has delivered by way of explaining the nature of the living world. It certainly warrents a slightly more detailed examination than has been given it so far in this book.

The essence of selection theory

For Darwin, natural selection was the cause of adaptations and species transformation because of differences resulting from those variations in survival and reproduction. Beyond that he provided no detailed analysis of the concept of selection. As has already been mentioned with regard to the likes of Huxley, Roux, James and Baldwin, and as will be considered in the next section of this chapter as well as in later chapters, the notion of selection being an explanation for change in spheres other than species transformation, has not been uncommon. Yet until relatively recently, little detailed attention was paid to the concept of selection itself, and whether its application to forms of change other than speciation meant that there was communality of causal structure in its multiple instantiation – in the language of Chapter 1, whether the processes involved in selection are the same, even though they are embodied in different mechanisms.

Broadly speaking, there have been two ways of dealing the "expansion" of selection theory. One was to consider Darwin's usage, and that of the neoDarwinists, as being archetypal and one that should be applied when it is considered appropriate with as little alteration and expansion as possible to other forms of change. An example of this approach has been that of memetics as a form of the application of selection theory to the understanding of cultural change (see Chapter 5). The other has been to try and develop a more universal form of the theory, a search for "general selection processes" in David Hull's words, which can be applied to all forms of change caused by the operation of selection. It is the latter that is being considered here.

It was the psychologist B.F. Skinner who wrote that "Darwin discovered the role of selection, a kind of causality very different from the push-pull mechanisms of science up to that time" that difference being the reason, Skinner suggested, why Darwin's theory appeared so late in the history of thought. It is debateable, at the very least, whether "push-pull" mechanisms of causation are absent from selection. They surely are not. But the way that they are put together in the selection process does indeed make selection different from other forms of change. The immediacy of instruction or association is insufficient for selection as a process: selection has a necessary temporal dimension that introduces an historical component to the process.

In a seminal paper of 1970 R.C. Lewontin argued that Darwin's conception of selection as the force driving evolution "embodies three principles" (in laying out his principles, Lewontin was applying his ideas in the first instance to evolution of species as classically conceived by Darwin, hence the language he used): The first is the principle of variation, in which different individuals in a population have different morphologies, physiologies, and behaviours; the second is the principle of differential fitness, in which different phenotypes have different rates of survival and reproduction in different environments; the third is the principle of heritable fitness, in which there is a correlation between the parents and offspring in the contribution of each to future generations. "It is important to note" wrote Lewontin "a certain generality in the principles. No particular mechanism of inheritance is specified, but only a correlation in fitness between parent and offspring. The population would evolve whether the correlation between parent and offspring arose from Mendelian, cytoplasmic, or cultural inheritance".

In 1989, Darden and Cain published a somewhat more formal analysis of selection theories, in which they presented selection theories as having two aspects. The one is what will be referred to here as their structural features, which correspond closely to Lewontin's principles. The other is the teleological aspect of selection theory; selection processes must be invoked as causal when the product has the appearance of being designed. Mayr once remarked that Darwin had solved the problem of teleology. By that he meant that Darwin had shown how the seeming goal-directed nature of adaptations as moulded by the effects of natural selection are a consequence of the history of successive selection events. The ancient idea of Aristotle's final cause, which subsequent religious doctrines attributed to the wisdom of an omniscient Creator, could now be explained not by such *a priori* causation, but by the scientifically acceptable *a posteriori* causation of the repeated action of selection. Darden and Cain were quite explicit in their claim: "Selection theories solve adaptation problems by specifying a process through which one thing comes to be adapted to another thing". Selection is a process that has an effect, and that effect is beneficial in establishing a relationship of fit between "one thing" forming an adaptive relationship with some other thing. Darden and Cain argue that the "language of 'benefit' is desirable for constructing an abstraction that can apply at different levels in an organizational hierarchy within an evolutionary theory context". This is an important point. If selection theory is to have any generality, then it must be possible to account for selection occurring at different organizational levels, and as will be apparent in later chapters of this book, that organization is usually conceived as being hierarchical in nature. The obvious implication is that the concept of "benefit" must then be applicable at these multiple levels, "benefit" being measured by conservation over time.

The issue of design, end-directedness and final cause – adaptation in the parlance of biology – is fraught with difficulties that go back, as mentioned above, thousands of years to ancient Greek philosophy, and which were brought to prominence in the 19th century by the English theologian William Paley. Not least is the problem as to how certain claims can ever be made that some feature of a phenotype is indeed an adaptation, and as such adds to the fitness of that phenotype. It might be noted that Lewontin himself has been at the centre of recent controversy surrounding the concept of adaptation. One way of resolving the difficulty is to move away from definitions dependent on demonstrations of fitness, which is seldom shown, much less measured quantitatively, and towards the notion that adaptations are products of a specific process. This process is what comprises the structural features of the selection process.

Darden and Cain's structural features that selection theory must have closely resemble those of Lewontin. The first is variation among a set of entities, all sharing an environment with the critical factors that provide a context for the interaction of those entities with those specific features of the environment. This provides the context for understanding the notion of "one thing", something within the varying entities, that forms an adaptive relationship with some "other thing", which is some aspect or aspects of the environment. The second is the interaction itself between the entities and the environment. Because they show variation, different entities will interact differently with the same features of the environment. The result of the interaction in the first instance is change which will be short-range with some entities showing "benefit" whilst others "suffer". Such subjective terminology will be translated into measurable effects such as endurance in time – some entities will be perpetuated in time, and others will not. Such short-range changes will then result in medium-range effects, such as differences in reproduction, and even longer-range effects such as alterations in lineages of the entities.

There is one other feature of Darden and Cain's analysis of selection that needs emphasizing. This is that in addition to variation and interaction, the varying entities must interact with some shared features of the world. A similar point had been made a few years earlier by Elliott Sober, who noted that if two populations at opposite ends of the universe differ in their rates of reproduction, there is no sense in which they could be argued as having evolved relative to one another if they have not been subject to common causal influences in the environment. In other words, variation and interaction must occur within a shared environment.

In a more recent analysis of selection theory, Hull, Langman and Glenn provide a very similar analysis to Darden and Cain. For them selection theory must specify variation ("if there is no variation, then there are no alternatives to select among"), replication (in the form of iteration or repetition), and environmental interaction (in which the varying entities are affected by the conditions of the environment, and now with niche construction in mind, also act to alter the environment with which they interact). For Hull and his colleagues, selection is defined as "repeated cycles of replication, variation, and environmental interaction so structured that environmental interaction causes replication to be differential".

Selection, then, is a process that leads to the design of living forms; and it is a process of specific structure in the form of a continuous cyclical generation of variation, the interaction of the variants with the environment, including alterations of that environment, and the conservation through replication of some of the variants, including the factors that cause the variation, the replicators, and their embodiment in phenotypic form, the interactors. This is a highly abstract characterization of the selection process, but abstract is what it must be if it is to serve as a general theory of design change that goes beyond Darwin's theory of species transformation.

The expansion of selection theory outside of species transformation

The Austrian physicist and mathematician Ernst Mach had wide philosophical interests, including a keen concern as to how scientific and individual knowledge is gained. Like Spencer, he believed that the adjustments of our thoughts and knowledge in the light of individual experience is a continuation of the process of evolution by which species are transformed. For Mach this was not merely a vague analogy, but an expression of a universal process. And unlike Spencer, the process he favoured was close conceptually to Darwin's notion of what drives the transformation of species rather than that espoused by Lamarck. In his inaugural lecture on being appointed a Professor of the history and theory of inductive science at the university of Vienna in 1895, Mach's theme was "on the part played by accident in invention and discovery". Contrary to the view that all "problems are held to be soluble and fundamentally intelligible on the first appearance of success", it was Mach's opinion that knowledge is a process of gradual accumulation, a hard won achievement carved out of continuous practice and use: "The majority of the inventions made in the early stages of civilization, including language, writing, money, and the rest, could not have been the product of deliberate methodical reflexion (sic) for the simple reason that no idea of their value and significance could have been had except from their practical use". This is a criticism of the empiricist epistemology outlined in the previous chapter. Knowledge may have its beginnings in the sensory surfaces, though there is more than a hint in Mach's thinking of a belief in the existence of innate knowledge. More to his point, though, Mach was saying that knowledge may begin with the senses but this is not enough. Knowledge also begins with doing, and pondering on the consequences of action. Half a century later the psychologist Jean Piaget made the same point when he avowed that "in the beginning was the response", a view which will be taken up in the following chapter. Mach's was a similar point. A human being, and it was humans that Mach was speaking of, makes something, an artefact, or a method, and then ponders on what that artefact or method achieves, and how that can be altered and improved on: "But more is required for the development of *inventions*. More extensive chains of images are necessary here, the excitation by mutual contact of widely different trains of ideas, a more powerful, more manifold, and richer connexion of the contents of memory, a more powerful and impressionable psychical life, heightened by use."

A purely analytical approach, however, is not enough. What Mach referred to as "accidental circumstances", and the comprehension of how those accidental circumstances can be incorporated into the invention of new ideas, is essential to the growth of knowledge. "In such cases it is a psychical accident, an intellectual experience, as distinguished from a physical accident, to which the person owes his discovery". Mach ended his lecture with a reference to his hero Newton and how, when questioned as to his method of work, replied that "he was wont to ponder again and again on a subject". Scientists and artists alike recommend persistent labour which affords "opportunity for the interposition of advantageous accidents" and the gradual relegation to the background of all things that are inappropriate: "then from the teeming, swelling host of fancies which a free and high-flown imagination calls forth, suddenly that particular form arises to the light which harmonizes perfectly with the ruling idea, mood, or design. *Then it is that which has resulted slowly as the result of a gradual selection, appears as if it were the outcome of a deliberate act of creation.* Thus are to be explained the statements of Newton, Mozart, Richard Wagner, and others, when they say that thoughts, melodies, and harmonies had poured in upon them, and that they had simply retained the right ones."

Mach was making an almost identical point to that of William James of 1880, and both were followed by a succession of others, all mining a similar notion of the growth of knowledge. Prominent amongst these was the philosopher of science, Karl Popper. First published in 1934, his *Logic of Scientific Discovery* argued that what defines science and makes it different from pseudosciences like psychoanalysis is the condition of falsifiability: the importance of being able to specify the conditions under which a theory can be tested and refuted. The condition of falsifiability was for Popper the selective process by means of which scientific knowledge grows: "the growth of knowledge proceeds from old problems to new problems, by means of conjectures and refutations" was how he put it in his, ironically, Herbert Spencer lecture delivered in Oxford in 1961. In that lecture he formulated a more general theory of knowledge as follows:

> "All this may be expressed by saying that the growth of our knowledge is the result of a process closely resembling what Darwin called 'natural selection'; that is, *the natural selection of hypotheses*: our knowledge consists, at every moment, of those hypotheses which have shown their (comparative) fitness by surviving so far in their

struggle for existence; a competitive struggle which eliminates those hypotheses which are unfit.

This interpretation may be applied to animal knowledge, pre-scientific knowledge, and to scientific knowledge. What is peculiar to scientific knowledge is this: that the struggle for existence is made harder by the conscious and systematic criticism of our theories. Thus, while animal knowledge and pre-scientific knowledge grow mainly through the elimination of those holding the unfit hypotheses, scientific criticism often makes our theories perish in our stead, eliminating our mistaken beliefs before such beliefs lead to our own elimination."

In that same lecture, Popper went on to say that while what he was saying makes use of metaphors, he was not merely speaking metaphorically: "The theory of knowledge which I wish to propose is a largely Darwinian theory of the growth of knowledge. From the amoeba to Einstein, the growth of knowledge is always the same: we try to solve our problems, and to obtain, by a process of elimination, something approaching adequacy in our tentative solutions."

The evolutionary development of science by way of a selection process was an approach subsequently taken up by others, like Stephen Toulmin. But it was the philosopher of science, David Hull, who pursued this idea most thoroughly and in a detail that was far in advance of the vague stances of the likes of Mach and Popper. Hull's views, broadly speaking, come in three parts. The first is an analysis of science as a system of ideas that evolves by way of an explicitly stated set of processes; the second is a careful evaluation of the disanalogies between evolution as traditionally understood, and the evolution of scientific knowledge; the third is a consideration of the complexity of the selection process operating within a science. Hull was aware that a truly general theory based on selection had to be based on a conceptualization that freed itself from traditional Darwinian and neoDarwinian entities of genes, organisms, demes, populations and species. He opted for the Dawkins/Williams framework of replicator theory as the basis for a substrate-neutral account of selection, as outlined in the previous section of this chapter. Thus, a replicator is an entity that passes on its structure largely intact across successive replications; and an interactor as an entity that interacts as a "cohesive whole" with its environment such that the interaction causes replication to be differential. Selection, Hull defined, as "a process in which differential extinction and proliferation of interactors *cause* the differential perpetuation of the replicators that produced them". The resultant entity is a lineage "that persists indefinitely through time either in the same or an altered state as a result of replication".

Hull was less than explicit as to the source(s) of variation, and the manner in which variable replicators give rise to variant interactors in some way analogous to the manner in which genes by a complex cascade of development result in variable phenotypes. It is easy enough to envisage in rough outline that Hull was addressing conceptual evolution within scientific communities in which the replicators are concepts, hypotheses or theories; the interactors are scientists or whole research teams testing those concepts by way of experiments and observation; and the results of those tests is a selection of some of those concepts and the discarding of others that fail the selection process. However, which precisely is what, and how variation arises, remains, twenty years on, work that needs to be done.

In two respects, though, Hull was far more explicit than any of his predecessors. The first was in paying attention to the disanalogies between biological and conceptual evolution. Some disanalogies that commentators have raised he quite rightly dismissed. Supposed rates of evolution are one such. The range of rates of evolutionary change in biological systems is enormous, and can be very rapid in viruses; by comparison, the changes in conceptual systems are approximately intermediate by comparison with evolution of organisms. Claims about sizes of replicators and interactors and the extent to which they are particulate are also easy to dismiss, as well as the assertion that conceptual systems may have multiple parents, whereas biological evolution always involves a bi-parental system. This is simply incorrect. As he points out, whilst some organisms are bi-parental, most are not; and whilst multiple parenting may seem to be the norm in conceptual evolution, it is not necessarily universal. Even cross-lineage borrowing may not constitute a serious disanalogy, because, as so often, the devil is in the detail of what is actually happening in complex systems. Hybridization, for example, is common in plant evolution. Recently it has been suggested it is often a significant source of species change in animal evolution. However, this was not "borrowed" from plant evolutionists. It derived from detailed observational studies.

On some issues, though, the disanalogies may be more significant because attention to them may point the way to where the analysis of scientific change as evolutionary needs to be focussed. It is often claimed that conceptual evolution is Lamarckian whereas biological transformation in its traditional form, not in the epigenetic sense of Jablonka and Lamb, is Darwinian. Thus, it is stated, when a scientist, or a group of them, acquire a particular concept and then pass it on to others this is the inheritance of acquired characters. However, the claim is based on the certainty we have about the distinction between genes and the phenotype in biological systems and the easy assumption that no such distinction holds for conceptual change. This assumption is easy to challenge by asking just what are the conceptual replicators, and what are the conceptual interactors, the analogs of the phenotype? Is the set of neural networks that constitutes the representation of string theory in a scientist's brain different from the printed page of a journal or book in terms of the causal role they play in conceptual evolution? Until key questions like this are identified and answered with certainty, no strong claim for disanalogy can be made.

Intentionality is another possible disanalogy between biological and conceptual evolution, but as with the issue of the inheritance of acquired characters, it points to the lack of real understanding of conceptual evolution as an evolving system. Hull does admit to intentionality seeming to play an important part in conceptual change, and the obvious absence of such a force in biological evolution. Related to the role of intentionality is one other possible disanalogy, and this concerns the notion of progress. Despite the occasional attempt, no clear case has ever been made for progress existing in biological evolution whereas such is clearly the case for most areas of science. Our understanding of disease and how to combat it, for example, is a clear case of a progression in our conceptualization of what causes many diseases. One way of dealing with this apparent difference lies in the characterization of selection theories that Darden and Cain made, and which Hull did not place at the centre of his analysis: this is that "selection theories solve adaptation problems", the notion of adaptation not being prominent in Hull's analysis of conceptual evolution.

As noted in the previous section of this chapter, what is or is not an adaptation, how an adaptation can or cannot be measured, and what role they play in evolution, are some of the most fraught and controversial questions in biology. Nonetheless, design is the most strongly associated condition of adaptations. Design is the product of selection operating in specific environments, and because environments are so variable, and often subject to constant change, the single condition common to all biological adaptations is that they constitute a relationship of fit between some characteristic of the phenotype and a specific feature of the environment, but exactly what that relationship of fit is will vary from adaptation to adaptation. In a similar way, conceptual evolution comprises a relationship of fit between a concept or a theory, and some feature of the world. And as science seeks to understand, that is form a relationship of fit between its concepts and every feature of the world, so there are many very different forms of concept. As noted in Chapter 1, the comprehension that planets have elliptical orbits has little bearing on the understanding of how photosynthesis binds the energy of the sun into the chemical structure of plants. However, the relationship of fit in conceptual evolution does bind all of science together within an easily generalized condition: this is that there is a common truth value to all of science.

Appeals to the notion of truth are never secure: truth may often be relative and always only partial. Nonetheless, that so many people can be saved from death in the twenty first century caused by diseases that in the none-too-distant past were invariably fatal is powerful evidence that there is a strong element of truth in the medical sciences that is constantly expanding; in this specific case truth is a correct conceptual understanding of the causes of disease. The same holds in diverse areas of science, including matters as different as the birth of stars and the formation of human memory. So there has indeed been progress in wide areas of science, and while science is a collective of many different kinds of truth, that is many different kinds of relationships of fit between concepts and what is out there in the world, the shared aim of all science can indeed be characterized as a kind of shared intentionality of seeking such truth. Such is the relationship of fit between scientific concepts and what is our there in the universe. As will be pointed out in Chapter 5 when a wider form of shared knowledge, culture at large, is considered, shared intentionality has an important part to play in all forms of culture. But the important point being made here is that something like an adaptive fit resulting in progress exists in conceptual evolution, and this is analogous to the notion of adaptive fit increasing the likelihood of survival and reproduction in biological evolution.

The third aspect of Hull's analysis was his contribution to understanding some of the complexities of the selection process at it operates in science. Earlier in this chapter when reviewing post-synthesis changes to the theory of evolution, the contributions of Hamilton and G.C. Williams in terms of kin selection and inclusive fitness were considered. In his book on science as a process Hull provided considerable evidence for science as a complicated social phenomenon involving conceptual inclusive fitness and the demic structure of science. As he points out, science is at once a cooperative and a competitive social process as individual scientists strive to get others to adopt their views and ideas. Hull's observations regarding this aspect of the evolution of science are excellent, but as they are tied very specifically to the way science works, they have little to tell us about a general theory of selection beyond the necessity of the processes of selection always being inserted into the specific demands of different forms of change.

The ever widening application of selection theory within the spheres of epistemology, anthropology, economics, and culture in recent years will be taken up in succeeding chapters. This chapter will end with a brief survey of the earlier application of selection theory to change other than that of species transformation, specifically in the functioning of the immune system and its possible application to understanding the development of the nervous system.

In the early part of the last century Paul Ehrlich, a pioneering biochemist and bacteriologist, was the first to suggest that the vertebrate immune system makes specific entities, which came to be termed antibodies, *before* encountering the antigens against which they defend the organism of which they are a part. His proposal was a clear statement that the immune system functions by selectionist principles. Ehrlich's idea was subsequently rejected in favour of the notion that the immune system contains units, lymphocytes, whose highly malleable structure is moulded into specific antibody form by the structure of invading antigens *after* the antigen is encountered. Ehrlich's opponents were in effect offering a Lamarckian, instructionist, account of how the immune system functions. We now know that Ehrlich was correct and that a significant part of the vertebrate system, that which develops immunity to specific antigens, operates as a Darwin machine embodying a within-organism selection engine of massive proportions. The immune system is, insofar as comparison is possible, as complex as the nervous system. There are in the region of ten times as many lymphocytes in our bodies as there are nerve cells which are manufactured in or circulate through bone marrow, lymph vessels and nodes, spleen, thymus, appendix, and the blood circulation system. Both the nervous and immune systems are diffuse organs that are dispersed through most of the tissues of the bodies of vertebrates. In humans the immune system is estimated to contain about a trillion lymphocytes which make around 100 million trillion molecules comprising the antibodies, about one million of which are needed to provide protection against the vast array of pathogens that threaten the average human life-span. These are astronomical numbers that indicate a system capable of generating variation on a massive scale. How it does so, as a Darwin machine, was revived from Ehrlich's conception by Niels Jerne in the 1950s in what Jerne referred to as the natural selection theory of antibody formation, and then developed further by F. M. Burnet in what he called the clonal selection theory of immune system function.

The precise mechanisms of antibody formation are embodied in complex molecular mechanisms involving nucleic acids, amino acids, proteins and polysaccharides that cells express as surface receptors on the cell membranes. The clonal selection theory postulates that cells express massive variation in receptor surface which, on encountering external antigens (non-self) the B lymphocytes are stimulated to produce specific antibody responses, the formation of immunological "memory" by the selective expansion of lymphocytes with specific membrane structures that not only endure, but "learn" by expressing antibodies with a high affinity for specific antigens improved through the immunological response by the selection of cells. As Rajewsky states in his review of how the antibody system learns: "Both naïve B cells and somatically mutated memory cells are produced by a process involving cell proliferation accompanied by stringent cellular selection, so that only cells of the desired phenotype survive".

In their review of selection as a general process, Hull, Langman, and Glenn note that the two most striking features of selection processes, whether operating between organisms as Darwin conceived, or within organism as in the case of the immune system, is that "they are incredibly wasteful and yet able to produce genuine novelty and increased organization". They conclude, correctly, that the efficacy of selection in leading to novelty and organization lies precisely in the wastefulness of the process. It is an inherent feature of how most processes of selection work.

One of the significant figures in the understanding of the molecular mechanisms underlying immune system function was Gerald Edelman, and it is thus unsurprising that Edelman went on to become an important figure in the further expansion of selection theory by applying it to the development of the brain. Edelman, however, was not alone in this. For example, the French neuroscientist Jean-Pierre Changeux from the 1970s onwards was a strong advocate of the application of selection theory both to the general development of the central nervous system and to its role in adult learning. It remains the case that the neuronal mechanisms that determine learning are largely unknown in any detail. More is known about brain epigenesis, especially when neurons and their synaptic connectivity is established. For Changeux, "since cell division mostly takes place in mammals before birth … the theory proposed deals with the outgrowth and stability of synapses. It postulates that, to some extent, a Darwinian selection of synapses contributes to the final establishment of the adult organization". There is, indeed, no doubt but that neuron numbers, and even more dramatically, synaptic connectivity, is reduced during the development of the brain, but whether it is indeed a selectional process that falls within the theoretical requirements outlined by Darden and Cain or Hull and his colleagues cannot be claimed with any certainty.

Edelman's account of "neural Darwinism" is much more explicit in terms of detailed mechanism. His theory is framed within a conception of "neuronal group selection" based on the reasonable assumption that the unit of selection in neural development is not the individual neuron but groups of neurons whose incorporation into neural networks comprise the basic functional units of brain organization. Edelman, probably because of his history as a molecular biologist, has little time for those who "confound principles with mechanisms and indulge glib analogies". His is an account of brain development couched within a framework of specific molecular mechanisms. He takes it as read that what determines brain organization in terms of neural networks is a complex developmental process of neural network selection based on the constant input of sensory information; the experienced world interacts with already developed neural networks to determine further brain organization. He posits two kinds of selection events. The first, the "primary repertoire", is the result of epigenetic processes of cell adhesion, cell movement, differential neuronal growth, cell division and cell death. He puts forward what he terms the "regulator hypothesis", which is a complex of ideas relating to cell and surface adhesion molecule gene expression, embryonic induction forces, and the notion of heterochrony (the timing of developmental processes), as the central hypothesis of developmental mechanism by which the primary, fundamental, circuitry of the brain is established. The central conception is how, from a potentially astronomical number of possible neural networks, a much smaller primary repertoire develops to form the core of brain function, at least as far as perception and learning is concerned. Upon this is built the secondary repertoire by way of a specific hypothesis of synaptic interaction which, while it does not alter the pattern of connectivity laid down by the primary repertoire, results in the neural circuitry unique to the experience of each individual. The secondary repertoire corresponds to the psychological notions of representations and concepts, though Edelman prefers the term "maps". These become interrelated by way of "re-entrant" signalling between selected neuronal groups such that the "mappings" or representations become integrated into ever-more complex architectures of brain circuitry underlying ever-more complex psychological functioning.

Edelman's is much the most complex account of a possible selectional process in terms of the mechanisms that underly the development of the brain. However, the evidence that brain development is indeed caused by a process of selection is lacking when compared with the supporting evidence for the claims that science and immune system function should be understood in these terms. In the case of the immune system, there is overwhelming evidence for the existence of variation in lymphocyte structure on a massive scale; and equally strong evidence for the perpetuation of specific lymphocyte forms following their interaction with antigen: all the components of the Lewontin-Hull formulation of the selection process are present. There is a differential perpetuation of certain replicator structures out of a vast pool of such potential replicators of variable form, the receptor surfaces serving as the interactors for the genetic replicators; and the Darden and Cain requirement of the presence of adaptive fit of the selected lymphocyte structures to specific antigen is clearly in evidence with the effectiveness of lymphocytes in combating specific invading antigen.

The case for conceptual evolution in science is less strong, but nonetheless persuasive. Ideas, concepts and theories arise in variable form in the minds of individual scientists or groups of scientists. Hull is correct to point to the complexities of social interactions in conceptual evolution. The translation of possible ideas (the atom is a single solid entity or it is mostly empty space, as in the famous case of Rutherford's work on the structure of the atom) into empirically testable forms (observing the behaviour of particles fired at extremely thin sheets of zinc sulphide) resulting in certain variations of an idea, the replicators, being perpetuated and finding yet further testable forms in empirical interactors, conforms well the notion of science as a selection process – a constant interaction between variable concepts, potential replicators, with empirical observation, the interactors, to result in the differential replication of some concepts at the cost of the demise of others. And as noted earlier, the presence of adapted fit is attested to by the inexorable increase in the truth-value of the sciences: scientific replicators are adaptive insofar as they increase our understanding of the world, as proven by progress in medicine, the landing of men on the moon and doubtless on Mars in coming decades, and the interfacing of human brains with computers, to mention just a few instances of scientific advance.

So the astonishing achievements of molecular biology, yet another case of science's increasing truth-value, provides undoubted support for viewing immune system function as the operation of a selection process. The relative ease of observation of how science works gives strong backing to the case for viewing science as operating by way of a selection process. But for the present, we just cannot yet observe enough of how neural networks are formed and how they are the substrates to specific functions like perception to be able to say with any certainty that Changeux and Edelman are correct, even though Edelman points the way in terms of mechanisms to how we should proceed. The notion of adequate or even optimal brain development is too diffuse and vague to support Darden and Cain's necessary condition that selection theory must embrace adaptive fit.

Closely related to the problem of brain development is the primary function of the brain in many animals, namely learning and cognition, and it is to these issues that we now turn.

Chapter 4

Evolutionary epistemology

No serious scientist now doubts that all living forms are the products of an evolutionary process, whatever that process is, and even non-Darwinists like Stephen Jay Gould accepted the causal role of selection in the formation of adaptations. Whatever it's causal role, selection is an essential part of evolution. As noted in a previous chapter, the generation of variation is a necessarily wasteful process. Even viruses, with their very limited core of nucleic acid, are able to parasitize host cells and use their hosts' molecular structures to generate the variation necessary for the evolution of such relatively simple organisms. Multicellular organisms, including those with relatively small numbers of genes, are able to generate diversity by way of epigenetic processes that lead to significant variation on which selection can act. The same applies to within-organism selection, like that of the vertebrate immune system, which operates on variation of a truly astronomical scale. With, at least in most vertebrates, nerve cells numbering thousands and, often enough, millions, providing a potential connectivity to be numbered in billions, if selection is a process responsible for change driving specific central nervous system function, there is variation aplenty to fuel that process. One central nervous system function that has been considered as a potential candidate for being driven by a selection process is learning.

The psychologist Donald T. Campbell coined the phrase evolutionary epistemology to describe the application of selection theory to some forms of individual learning, amongst other kinds of knowledge gain. He did this in part because he thought that a process that gains knowledge at both a population and an individual level might indeed be the basis for a general theory in biology and that a grand phrase like evolutionary epistemology would be an appropriate description for so ambitious an undertaking. But he was also aware that learning itself is a word too narrow and limited in scope when what he wanted was an approach that naturalized epistemology along the lines pursued by the philosopher W.V.O. Quine in the 1950s and 1960s, which itself leaned on Campbell's own early writings; and because he wanted to encompass more than the narrow acquisition of information through learning by the individual. In addition he also wanted words that would take in the writings of, amongst others Karl Popper, on what distinguishes science from other forms of unscientific knowledge claims. Campbell's own grand scheme will be considered later in this chapter. First, though, it is to a distinction drawn by Popper himself with which we need to begin.

In an essay entitled "evolutionary epistemology" of 1984, borrowing the phrase from Campbell's essay of ten years before which paid homage to Popper's own work, Popper himself offered two theses upon which such a potential general theory in biology should be built. The first, which he described as "almost trivial" is that the "human ability to know", including that gained through scientific knowledge, is itself the "result of natural selection". The second thesis is that knowledge is gained through a Darwinian process of selection. The latter has been the focus of thought by almost everyone considering individual knowledge gain, learning, within the context of a broader biological theory. However, Popper's first thesis is, in fact, far from trivial and has very significant implications. The first of these concerns Darden and Cain's (see previous chapter) insistence that selection theory always applies when the product of a process has teleological design; when there is an adaptive fit between a feature of the world and the organization of some aspect of the phenotype. The second has importance in settling the old argument, briefly described in the second chapter of this book, amongst epistemologists between the contrasting claims of rationalism and empiricism. Thus it is to this teleological aspect of evolutionary epistemology that we first turn.

Learning as an adaptation

As noted in Chapter 2, the world is in a state of endless change. Were this not the case, evolution would have driven the organic world to some constant set of optimal forms and then retained them unchanged across time. This, of course, has not occurred. The continual evolution of living forms across thousands of millions of years is evidence for the pervasiveness of change, and is itself a source of such endless change. Evolution is at once the response to change, and an engine of change.

Inherent in change is uncertainty. If flux always means a constant cyclical reversion to some previous state then that would itself be a form of constancy without any uncertainty. Uncertainty defines change, and as Waddington put it in his seminal 1969 piece referred to in Chapter 1, "the systematic exploration of the evolutionary strategies in facing an unknown, but usually not wholly unforecastable, future would take us into a realm of thought which is the most challenging and very characteristic of the basic problems of biology. The main issue in evolution is how populations deal with unknown futures". Waddington was absolutely right. The unknown futures problem is one of the central theoretical problems of biology, and the evolution of learning was one response to this problem, as was the evolution of the immune system. In vertebrates, these are functionally related systems. Both evolved to deal with uncertainty.

Waddington's unknown futures problem is, of course, rooted in the pervasiveness of change, but it is also the product of the systemic characteristics of the succession of multicellular organisms drawing upon the instructions contained within their gene pools. "Pools" of genetic "instructions" are metaphors, but they do give us a broad conceptual hold on how complex living systems work.

At conception, every multicellular organism comprises a sampling of the genes from its breeding population. However complex the subsequent cascade of developmental processes are which transforms each genotype into a functioning phenotype, that sampling of genetic instructions, apart from mitochondrial DNA, is all that each organism has from which to begin to construct itself. If the world were an unchanging place, then the only significant limitation on the competence of the process in supplying organisms with their needed adaptations would be the adequacy of the sampling of genetic instructions from the gene pool. But in a world that is subject to change, there is a problem that the ethologist Konrad Lorenz referred to as generational deadtime. This is the lagtime that is an invariant feature of any system whose construction takes some finite period of time based upon a set of instructions that cannot be continually updated. In the case of sexually reproducing multicellular organisms, each organism is cast off from its gene pool with a fixed set of instructions that it cannot alter and augment in response to the changes in the world that may occur in the period from conception to the point in time when it is sexually mature and able to feed its own genes back into the gene pool of the breeding population. Generational deadtime cannot exceed the length of an organisms own lifespan. In a relatively small percentage, notably vertebrates, it may come close to equalling it. In primates, generational deadtime may be measured in years. This is a length of time sufficient for significant change in the world to have occurred with regard to conditions that have a direct effect on the fitness of these creatures: these may range from changes in the pathogens to which they might be subjected, to alterations in the spatial position of vital resources like food and water and to shifts in alliances in social species. The functional relationship of the immune system and those parts of the central nervous system that subserve the acquisition of information is clear. Both are responses to the unknown futures problem. In the case of learning, what is acquired is information about changes that might occur during generational deadtime that are concerned with the physical and social worlds of the learner. There is no doubting that epigenesis and the degree of developmental plasticity to which it may give rise, especially in plants, is also a response to the unknown futures problem. Despite a strange controversy of some decades ago, there is no evidence whatever that any species of plant can learn. Learning is *sui generis* as a process in some animals that leads to lifelong knowledge acquisition.

In his book on *Neural Darwinism* in which Edelman argued for the development of the central nervous system as being governed by the process of selection, the opening paragraph contained an arresting statement on how the world presents itself to any newborn organism, including humans: "the world is initially an unlabelled place. The number of partitions of potential 'objects' or 'events' in an econiche is enormous if not infinite". There can be no more important observation to any science or philosophy of knowledge than Edelman's point that any creature, even those with limited sensory inputs, are faced with the massive epistemological problem of how to know a world that is so filled with what there is that might be known. How, for example, does a newborn infant divide up and link together which aspects of the world it experiences: which visual events relating to orientation, texture, or colour go with which auditory qualities of pitch or loudness, and which relate to cutaneous sensations of touch and temperature, and how to accommodate different olfactory and gustatory qualities to any of these features of the experienced world? Whether one adopts some form of Humean associationist stance on what is central to learning, or a Piagetian constructivism as the heart of the learning process, the number of things that might be learned is huge. This is the central problem of any epistemology; let us call it the first problem.

The second problem is that if any and every form of learning, of knowledge gain, has evolved as an adaptive solution to Waddington's unknown futures problem, then it is a requirement that the process operate on a time scale much reduced from that of the main evolutionary programme which has given rise to it. Learning must be fast and frugal, to use the biologist Gerd Gigerenzer's phrase. But how can learning be fast and frugal if the number of potential forms of knowledge is "enormous if not infinite"? The answer to this question is that learning can only be fast and frugal if the learner comes into the world knowing something of what it has to learn. This is the only possible solution to the combination of the first and second problems just outlined. If learning occurred by way of the chance sampling and matching of all possible combinations of sensory input, then it would be, on average, a very slow, fumbling and inefficient process. It would not achieve the teleological results that were the reason for its original evolution. Only if the mechanisms of learning are pointed to a greatly restricted portion of all the possible things that could be learned, would the learning process do what it was evolved to do.

It is no coincidence that one of the first persons to point the way to the solution to these problems, the ethologist Konrad Lorenz, was an ardent Kantian steeped in the notion of Kant's *a prioris*. Lorenz was also a convinced evolutionist and one of the founding fathers of ethology – the study of behaviour as it occurs in the natural environments within which it evolved. Early in his writings, Lorenz drew a sharp distinction between instinctive or innate behaviours, the products of evolution, and acquired, learned behaviours. It was a distinction which, after the second world war when the work of the ethologists became more widely known, was to become the focus of a sustained conceptual attack led by Daniel Lehrman and T.C. Schneirla. At the heart of the criticism of Lorenz's ideas was that instinctive behaviours, like all behaviours, do not emerge invariantly and inevitably. Like all behaviours, those labelled as instinctive by Lorenz are the product of a complex cascade of developmental processes, some of which includes learning. Thus the distinction between learned and instinctive behaviours is false, they argued. "Analysis of the developmental process involved shows that the behaviour patterns concerned are not unitary, autonomously developing things, but rather that they emerge ontogenetically in complex ways from the previously developed organization of the organism in a given setting" wrote Lehrman.

The criticisms of Lorenz's innate-learned dichotomy were essentially of a developmental nature. They paid little heed to the evolutionary foundations of Lorenz's position. They were also very strongly stated and verged on the personal. (A more detailed review of this important argument can be found in Chapter 4 of this author's *Necessary Knowledge*). They forced Lorenz to rethink his stance and the result is to be found in the reformulation of his position on learning and instinct, which was first published in his 1965 monograph on *The Evolution and Modification of Behaviour*. He conceded that his critics were partly correct. The distinction he had drawn between innate and learned behaviours was indeed incorrect. However, the reason he gave, and the resultant conception that he drew was completely original and theoretically very powerful.

Learning, in both humans and other animals, had been subject to experimental study and theoretical analysis for more than 65 years when Lorenz stated what no one had noticed before: "The amazing and never-to-be-forgotten fact is that learning does, in the majority of cases, increase the survival value of the behaviour mechanisms which it modifies". One of the reasons that this had for so long gone unremarked, he suggested, were the unnatural conditions of laboratory experimentation. It is only when behaviour is observed in the natural environments of animals by scientists "tolerably versed in biological thought" that the adaptive nature of learning is apparent. However, Lorenz was quite wrong in one respect. At the time of his writing his monograph, there was absolutely no evidence that learning is always adaptive in outcome. But his theoretical claim, empirically unsubstantiated though it was, was correct. If learning is fitness enhancing, then it can only be so because it is a product of evolution. Learning, generically, is an adaptation, a product of evolution, and hence genetically part-caused. In other words, learning itself is an instinct. Thus did he collapse his previously drawn dichotomy into a singularity.

In an essay of 1969 he expanded this argument into a broad form of evolutionary epistemology as follows:

> An amazing number of scientists, otherwise biologically minded people among them, seem unable to grasp the fact that the stratified structure of the whole world of organisms absolutely forbids the conceptualization of living systems or life processes in terms of 'disjunctive' – that is to say, mutually exclusive – concepts. It is nonsense to oppose to each other 'animal' and 'man', 'nature' and culture', 'innate programming' and 'learning', as if the old logical diagram of alpha and nonalpha were applicable to them. Man … is still an animal; human nature persists in and is the basis of culture; and all learning is very specifically innately programmed.

Like Donald Campbell (see below) Lorenz saw the possibility of a truly general theory in biology rooted, at least in part, in an evolutionary epistemology. Awarded the Nobel prize just a few years later for his work as an ethologist, his ideas on the relationship between evolution and learning would have alone justified the honour.

The early work on trial-and-error learning in cats by Thorndike and Pavlov's studies of classical conditioning in dogs committed psychology to the notion of a general process, or a small number of general processes, of learning that somehow obscured the possibility that no matter how general learning is as a process, it is almost always restricted in its scope of knowledge gain to specific features of the environment. The possibility of constraints on learning had not been entertained prior to Lorenz's monograph, and there was no evidence that such existed. This was to change rapidly after the publication in 1966 of the work of John Garcia, whose debt to Lorenz was considerable, and his colleagues showing that aversive conditioning to nausea in rats has seemingly unusual temporal characteristics and is confined to associations between specific forms of stimuli. Within a few years it was shown that what was termed the restriction of "cue to consequence" learning in quails is quite unlike what occurs in rats; a finding in line with the dietary differences between these animals. What was being reported are adaptive constraints on learning that accord with the life history strategies of different species. Within a few years notions of preparedness, species-specific reactions, adaptive specializations and constraints on learning were terms being regularly applied in highly respected journals devoted to the experimental study of learning, and numbers of conference proceedings and other forms of anthology concerned with species-specific learning differences were published.

Here, then, was the answer to the puzzle posed by Edelman and the reason why learning is indeed fast and frugal. It is because evolution has "pointed" or directed learning to specific features of the world that must be learned. Learners come into the world knowing what it is they must learn about. In his 1965 monograph Lorenz had pondered what might be responsible for the adaptive nature of learning and had speculated that some kind of skewing of attention might be the mechanism principally responsible. How is it that chaffinches in an English garden come to have the song of their species and not that of other birds whose song is also to be heard by the young birds? How can sex differences in spatial learning in different species of vole be understood in the context of whether they are monogamous or polygynous? And why is it that human newborns pay significant visual attention to faces? In each case, and the many, many, others that have been documented, the explanation lies in learners coming into the world with their learning mechanisms "tuned" to very specific features of their sensory experience. There is what Andy Clark termed a minimal nativism attached to most kinds of learning, which can only take the form of fragmentary representational knowledge that drives attention to specific features of the experienced world. Thus does learning, nurture, itself have nature, as Lorenz decreed. There is no other way of explaining why learning is of necessity fast and frugal, and why there is now a mass of empirical evidence for constraints on learning in so many different species of learners.

The adaptive characteristic of learning fulfils Darden and Cain's requirement that the process underlying learning must have a teleological basis, one of fit between the mechanisms of learning and specific features of the world, and which might be driven by selection. It also has a bearing on the very old philosophical problem considered in Chapter 2. Plato's and Descartes' rationalist belief in the existence of innate knowledge at birth that owes nothing to the senses has now been shown to be correct. The notion of the mind as a blank slate at birth is a biological nonsense. Something akin to Immanuel Kant's *a prioris*, knowledge that transcends experience and which cannot be inductively inferred from experience, do exist. That is the significance of Lorenz as a Kantian and the importance of his also being an evolutionist because it was as the latter that he was able to discern an error in Kant's notion of the *a prioris*. Kant thought, precisely because they transcend experience, that the *a prioris* do not relate in any meaningful way to the world as it really is – indeed they may actually stand as obstacles to any direct knowledge of the world. In an early paper, Lorenz combined his evolutionism with his Kantian convictions when he asked the question "is it at all probable that the laws of our cognitive apparatus should be disconnected with those of the real world?" His answer was no, of course not. In this Kant was wrong. The cognitive processes of any creature able to acquire knowledge of the world through those processes must bear a positive relationship to the experienced world. Hence the necessary existence of innate knowledge, and its importance, contrary to Popper's view, to an evolutionary epistemology.

Cognition as a selection process

Cognition is a generic word for the gaining of information, whether it be by way of experience and the senses, or through thought. One of the oldest words within the new science of psychology, it was banished by the puritanism of behaviourism early in the 20th century because it allowed in thought which might not find expression in behaviour. Learning, defined as a change in behaviour originating in experience and excluding any causes rooted in maturation or temporary alterations of state such as fatigue, replaced it in standard psychological writings. Restored in the 1960s by a psychology that conceded that thought does indeed occur and may have a causal role in the acquisition of information, cognition and learning will be used here as interchangeable terms.

Anecdotes of learning in animals were present in Darwin's *Descent of Man*, as well as in the writings of his successor George Romanes. Conway Lloyd Morgan described some crude experimental studies on learning in non-humans, but it was an American, Edward Thorndike, who performed the first really rigorous studies of learning in a laboratory setting, mostly using cats as subjects though some of his work included dogs and monkeys. Thorndike constructed what became known as "puzzle-boxes" which had doors secured by latches that would be released if a rope were pulled, or a lever depressed, or both acts (and in some experiments as many as three actions) performed. The animals could then escape from the box and gain access to some food placed outside of the enclosure. Varying the complexity of the acts required for escape from the puzzle-boxes, Thorndike recorded the activities of his subjects and the time that elapsed before the animals' behaviour resulted in the doors being raised. With repeated trials, initially seemingly random behaviours became more focussed actions leading to ever more rapid escapes from the boxes. Eventually even quite complex behavioural sequences would be performed with skilled rapidity resulting in quick release from the boxes and access to the food.

In his earliest writings of 1898 Thorndike considered that what he was observing was some form of association between sensory impressions and what he labelled as "impulses to action". The resultant association he referred to as a "bond" or "connection", with Thorndike asserting that what he was developing was a "bond psychology" or "connectionism" – a curious anticipation of the label developed some 80 years later by neural net modellers. Later writings, both by Thorndike and others, emphasized that what he was observing was a form of trial-and-error learning, or instrumental learning, in which the learner initially performs a relatively large and random form and number of behaviours, which become pared down as a consequence of their leading to a goal, eventually resulting in the efficient execution of the minimum amount of behaviour that leads to that goal. A number of "laws of learning" were drawn up by Thorndike, such as the law of readiness (a crude anticipation of what later would be termed constraints on learning), the law of exercise (concerned with the strengthening of connections with practice), and most importantly the "law of effect", which encapsulated the strengthening or weakening of a connection between a behaviour and its consequences, which would subsequently come to be termed as reinforcement and the specific conditions under which reinforcement acts. These were early attempts to provide a formal theory of learning.

What was not remarked upon at the time was the resemblance in the process that Thorndike was observing as learning by an individual animal, and the process of evolution by selection described by Darwin. What Thorndike reported was that in an unfamiliar environment his cats were generating a range of diverse behaviours, with his subjects gradually narrowing down the extent of these behaviours by some kind of internalized selection mechanism which preserved those behaviours that resulted in favourable consequences for the animal (positive reinforcement) and eliminating those that had no, or negative, effects (negative reinforcement). As this author has noted elsewhere, had Darwin been the psychologist carrying out these experiments, not Thorndike, he might have written a book entitled *The Origins of Behaviours by Means of Internal Selection or the Preservation of Favoured Acts in the Struggle for being Remembered.* Later generations of theoretical biologists interested in the transformation of species in time might have seen the similarity between such individual instrumental learning and speciation, and fantasized about what might have been had Darwin been a biologist and how he might have writen a book with the title *The Origin of Species by Means of Natural Selection or the Preservation of Favoured Races in the Struggle for Life.*

Around the same time that Thorndike was experimenting with his cats, in Russia the physiologist Ivan Pavlov stumbled upon a form of learning in dogs that was to be termed classical conditioning. Whilst working on the functioning of the digestive system, Pavlov accidentally observed salivation to stimuli that regularly preceded the presentation of food. He began a systematic study of the phenomenon, and found that if a food powder, what he came to term the unconditional stimulus, is placed in the mouth of a dog, it salivates; and if some arbitrary stimulus, such as a bell ring or the beating of a metronome, regularly precedes the presentation of food, that salivation will, after some number of pairings, occur to that arbitrary stimulus, which was labelled as a conditional (or conditioned) stimulus, even in the absence of the unconditional stimulus. Pavlov later referred to conditioned salivation as "psychic" in order to distinguish them from unlearned physiological responses.

Pavlov's observations laid the foundations for a long history of the laboratory study of associationism. The work became famous because it was a science whose ancient conceptual foundations began with the writings of Aristotle, and later advanced by the philosophical analyses of Locke, Hobbes, and other empiricists, and especially by Hume who had envisaged a science of the mind based on associationist principles which would mirror in its empiricists' precision a kind of mental mechanics to rival that of Newton's science of matter.

The psychologist David Premack coined the interesting phrase "arbitrary causal relations" to express the uncertainty of the physical and social world. Whilst we can never be certain, it is more than likely that learning evolved hundreds of millions of years ago, perhaps not long after the evolution of a central nervous system comprising a small aggregate of nerve cells, as a means of establishing local cause-effect relations in response to this specific aspect of Waddington's unknown futures problem, Premack's arbitrary causal relations. Relatively unspecified mechanisms for establishing arbitrary causal relations, sensitive to and hence pointed towards the detection of events that are associated in time and space that comprise such causal relations would bestow significant fitness benefits on the learner. What Thorndike and Pavlov did was capture within an experimental setting two seemingly different forms of learning about the world's arbitrary causal relations. As noted earlier, there has never been any evidence of learning in plants that has stood up to close scrutiny. And there is no certainty how widespread such forms of learning are in a world that encompasses tens of millions of species of animals, but it is clear that learning of the kind described by Pavlov's and Thorndike's experiments are common in vertebrates, and also present in many invertebrate species such as arthropods (especially insects like bees whose characteristics of conditioning are remarkably similar to that of humans), some species of mollusc (cephalopods such as squids and octopuses) and a variety of flat worms and segmented worms. Whether learning occurs in single celled animals is controversial.

Despite advances in neuroscience over the last century, especially with regard to understanding the mechanisms of the action potential (the nerve impulse) and synaptic transmission, there is as yet no clear understanding of the physiological mechanisms that are the physical basis for any form of learning. In this regard our understanding of learning is not unlike that of evolutionists in the days prior to the discovery of genes. In other words, what the science of learning has given us is an ever more detailed understanding of the processes by which learning occurs, but nothing about the mechanisms embodying the processes. In this regard, the two forms of knowledge gain that we have dealt with here, instrumental learning and Pavlov's classical conditioning, bear both broad similarities, and some important difference.

Cause-effect relations by definition are relations of association. In classical conditioning, the learner associates events in the world over which it may have no control. In Pavlov's original studies, the dogs controlled neither unconditional nor conditional stimuli, but nonetheless came to associate the latter with the former. There was some discussion as to whether the animal's salivation prior to the presentation of the meat powder might not have been instrumental in preparing the dog for the meat powder, and thus showing that the Thorndike and Pavlov experimental arrangements were not essentially different. Others were to argue that the real point of Pavlov's experiments is that they demonstrated that what the dogs were able to do was predict the occurrence of the unconditional stimulus through the appearance of the conditional stimulus. The word prediction does not mean that the animals made a conscious prediction; it meant merely that some form of anticipation of a future event was demonstrated by the behaviour of the animals. It was "as if" classical conditioning resulted in their predicting a future event. Again, the notion of prediction was never taken to mean some form of reasoning or thought process about future events on the basis of what had occurred in the past, because often regular sequences of events observed in natural environments are correlative, not causal, but that does not negate the possible positive effects of predicting events. The sensory impressions of essential nutrients and fluids do not "cause" their beneficial effects, but that is irrelevant to the positive effects that derive from associating, and hence anticipating, the one from the other. In effect, classical conditioning places the learner in the position of being Hume's ideal believer in cause-effect relations as a "habit of mind".

A century of experimentation has revealed learning mechanisms sensitive to just those variables that one would expect it to be sensitive to had conditioning evolved as a means of detecting physical causal relations. Both temporal and spatial contiguity are indicators of causal relationships. It has been repeatedly shown that the temporal relationship between conditional and unconditional stimuli is a crucial determinant of conditioning, the magnitude of that temporal relationship varying with the nature of the unconditional stimulus, as the constraints on learning literature shows. Spatial contiguity has also been shown to be a factor in enhancing conditioning. However, contiguity is not enough. In the 1960s, American psychologists showed that contingency is also a critical variable in determining whether conditioning occurs. Defining contingency as the probability that event B is preceded by event A being greater than the probability that event B occurs when it is not preceded by event A, Robert Rescorla and his colleagues were able to show that this means that in a complex and uncertain world, invariant pairing is not a necessary condition for conditioning to occur; but also that if the contingency is lost amidst the swirl of uncertain environmental events, then conditioning will not occur. Under conditions when the linkage between events becomes so loose that uncertainty makes it unlikely that an association will be formed, the measure of contingency is an objective and quantifiable measure as to where and when that point occurs. In effect, contingency is a measure of the extent to which the first event, the conditional stimulus, is a measure that predicts the likely occurrence of the second event, the unconditional stimulus. Thus it was that a cognitive element entered into the animal learning literature with words like prediction, expectation, and surprise becoming common explanations of the causation of causal understanding in animals. It became acceptable to say that Pavlov's dogs were surprised by the bell, the conditional stimulus, and that once conditioning had occurred adding a second stimulus would have little power of association between that additional stimulus and either of the first two stimuli because the bell adequately predicts the occurrence of the unconditional stimulus and hence there is no strong contingency attaching to the second stimulus. What has come to be called the Rescorla-Wagner model is remarkably simple and states that it is the mismatch between past and presently experienced paired events that determines conditioning.

Thus it is clear that contiguity and contingency are central to the process of establishing associative learning because it is predictability that lies at the heart of learning about physical causality. This is no coincidence that has come about through chance, but just another example of the teleonomic nature of adaptations: associative learning is the adaptive response to the advantages of acting upon perceived cause-effect relationships.

Instrumental learning places the learner within a much more direct framework of cause-effect relationship because it is the behaviour generated by the learner itself that becomes causal to its effects. Thorndike's puzzle-boxes gave way in the 1930s to the apparatus designed by B.F. Skinner, the so-called Skinner box, in which depressing a lever in the case of a laboratory rat or pecking at a plate if the subject is a pigeon, resulted in the delivery of a small quantity of food, the reinforcement. Skinner boxes led to a period of unprecedented experimentation on learning, and it is not surprising that Skinner was one of the learning theorists, as noted in the previous chapter, who emphasized the importance of selection as a process of learning, because instrumental learning involves a strong element of the learner, seemingly by way of some form of internal selection process, associating effective behaviour with good outcomes for the learner in the form of reward or reinforcement. But can one assert that what Skinner's rats and pigeons were learning was knowledge of cause-effect relations between the learner's behaviour and its outcome, in some manner comparable to what occurs in humans placed in similar situations, and both cases being comparable to the learned associations observed in Pavlov's classical conditioning studies? A series of experiments at Cambridge University in the 1990s indicate that the answer to this question is a "yes", that there is indeed an identity of what is being learned in all these cases. In a complex series of experimental observation, it was shown that human subjects make judgements about causal relationships and act instrumentally to maximize payoffs to themselves that shows a sensitivity to both contiguity and contingency identical to that demonstrated by the behaviour of animals like rats or pigeons in Skinner boxes and Pavlov's dogs. In other words, they seem to demonstrate that non-human learners acquire behaviours instrumentally in seemingly identical manner to humans, and that the causal judgements in humans and the instrumental behaviours in animals are affected in the same way through the manipulation of the same relationships of contiguity and contingency. Whether or not these are Humean illusions of causality or insights into real causal connections, it appears that they are instilled by exactly the same conditions in different species of learner.

Nonetheless, whilst the establishment of causal relations might bind together all forms of associative learning, there remains a strong case for assuming some differences in process between establishing causal relationships between events in the world over which the learner has no control, so-called stimulus associations, and the links between the behaviours generated by the learner and that behaviour's outcome, instrumental, or operant learning. This brings us back to the views of Skinner and others whose focus has been on the latter forms of learning and the idea that selection is an important part of those forms of learning process. In a 1960s paper in *Science*, Skinner, not for the first time because he had first used the "evolutionary analogy" as early as 1953, drew parallels between selection operating at what he called the phylogenetic level in the evolution of behaviour, and the ontogenetic level in the development of individual behavioural repertoires based on the contingencies of reinforcement: "... the rat must press the lever at least once 'for other reasons' before it presses it 'for food'. There is a similar limitation in phylogenetic contingencies. An animal must emit a cry at least once for other reasons before the cry can be selected as a warning because of the advantage to the species. It follows that the entire repertoire of an individual or species must exist prior to ontogenetic or phylogenetic selection, but only in the form of minimal units." Skinner was plainly moving towards the view of the same process of selection operating at both the Darwinian level of evolution, the process that leads to speciation, and that of individual knowledge gain through operant or instrumental learning which results in behavioural change. Some 15 years later, Skinner writing in the same journal suggested that "selection by consequences" is a causal mode unique to living organisms that began "when a molecule came into existence which had the power to reproduce itself". In fact, Skinner was less concerned with any possible generality of process, and more with what he considered to be the lack of appreciation of the power of learning by selection: "Since a species which quickly acquires behaviour appropriate to a given environment has less need for an innate repertoire, operant conditioning could not only supplement the natural selection of behaviour, it could replace it". This was a serious overstatement of the powers of learning because it completely overlooked the necessity for learning mechanisms to be pointed at what it is that must be learned, and that pointing occurs by way of natural selection, which cannot be "replaced" as a causal force in establishing such learning constraints. Nonetheless, Skinner was clearly headed towards something like a general theory based on selection.

There is an odd aspect to Skinner's writings, which was a consistent failure to reference the work of others. It is possible that Skinner simply used the ideas of fellow scholars without feeling any need to acknowledge their precedence, or perhaps he was a strangely conceptually closed scientist who seemed to have no knowledge of what others were writing at that time, or had written in the past; in any event, some kind of credit is due to him for recognizing in that 1981 paper that "there is a third kind of selection by consequences, the evolution of social environments or cultures". He concluded that "human behaviour is the joint product of (i) the contingencies of survival responsible for the natural selection of the species and (ii) the contingencies of reinforcement responsible for the repertoires acquired by its members, including (iii) the special contingencies maintained by an evolved social environment". Thus did Skinner himself move ever so slightly towards the notion of some form of general theory in biology.

Recently Sigrid Glenn, as part of the Hull et al. 2001 paper on "a general account of selection", provided a much more explicit analysis of operant learning as a selection process than ever did Skinner himself, and drew a number of parallels between changes in behaviour occurring through operant learning and the processes of selection as conceived by evolutionists. She drew attention to the way in which operant behaviours are structured in time and related one to another: "An operant repertoire is made up of interrelated behavioural lineages, each having its origin at a different time in the history of the organism, and each having its own history. As in the case of the evolution of life on earth, understanding the process requires focussing on particular lineages. Each behavioural lineage evolves in relation to its local environment, and changes in one lineage can impact other lineages in the organism's repertoire". Glenn also wrote of the need to understand the relationship between CNS mechanisms of retention and replication and the generation of variation of operants, and how these compare with the genetic and epigenetic mechanisms of information storage and variation as these occur in conventional evolutionary accounts. In addition she drew explicit parallels between behavioural responses, the evolving operants, and the interactors (or vehicles as Dawkins would prefer) of modern evolutionary theories. The analysis of operant learning in terms of variation of interactors and their differential replication resulting in lineages of adaptive behaviours is the closest thing we have to an expansion of selection type theory into the sphere of individual learning. To repeat the point made earlier, the stimulus-stimulus associations formed by classical conditioning may share with operant learning the establishment of causal relations, but there is nothing to support the case for conditioning being driven by selection processes: indeed, if anything, conditioning has the appearance of being an instructional process of the kind written about first by Lamarck and subsequently adopted by Spencer (see Chapter 2).

It should also be noted that any complete account of explicit claims to the identity of the processes underlying evolution and instrumental or operant learning would have to include the writings of a number of others who noted and wrote about such similarities. Prominent amongst these was the British zoologist J.Z. Young, who explicitly compared learning "as the setting up of effective ordered states of the nervous system by selection among a range of possibilities", his inclusion of habituation and sensitization as forms of selective learning as well as general CNS development suggesting a rather undiscerning generalization; the American psychologist John Staddon who wrote extensively about operant learning; Herbert Simon, early doyen of artificial intelligence who considered human problem solving to be a form of natural selection; and the philosopher Daniel Dennett, who wrote that "the Law of Effect and the principle of natural selection are not just analogues; they are designed to work together", exactly as the constraints on learning literature shows. These are just a few of those who noted parallels and possible identities of process between evolution and other biological forms of change.

In more recent years, the suggestions for viewing at least some forms of learning as products of processes of selection has broadened. As noted in the first section of this chapter, the learning of species-specific song by songbirds was one of the most potent forms of evidence for the necessity of constraints on some forms of learning, though the early literature on birdsong was dominated by the instruction model of learning. But now one of the pioneers of the literature on learning of birdsong, Peter Marler, has published evidence that "song dialects, a common consequence of vocal learning, can be achieved by overproduction of previously memorized songs and the selective attrition of those that fail to match the dialect of interacting males". And as Marler notes, "the distinction between instructive and selective mechanisms for the nature of the underlying neural mechanisms" may be a significant advance in establishing those mechanisms. Little, as noted earlier in this chapter, is known about those physiological and biochemical mechanisms that underlie learning in any of its forms, but Marler's point is partly made by some recent published studies on the neurological basis of learning. For example, a 2007 paper in *Science* by Jin-Hee Han and others describes evidence for a selective mechanisms in the recruitment of cells into neural circuits that constitute the memory traces for fear conditioning. Fear conditioning has all the appearance of having an instructive rather than a selective process at its heart. If Han and colleagues are correct in their deduction then it is possible that selection as a process is more widespread than surface, behavioural, appearances of the learning paradigms suggest.

The curious case of Piaget's genetic epistemology

No discussion of any naturalized epistemology would be complete without reference to the work of Jean Piaget. Piaget was one of the giants of 20th century psychology. He carried forward the insights of James Mark Baldwin on cognitive development in children as a progression through a distinctive series of development stages, and was the founder of constructivism, the constant and dynamic interchange between organism and environment in which autoregulatory and self-organizing processes lead to the construction by the knower of the world to be known as well as the cognitive processes themselves by which knowledge acquisition occurs, which in recent years has undergone a significant revival. The scope of Piaget's thought and writings are unrivalled in the psychology of the last century, a measure of which can be gained in the many contributions to the Modgils' anthology listed in the bibliography. Whilst he provided a significant form of general process theory he resisted the associationism of empiricist psychology and would have nothing whatever to do with the absurd ant-theoretical stance of the behaviourists. But more than being a general process theorist within the field of cognitive psychology, Piaget attempted to build a truly general process theory that attempted to synthesize cognition, development and evolution within a single general theory. His earliest work had been as a zoologist and much later in his life an interviewer asked him: "You have just used the word 'biology'. Have you come back to biology?" to which Piaget responded "Well, I haven't come back to it – I've never left it".

In order to achieve such a broad theory, Piaget adapted a specific form of the highly abstract system called structuralism. Piaget's scheme was thus a somewhat broader instance of the school of thought that was developed primarily in France within the human sciences of anthropology and linguistics in the 1950s and 1960s, and which was based on the earlier work of Ferdinand de Saussure, the founder of structural linguistics. Claude Lévi-Strauss is generally acknowledged to be the founder of modern structuralism, which is based on the notion of a closed system of elements and rules that accounts for the production and social communication of meaning. What Piaget attempted, though, was much broader than a framework for understanding meaning by and between humans; his concern, as noted above, was to incorporate human cognition within the general framework of a theoretical biology that included evolution. In his monograph entitled *Structuralism* he defined it as "a system of transformations ... that involve laws; the structure is preserved or enriched by the interplay of its transformation laws, which never yield results external to the system nor employ elements that are external to it. In short, the notion of structure is comprised of three key ideas; the idea of wholeness, the idea of transformation, and the idea of self-regulation".

The titles of three monographs, *Biology and Knowledge, Adaptation and Intelligence,* and *Behaviour and Evolution* all written in the 1960s and 1970s indicate the breadth of his thinking; in all three his "key ideas" dominate, especially transformation and self-regulation. At the heart of his system was a rejection of chance variation and selective retention of the selection theories that dominated the evolutionary literature after Darwin. He advocated instead an unending two-phase process of assimilation and accomodation which results in transformation of adaptive structure: the combined effects of assimilation and accommodation is a continual process of adjustment and regulation to the changing conditions of the world. Assimilation is the incorporation of the demands of the world into organic structure; accommodation is the adjustments that must be made to those structures on the basis of already existing structure. All adaptations are the outcome of a constant dynamic and endless interplay between assimilation and accommodation in order to achieve a state of equilibrium between adaptive structures and the state of the world, and both are present at all levels of adaptive organization – genetic, epigenetic and individual cognition, including the logico-mathematical levels that were the focus of so much of his work on human cognition.

Piaget believed that "all knowledge at all levels is linked to action" and he placed considerable emphasis on the role of behaviour in evolution. His was a truly synthetic and general theory. However, in one respect, Piaget's genetic epistemology is deeply flawed. Much influenced by the work of Waddington, whose work on genetic assimilation Waddington himself always placed within a strict Darwinian framework of explanation, Piaget repeatedly reverted to a form of Lamarckianism of the inheritance of acquired modifications.

For example, in the introduction to *Behaviour and Evolution* he states that that new forms of behaviour are frequently produced during individual development and that these have a causal force if one "adopts the Lamarckian view that phenotypical variations are transmitted by heredity". Thus Piaget was no Darwinist and so cannot be counted as a contributor to any general theory based on selection; Lewontin scathingly referred to his notion of adaptation as a "pseudo-Lamarckian response". That he was not a Darwinian evolutionist is a conclusion that his own disciples agreed with. For example, in her review of Piaget's position with regard to evolutionary epistemologies, Christiane Gilliéron asserted that "evolutionary epistemology relies on the 'blind-variation-and-selective-retention theme. Genetic epistemologies do not".

Piaget was deeply sceptical of the notion that chance events lie at the heart of the evolutionary process. Contrasting conventional evolutionary theory with his own position, he argued that "the choice is between an alarming waste in the shape of multitudinous and fruitless trials preceding any success no matter how modest, and a dynamic with an internal logic from the general characteristics of organization and self-regulation peculiar to all living things". It is revealing that Jablonka and Lamb (see Chapter 1), as exemplars of an expanded, post-Darwinian theory of evolution, do not once reference Piaget's work or ideas.

The evolutionary epistemology of Donald Campbell

Donald Campbell was a social psychologist who rose to considerable eminence within mid-20th century academic psychology of the United States. His writings on evolutionary epistemology began in the late 1950s with his best known paper, *Evolutionary Epistemology*, being published in 1974. That 1974 paper contained the most extensive listing ever published until then on evolutionary approaches to epistemology; just 13 years later Campbell and colleagues produced a bibliography containing some 500 additional contributions – that is a 40 fold increase in publications, and much of this was inspired by Campbell's work. He may truly be considered the father of evolutionary epistemology.

As noted in a previous chapter, the beginnings of an evolutionary epistemology based, necessarily, on process accounts of evolution since nothing was then known of possible mechanisms, go back to the writings of Huxley, James and Baldwin in the 19th century; and parallels between evolution and the way science gains knowledge were drawn by Mach and Popper amongst others. However, as we have seen earlier in this chapter, few within the expanding field of learning, especially the study of learning in non-humans, considered the possibility of significant similarities between learning and evolution in the first half of the 20th century that might reveal any generalities of process. Then in 1951 J.W.S. Pringle published an abstract analysis "on the parallel between learning and evolution" cast largely within the context of the laws of thermodynamics and notions of complexity. Starting with the physicist Erwin Schrodinger's observation that living creatures should be regarded as machines that "feed on negative entropy", he argued as follows:

> By contrast with non-living systems whose complexity remains constant or decreases, biological systems may show a progressive increase in complexity such, for example, as occurs in evolution. It is here suggested that this increase in complexity in living systems takes place through the agency of a particular type of process which occurs in living organisms and which confers on them the most characteristic property of life. The parallel between learning and evolution arises as a corollary to this principle since it can be shown that both in evolution and in learning there is an increase in the complexity of the organism; a similar type of process may therefore be at work in the two cases.

This process is the natural selection of random variations, which Pringle suggested "should more accurately be described as the selection of improbable variations". What was unusual about Pringle's paper is that, working on the assumption that all forms of learning lead to increases in behavioural (and the underlying neural structural) complexity, he applied his model to every known form of learning, including habituation and classical conditioning. At almost the same time, W.R. Ashby's book *Design for a Brain* presented a remarkably similar case.

It was Campbell, beginning with a paper in 1956 in which he argued for the application of the "blind variation and selective survival model" to "perceptual processes as substitute trial and error", who really began the movement for a truly general process account of a naturalized epistemology. Intuiting that the word "blind" may lead to difficulties, he suggested that "the term 'nonprescient' is perhaps most appropriate". Then, just three years later, Campbell published a paper in *Inquiry*, in which he massively expanded the variation and selection process model to an extraordinarily wide range of knowledge gaining processes including imitation, linguistic instruction and social decision making; a paper, as he said in a personal communication, "written before I'd read Popper". He followed this up with a 1960 piece entitled "Blind variation and selective retention in creative thought as in other knowledge processes" published in the *Psychological Review*. He went on to publish some 30 or more papers in a variety of settings, all on the same, or an expanded, theme. Perhaps the best known, and the one to be concentrated on here is his 1974 review in the volumes written and published as a tribute to the work of Popper, whose writings, and their relevance to Campbell's evolutionary epistemology, he had by the 1970s certainly discovered.

A truly general evolutionary epistemology should not be human-centred, but Campbell realized that, at least initially, any approach to epistemology would have to be tied closely to our own specie's capacity for gaining knowledge. Thus it was that his first sentence in that seminal review stated that an evolutionary epistemology would have to, at a minimum, take cognizance of, and be compatible with, the status of human beings as products of biological and social evolution. It was his second sentence that signalled a profound shift in emphasis: "… evolution, even in its biological aspects – is a knowledge process", and, in line with Pringle and his other predecessors, that "the natural selection paradigm for such knowledge increments can be generalized to other epistemic activities, such as learning, thought, and science". (It should be noted that Campbell wrote that such an epistemology was owed primarily to the work of Popper. This was a serious overstatement that arose in the context of the occasion for the writing and publication of the paper, which was an examination and celebration of Popper's work. In the overall context of Popper's own writings, the possibility of a truly general theory in biology that incorporates a naturalized epistemology, in truth, plays only a very small part. In his 1969 review of "epistemology naturalized", for example, the philosopher W.V.O. Quine makes no mention of Popper. That is why, in this specific context, Campbell is the more significant figure.)

Campbell's initial argument is grounded in Popper's acceptance of Hume's scepticism of induction (see Chapter 2 of this book), and the recognition that if there is a process that has any epistemological generality then it must be something other than induction. What Popper had advocated instead was a form of non-inductive generalization from some specific single experience and not from repeated exposure to the same events; and so what Campbell too was looking for was "an epistemology capable of handling *expansions* of knowledge, *breakouts* from the limits of prior wisdom" that might encompass all forms of knowledge gain from the most simple, and perhaps oldest, to the most complex and recent. His solution was a nested hierarchy of selective-retention processes. "Blind-variation-and selective-retention process is fundamental to all … increases in knowledge, to all increases in fit of system to environment". Thus did he advance the view that knowledge of any and every form is a relationship between some form of organization of the knower and some feature of the environment – the characteristic of teleonomic fit that Darden and Cain require for selection type theories.

The essential features of any process of knowledge gain are the, now familiar to the reader, means of generating variation, consistent selection from amongst the variants, and a way of preserving and propagating selected variants. Intrinsic to the notion of a nested hierarchy is the possible presence of processes that "shortcut a more full blind-variation-and-selective-retention process", which are themselves products of the process of variation and selective retention. Here Campbell was presenting the basis for what earlier in this chapter were referred to as the constraints on learning, a form of shortcutting in the process of knowledge gain. One form of this is any instance of "substituting for overt locomotor exploration or the life-and-death winnowing of organic evolution".

In the 1974 paper Campbell was again sensitive to the problems raised by the phrase "blind variation". He clearly understood that variations could not be "blind" in the sense of being disconnected from the mechanisms that generated variations in the past. But for him the "essential connotation of blind is that the variations emitted be independent of the environmental conditions of the occasion of their occurrence" and that any variation not be a "correction" of some previous trial. It should be noted that the issue of just how "blind" variation can be has remained a controversial issue, especially in the light of Campbell's own notion of "shortcutting", and the literature on the constraints of learning and the seemingly purposive nature of much of cultural evolution. This is an issue that will be returned to later in this chapter, and in the next chapter.

Campbell was sensitive also to the possible criticism that the hierarchy of knowledge processes that he then presented would go beyond the bounds of what would be considered "reasonable in extremity, dogmatism and claims for generality", and would alienate readers. However, Campbell clearly thought that a general theory needs wide scope. What follows is a brief summary of his hierarchy of knowledge processes.

The first level is "nonmnemonic problem solving" by blind variation of locomotor activity until a setting is achieved that is nourishing or nonnoxious. At this level there is no memory and hence no possible using of old solutions; he also thought that such a level might operate without exteroceptors – a literally blind level of knowledge gain.

His second level is "vicarious locomotor devices" where distance sensory receptors, like vision, substitute for actual locomotor trial-and-error. There is an obvious lessening of energetic cost when distance receptors reduce the need for overt locomotor activity, but whether these first two levels involve "knowledge" gain might be considered questionable because Campbell does not attach either to the primary (Darwinian) evolutionary level which is where the knowledge gain must be occurring.

The third and fourth levels take us into the more familiar spheres of habit and instinct. His assertion that the "epistemological status of the knowledge, innate or learned, (is) no different" is biologically odd, given the clear separation of his first two levels from either of these, but perhaps reflects Campbell's epistemological concerns rather than any real biological basis. It should also be remembered that he is presenting a nested hierarchy in which each level incorporates "lower" levels.

Level five is "visually supported thought", which he offered as the dominant form of problem solving in non-human animals and level six is "mnemonically supported thought" of the kind recorded in the writings of scientists and mathematicians like Mach and Poincaré many of whose conceptual advances came with a form of ruminative day dreaming as their thoughts generated variations of ideas, some small number being selected for further inventive thought. James' conception of creative thought as being analogous to Darwinian evolution is another instance of such mnemonically supported thought, though Campbell suggests that James paid less attention to "mental selectors" than he should have done and laid a misplaced emphasis on environmental selection.

Level seven is "socially vicarious exploration: observational learning and imitation". The evolution of such social learning is driven by the economy of substituting for individual trial-and-error learning the assumption of vicarious trial-and-error learning of others within a social group. In the last two decades social learning of many kinds has become the principal focus of experimental learning research.

Level eight in Campbell's scheme is language, in both humans and non-humans and is the most vulnerable of his epistemological levels to serious criticism with regard to its blind-variation-selective retention basis. No evidence or substantive analysis of the famous dance in honey bees by which the location of food sources is communicated, nor pheromone trail-laying by ants and termites, the two non-human examples that Campbell gives of "language", is provided which would begin to convince anyone that trail-and-error learning of any kind is causally involved; and his extension of such ideas to human language learning is a curious and unwelcome reversion to the Skinnerian notions of language learning of the 1950s, which Noam Chomsky and other linguistic scholars consigned to the trash bin of the history of human thought. It is obvious why the products of language as a signalling system acting as a form of vicarious trial-and-error selection finds a place close to social learning in a hierarchy of knowledge processes: in humans it is the dominating form of social communication by which vicarious learning is transmitted between individuals. But to imply that trial-and-error learning is one of the principal means by which humans acquire language, even if just the meaning of words, was a surprising claim on Campbell's part.

Levels nine and ten are cultural cumulation and science respectively. The two succeeding chapters of this book deal with the first of these, and as noted in the preceding chapter, there is a long history of viewing science as operating by way of a selection process.

The remaining sections of the 1974 paper are concerned with issues already taken up in this book, notably the means by which Kant's notion of the *a prioris* can be incorporated within an evolutionary framework, and specifically one which includes a hierarchy of knowledge gaining processes of the kind Campbell develops. No-one before Campbell, or since, has presented so ambitious a general scheme based on a hierarchy of selection processes. He rightly paid tribute to James Mark Baldwin's *Darwin and the Humanities* as one of the most ambitious of prior attempts to expand Darwinian theory by way of a naturalized epistemology in which Baldwin was "consciously inspired by the theory of natural selection" to develop his ideas of "'organic selection', functional selection', 'social hereditary', 'selective thinking', experimental logic', thoroughgoing 'naturalism of method', etc. Such views as these all illustrate or extend the principle of selection as Darwin conceived it – that is, the principle of survival from varied cases – as over against any vitalistic or formal principle", as Baldwin himself phrased it.

Thus may one conclude that Campbell was as much the successor to Baldwin as he was to Popper. He was aware that there is a conceptual risk in the grand nature of his hierarchy: "… a systematic extrapolation of this nested hierarchy selective retention paradigm to *all* knowledge processes, in a way which, although basically compatible with Popper's orientation, may go further than he would find reasonable in extremity, dogmatism and claims for generality. It may on these same grounds alienate the reader."

Well, perhaps. But Campbell was making much more of a philosophical than a scientific case. In developing a conception of so broad a hierarchy of knowledge processes, Campbell attempted to show the power of a synthesis, based on a supposed identity of process, of different forms of knowledge as a contribution to philosophy by way of science, rather than a scientific advance by way of philosophy. In short, a naturalized epistemology has, in Campbell's view, real philosophical clout. But whether it has had a similar degree of influence on the biological and social *sciences*, is debateable.

Evolutionary epistemology in perspective

Campbell's 1974 paper, and those that preceded it, certainly did have a galvanizing effect on the quantities of papers published, and the number of conferences devoted to, evolutionary epistemology. However, despite a surge in interest and activity, especially from the Austrian school led by R. Riedl and F.M. Wuketits, that large increase in published works on evolutionary epistemology needs to be seen in the context of what, historically, had been a very low level of scholarly output.

There were other reasons why, despite the bold ambition of Campbell's conception, evolutionary epistemology failed to make the significant impression that some had hoped for in terms of raising the possibility of a truly general theory in the biological and social sciences. The 1974 paper made few biological references. That the immune system works as a prodigious Darwin machine was by then well understood, but not referred to by Campbell; adaptation was mentioned casually, but was far from Campbell's main concern. Evolution, not epistemology, is what will drive a general theory, and Campbell's evolutionary epistemology was too much epistemology and not enough evolution. The balance was wrong. And it simply lacked the biological vision of, for example, Dawkins' notion of a universal Darwinism, or the bold argument for real generality of Lewontin's principles of variation, transmission, and selection by competition presented within a broader context than a series of unsubstantiated instances about knowledge gain. That was what allowed Chomsky to dismiss the whole approach as a "vague analogy".

There were other, more specific, criticisms. By the 1980s, Richard Lewontin was arguing that his own principles were not enough for a truly general theory, and that "the metaphor of adaptation (that) begins with a world in which an organism's environment is somehow defined without reference to the organism itself, but as a given to which the organism adapts itself" is deficient. As noted in Chapter 1, Lewontin's ideas were seminal in the development of Odling-Smee's conception of niche construction, and invited in the early 1980s to comment upon evolutionary epistemology, Lewontin applied his notion of the incompleteness of traditional approaches to adaptation in general to evolutionary epistemology specifically. Lewontin wrote that a view of the environment as "causally prior to, and ontologically independent of, organisms is the surfacing in evolutionary theory of the underlying Cartesian structure of our world view. The world is divided into causes and effects, the external and the internal, environments they 'contain'", whilst adequate for an explanation of the non-living world, "it creates indissoluble contradictions when taken as a meta-model of the living world". And that includes any conception of the ability of organisms to have knowledge, modelled upon the processes of evolution. Organisms, argued Lewontin, assemble their environments, alter their environments, transduce physical inputs qualitatively and modulate signals from the environment statistically: "The fundamental error of evolutionary epistemologies as they now exist is their failure to understand how much of what is 'out there' is the product of what is 'in here'". Evolution is as much a process of construction as it is of variation and selection; and for

Lewontin, Cambell's (and Popper's) evolutionary epistemology is modelled too much on conventional neoDarwinian lines. (It might be noted that Lewontin recognized the constructivism of Piaget's work as being, in his view, more appropriate to an evolutionary epistemology, but noted its neo-Lamarckian flaws.) Whilst not using Odling-Smee's phrase, what Lewontin was saying was that for evolutionary epistemology to have real generality, it must at a minimum be married with the conceptions of niche construction. This is a point that will be returned to in later chapters.

The criticism of the philosopher Paul Thagard focussed upon Campbell's insistence on the phrase "blind variation" and its application to many forms of knowledge gain, especially knowledge gain in science. Parallels between biological evolution and science are superficial, Thagard argued, with a clear correlation existing, throughout the history of science, between theories, hypotheses and ideas in science, and the conceptual environment of science. In Thagard's view Campbell's controversial claim for "blind" variation in all forms of knowledge gain could not be substantiated – indeed, is clearly incorrect. Despite his own recognition of "short cuts" in his hierarchy by which what might appear to be *a priori* knowledge being the result of *a posteriori* knowledge gain by a knowledge gaining process at a lower or more fundamental level, Campbell had been specific in his claim that blind variation meant variation "independent of environmental conditions of the occasion of their occurrence". Thagard simply rejected this notion as plain nonsense when applied to science, at least, and probably to other levels of Campbell's hierarchy. Scientists specifically, and other human problem-solvers, are intentional agents with very specific goals defined by existing knowledge in any area of science, or within wider cognitive problem spaces. When Rutherford and his colleagues attempted to understand the meaning of the unusual trajectories of alpha particles fired at aluminium foil sheets, it was the structure of the atom that all their conjectures were focussed on, not issues concerning the transmutation of base metals to gold. And what applies to scientific knowledge applies equally well to many other of Campbell's knowledge levels: "The difference between epistemological and biological selection arises from the fact that theory selection is performed by intentional agents working with a set of criteria, whereas natural selection is the result of differential survival rates of the organisms bearing adaptive genes". The last thing that scientists do is generate ideas independently of the circumstances within which they are subsequently selected or rejected.

Thagard also considered the differences in the dynamics of selection and transmission to be quite different, "a beneficial gene is replicated in specific members of a population, but a successful theory is immediately distributed to most members of a scientific community. Thus is science "progressive" in nature, whereas the notion of progress in evolution has largely been derided as a fallacy.

In a curious analysis of 1988, the philosopher Michael Bradie argued that evolutionary epistemology actually comprises two separate conceptual schemes. The one he labelled the "evolution of theories program", which treats all forms of knowledge as products of a single general process; the other, "the evolution of cognitive mechanisms program" concerns the evolution of human cognitive mechanisms, and is, David Sloan Wilson argued, a form of "psychological epistemology". There is, however, nothing in the analyses of Donald Campbell, or any other evolutionary epistemologist, that supports such a separation. Unless one adopts the unacceptable view that human cognition is evolutionarily separable from the cognition of other animals, in effect that it is not the product of evolution, there is no reason whatever, to take Bradie's distinction seriously. That X is a product of evolution does not in any way negate the statement that X itself operates by way of the same processes that govern evolution.

Based on Bradie's dubious distinction, D.S. Wilson then went on to draw an equally dubious distinction between the notion of adaptations as knowledge, which is inherent in the evolution of theories programme, and knowledge as an adaptation, which is a part of the evolution of cognitive mechanisms programme. Adaptations are forms of knowledge because they conform to Darden and Cain's criterion (see Chapter 3) that "one thing" comes to form a relationship of fit with "another thing"; the one thing and the other thing being features of the world apart from a specific organism and some aspect of the organization of that organism respectively. Within an evolutionary epistemological framework, that is what knowledge is. And the evolutionary epistemological argument is that this applies as much to the relationship between the thick coat of a bear and the temperature range within which the bear lives, and the neural networks of the bear that constitute what the bear knows "about" its own social group. Knowledge does not mean truth. It means a relationship of fit which is caused by a specific process or set of processes. Equating knowledge with truth is to commit the same error as non-biologists do when they regard adaptations as perfect. Perfection has no biological meaning, and neither does truth have cognitive meaning. That I can have knowledge of unicorns means merely that I have a neural network state that corresponds to a mythical creature; it does not mean that unicorns exist as a truth independent of those neural networks, and that is the case no matter how many other people also have neural network states that comprise the basis of the notion of a unicorn. Those neural networks are, however, real entities in the world, even if unicorns do not exist beyond those neural networks. To argue otherwise is to have no understanding of the nature of culture – but that is a matter for the next chapter.

A final judgement on evolutionary epistemology in terms of its claim that all forms of knowledge are the products of a selection process has to be tempered by the same sense of uncertain knowledge that led to the rejection in the previous chapter of CNS development as being the product of a selection process. As David Hull and his colleagues pointed out in their 2001 review, the "empirical facts remain too controversial" to support the broad claim that all forms of knowledge gain are caused by selection processes. We just do not know; and in many cases, like classical conditioning or habituation, it seems unlikely. But that does not negate the likelihood that some forms of knowledge gain are caused by selection processes, even if there are other forms of knowledge gain that cannot be included in a general theory of biology.

Chapter 5

Selection and cultural change

There has been a surge of opinion over the last 30 or so years that the processes of selection that drive the transformation of species are the same processes that cause the transformation of culture. The previous two chapters have considered a specific form of human culture, science and changes in scientific knowledge, within the framework of a general process theory of knowledge gain. What will be considered in this chapter is culture, both human and non-human, within a more general context of shared action, *general* knowledge, belief, and value outside of the specific confines of scientific knowledge. Science is an exacting process of careful empirical investigation leading to precise conceptualization about the nature of the world. It is a form of knowledge hard-won, even if it is won within a specific form of culture. Knowledge as it will be considered in this chapter is something much more "casual" and quotidian. It is the stuff of shared, ordinary, everyday experience, knowledge in the sense of internalized representations of the world outside of ourselves, which all humans gain as a result of relatively untrammelled and undisciplined interactions with the world about us.

There is a paradox here. Culture is the product of the lives that each of us experiences. However, human culture, despite its ordinariness to each and every one of us, is the most complex phenomenon on our planet. It is the stuff of money, patriotism, ideology, and religion, as well as unicorns and dragons, amongst many other things; and it is how these "things", these forms of social reality interact and change. Providing a scientific account of it is as challenging as anything that Ernest Rutherford's physics has had to face. And in order to examine the question of whether selection processes are responsible in any way for cultural change, we need to have a good understanding of precisely what culture is.

Because of its complexity, and because it is a phenomenon so central to human nature – and so central to the difficulties and dangers that our species faces – there are two common misconceptions that must be dealt with first before the principal aim of this chapter can be considered; which is just what culture is and whether selection is a process that drives culture in the same way that selection is a causal force in the transformation of species, immune system function, and some forms of individual learning, and the collective knowledge of science.

One of these misconceptions is that culture is a human-specific trait. It is not. Properly defined, culture is not an exclusively human attribute. However, it is certainly the case that particular forms of culture are some of the most, perhaps the most, dominating features of our species; and it is likely, though the evidence is as yet incomplete, that these particular characteristics of human culture are indeed unique to our species. Thus does this misconception break down into two issues: the first is the existence of culture in a small number of other species; the second is the question of what marks off human culture from the culture of these other species. Both are matters of some importance regarding the role of selection in culture, for which reason both will receive much attention in the following pages.

The other is an error which was the target of Lorenz's admonition quoted in the previous chapter; this is that in a causally stratified world, the conceptualization of living systems and processes in terms of mutually exclusive categories and concepts is a serious mistake. This is no place for a detailed history of the muddle and confusion, and worse in practical consequences, that arose when the likes of Francis Galton, Darwin's cousin, and his followers ascribed, if not all, then certainly the most important causal significance in the understanding and explanation of humans to "biology" and how the resulting schools of racial theorists and eugenics came into collision with the emerging discipline of cultural anthropology whose founding father, Franz Boas, was eventually goaded into the equally absurd and opposite view that social/cultural factors are the main forces that determine what it means to be human, these social and cultural forces having little causal relationship to biological forces. As this author has noted elsewhere, mankind's "natural" place is in culture, with culture being an essential part of our biology that allows us to enter into that culture. Thus any causal opposition between human biology and human culture is a wholly wrong conception of the causal structure of the world. The human capacity for culture is a product of human evolution and is as "natural" as our bipedal gait, or any other attribute that is part-caused by our genes. Culture is a part of our biological heritage. That, however, does not necessarily mean that cultural change conforms as a process to that which determines the transformation of species, the functioning of the immune system, or restricted forms of learning and conceptual/scientific change. The object of this chapter is to examine whether cultural change does or does not do so. In order to do this we will first briefly review the existence of culture in species other than our own; human culture and its unique forms will then be considered; the possible mechanisms necessary for human culture will then be surveyed; and finally the issue of whether human cultural change conforms to the processes of change reviewed in previous chapters will be examined.

Culture in non-human species

Within a biological context, culture is a form of non-genetic communicating and sharing of "something" – what that something is varies, though in non-human species that share through extra-genetic channels, that "something" is behaviour relative to specific aspects of the environment. Honey bees, for example, are able to communicate to fellow hive-members the position of food sources and possible sites for new hives. Another instance is the sharing of song forms and regional dialects in songbirds, which occurs through young birds hearing the song of adults of the same species and region. Devon chaffinches share variations in basic chaffinch song which is different from Berkshire chaffinches. In the United States, white crowned sparrows show a similar regional variation of white-crown sparrow song as a function of spatial position around the bay of San Francisco. Many empirical studies have shown with certainty that such regional variation is the result of young birds listening to and learning the characteristics of local song dialects of adults. According to our definition of culture, this is culture and cultural change and transmission of some kind. The first analysis of the cultural evolution of birdsong within the framework of memetics (see later in this chapter) was published by Lynch and others some 20 years ago; and it might be noted that in a series of papers in the early years of this century, Noam Chomsky and colleagues had suggested that recursion might lie at the heart of the human language faculty, but a report in *Nature* in 2006 by Gentner and others reported the existence of recursive syntactic pattern learning by European starlings.

If there is confirmation of the Gentner finding, then yet another supposedly unique human attribute will go by the wayside. One which did so some time ago is tool use in both apes and corvids, as recently reviewed by Emery and Clayton. The most convincing and impressive of these findings is work on New Caledonian crows which display significant cognitive skills in manufacturing tools for retrieving otherwise unobtainable food, such tools being made to standards of consistency indicating tool manufacturing behaviour shared between individuals within social groups. Here, then, is another example of non-human culture.

Corvids, like apes, have comparatively large brain sizes relative to body size. Just what relatively large brain size means in terms of cognitive capacity has been long debated: what is undisputed is that forms of culture are also widespread in Cetaceans, as reported in an extensive review of 2001 by Rendell and

Whitehead. Whales and dolphins, like crows, have much larger brain size than would be predicted from their body size, this being especially the case for dolphins, and forms of culture are widespread in these animals. The song of humpback and bowhead whales is a continuously changing characteristic of very widely dispersed individual members of these "cultures". Also shared are methods of attacking prey and forms of feeding. There are well recorded instances of adult cetaceans actively tutoring their young in terms of approaching and catching prey; there is also evidence available of the young of predatory felines like lions and tigers observing the hunting behaviour of adults, though whether this directly influences the hunting behaviour of the young animals has yet to be shown empirically.

The most impressive known cases of culture in non-humans are to be found amongst apes, especially chimpanzees and orang-utans. Christophe Boesch in 1996 reported the presence of leaf-clipping, leaf grooming, knuckle-knocking and drumming communication amongst wild populations of chimpanzees in central and west Africa. Then in 1999, a group of nine primatologists reported in *Nature* the results of seven separate long-term studies of free-living chimpanzees covering some 151 years of accumulated observation. A total of 39 different behaviours concerned with tool usage, grooming, signalling and courtship, are widespread and customary within different populations. Often entirely unique to specific populations, a behaviour like food-pounding, for example, is common amongst the Gombe chimpanzees, but never observed less than 200 kilometres away in the Mahale group. Amongst the west African groups of chimpanzees of the Ivory Coast one cracks open nuts by placing them on what is in effect a stone anvil and then striking them with a rock or wooden club, yet such innovative behaviour has never been observed in animals east of the Sassandra-N'Zo river, where nuts are as abundant as they are to the west. The authors concluded that such behavioural differences cannot be explained in terms of differences either of genetic constitutions or ecologies. These are behavioural differences confined to spatially isolated groups and can only be the result of members of each population observing innovative others within their social groups and then copying their behaviours. A subsequent report in 2001 in *Behaviour* by the same authors expanded upon the observed behaviours to include the likes of the throwing of objects and the use of clubs against other animals, and in *Nature* in 2005 the first author of these reports, Andy Whiten, together with two other colleagues documented an experimental study on cultural conformity of tool use by chimpanzees in controlled laboratory experiments.

These are just a small sample of a growing literature on chimpanzee culture. It is no surprise that similar studies and results have been reported for free-living orang-utan populations in Borneo and Sumatra involving dozens of different behaviours including gestures, tool-use, and vocal signalling, all showing significant correlations between geographic distance and cultural difference which cannot be attributed to near identical ecological conditions, and which do not accord with any possible genetic differences between populations.

The existence of non-genetically communicated and shared behaviours in our nearest living relatives is unsurprising given both that it clearly occurs also in bird species from whom we are separated by some 250 million years of evolutionary divergence, which suggests that common cognitive mechanisms and processes may not be necessary for behaviours to be shared in very different species of animals; and given also that apes like chimpanzees and orang-utans have been shown to have psychological capacities that include being able to act on what they can infer about the knowledge of others, are rational maximizers in games of choice played against human opponents in what is known as the ultimatum game, and are able to save tools for future use indicating an ability to remove themselves from their immediate circumstances, all of which are cognitive skills remarkably close to those which characterize aspects of human cognition. Whatever the cognitive requirements for cultural sharing of behaviours, and we do not yet know with any certainty what these are in non-human apes, they may well be common to both humans and others apes that demonstrate cultural sharing, but quite different to the mechanisms that underlie song sharing in songbirds. In other words, the capacity for cultural sharing may depend on an array of cognitive processes, only some of which we share with other animals. The mechanisms of culture may be more diverse than is usually thought.

There is, though, one issue regarding non-human culture and its causes that warrants a brief examination, and that concerns whether it has any adaptive value for the animals that enter into such shared activities. This is relevant insofar as any claims for the causal presence of selection processes in cultural change should be supported by the presence of teleonomic considerations, as Darden and Cain (see Chapter 3) specified in their analysis of selection theory; that is, there should be evidence of benefit, of adaptive gains, resulting from shared behaviours. But is there any evidence or at least supportive argument that this is the case?

The adaptive value of birds acquiring song which is characteristic of their species and region is surely rooted in the need to maintain within-species reproductive behaviours. Yet even this obvious conclusion is "theory based", and without empirical certainty. There are also no studies that have yet been reported that provide any evidence for adaptive gains resulting from other forms of shared behaviours. Given the relative paucity of studies showing that any behaviours increase the fitness of the animals exhibiting the behaviours in question, this is unsurprising. As in the case of birdsong and the more general case of behavioural adaptations, we have to fall back on argument and supposition. In the cases of honey bee dancing that leads other animals in the hive to food sources, and given the relatively high degree of genetic relatedness amongst hive members, there is an obvious case to be made that this is indeed an instance of behaviour that increases inclusive fitness. Even in the absence of any knowledge of genetic relatedness amongst corvids and, in most cases, cetaceans, there is a core argument to the effect that the sharing of behaviours that increase access to food might also be judged to have some adaptive value.

The same argument might apply to some of the shared behaviours recorded in apes, such as termite fishing in chimpanzees and seed extraction in orangutans. However, many of the shared behaviours such as scratching body parts or the dragging of branches in display are not suggestive of any adaptive value at all. It may be that whatever adaptive gains derive from copying the behaviours of conspecifics has resulted in the selection of underlying cognitive mechanisms the workings of which spill over into the copying of behaviours that have no effects whatever on increases in individual or inclusive fitness. In short, the benefits that derive from the sharing of some behaviours may outweigh the costs of sharing other behaviours that bestow no adaptive advantage, but which are not disadvantageous. Thus may it be that the cultural sharing of some behaviours may not conform to Darden and Cain's teleonomic criterion but are by-products of mechanisms that also support fitness-enhancing sharing. This is not strong science, but it is an argument that probably holds.

HOKS and the uniqueness of human culture

The sharing of specific actions observed in animal cultures is obviously present also in humans. Imitation has been observed in neonates, and from the use of implements like spoons and forks to the tying of bows and the use of precise gestures, the transmission of specific behaviours that are acquired by individuals observing the behaviours of others is a commonplace of human cognitive development and one that we share with our nearest relatives. It is possible that human culture as we now know it derives in part from such behavioural sharing. What is not possible, though, is any substantive understanding of human culture based only on such simple behavioural imitation. Whatever, human culture is, is it something much more, and quite different from, the acquisition of purely simple behavioural acts. Deciding exactly what it is, however, is a not insignificant part of establishing a science of culture; and "decision" it must rest on, because there is yet no compelling evidence or argument as to exactly what defines human culture.

Kroeber and Kluckholm 50 years ago reviewed over 150 different definitions of human culture, and a half century later the anthropologist Adam Kuper referred to culture as a "hyper-referential" word. That indeed is what it is, and if we cannot agree on what a word refers to, we cannot have a science that considers its structure, that measures it, and that provides a causal account of it. One way of beginning to extract ourselves from this morass of too many meanings is to think of culture as being essential to, perhaps directly causal in, providing the social adhesion that defines what it is to be human. This is not the sharing of gestures or even the making of tools and the wielding of implements; in these pages, the "assumption" is that culture is the capacity for sharing beliefs and values, a kind of social glue that holds individual humans together as a social group. Goodenough provided a broad covering definition as "a society's culture consists of whatever one has to know or believe in order to operate in a manner acceptable to its members". This is an ideational definition of culture and is thus "cognition-friendly"; that is, it provides a definition that is in principle understandable within a cognitive framework. Its virtue is also that it provides a notion of some form of "social force" that goes far beyond the simple motor acts of chimpanzees and orang-utans, and even beyond the conceptual knowledge of science: culture is not just knowledge but goes beyond knowledge and is something that binds human beings together. Culture is knowledge as a form of social glue.

In the long and often bitter history of the relationship between the "natural" or biological sciences and the social sciences, the accusation most often made against biologists indulging in destructive forays into the social sciences is one of over-simplification, usually in the form of some kind of "atomization" of culture by marauding biologists. "Unlike genes, cultural traits are not particulate", wrote Kuper. "An idea about God cannot be separated from other ideas with which it is indissolubly linked". Judaeo-Christian and Islamic monotheism is a different system of ideas from Greco-Roman polytheism, which in turn is different from Hindu polytheism; but all are linked within the broad conception of powers in entities that stand apart from humans. There is no simple, discrete, God idea, argue the social scientists; and biologists availing themselves of such a foolish stance also are usually guilty of ignoring the synergistic relationship between cultural beliefs and values and the matrix of material institutions that they give rise to, and which in turn support cultural conceptions. In short, if we are ever to get a scientific grip on human culture, and what makes it unique, we are going to have to move far beyond the notion of culture as we observe it in other species. How do we do this?

There is no certainty as to how human culture evolved. Behavioural imitation must surely be a part of that story, and the role of language remains, and ever will be, controversial, with some, like Philip Tobias arguing for the presence of some form of linguistic communication as early as *Homo habilis* some two million years ago, but most guessing – and it is a matter of guesswork - at its rise anywhere between 250,000 and 100,000 years ago with the appearance of *Homo sapiens*. We will probably never know. The only certainty we can have is to take culture as we now know it, and to consider its two most predominant forms, using these as stepping stones to the beginnings of an analysis as to whether human culture might be driven by a selection process. In everything that follows is the assumption that Goodenough's definition of culture, as that which people share with others in order to be accepted within a social group, is a correct approximation to what culture really is. The two most important constituents to be considered are what are referred to here as higher-order knowledge structures (HOKS) and social constructions.

HOKS are important components of semantic memory, which is the mass of information that each of us has of the world we live in. Such information ranges from the consequences of simple actions and the names of individual objects, which become bound together to form clusters of knowledge, which bind with other clusters of knowledge to form higher-order knowledge structures. Beyond the age of two or three years, all humans have complex semantic memory clusters which are at the centre of our understanding and communication. Telling a child that "the house must be kept clean and tidy" requires knowledge of what a house is, what the states of cleanliness and tidiness are, and how they are attained and maintained. Likewise, telling someone that shopping at a particular supermarket is good value for money hinges on the understanding of what shopping is, what a supermarket is, what money is, and what constitutes the condition of good value. And these are simple forms of HOKS and their communication. What it means to be a citizen living in a democracy, or to live a life without sin, are much more complicated. But the point being made is a simple one: all semantic knowledge can be joined to other semantic knowledge, and the clustering of such knowledge into higher-order entities is part of normal human cognition.

Interwoven into the process of creating higher-order semantic memory is the process of developing word meaning and using it for normal communication, such meaning forming concepts essential for exchanging information. Animate objects, for example, are an important cluster of things that we may eat or be eaten by, and children rapidly form semantic memory clusters around the categories of animals and plants, with subdivisions within each into, for instance, feathery birds and furry animals. Birds have specific characteristics; they sing and fly and have feathers and wings – though not always. We know from experimentation that people take longer to characterize penguins and ostriches than they do blackbirds and ducks because ostriches and penguins violate the assumptions about "birdness". There are opposing schools of thought about how a HOKS is formed; one proposes the existence of models comprising the necessary and jointly sufficient attributes, sometimes referred to as the "classic" theory of HOKS formation; the other, "prototype" theory, subscribes to the Wittgensteinian conception of the fuzzy exemplar, a family resemblance being slowly established about the common attributes of a particular concept. Whichever proves correct, the important point is that all humans, barring severe pathology, establish separate concepts about the experienced world which are bundled together into clusters of meanings, such as pets, or insects, which have complex relationships of overlap and separateness. Things really become complicated when animals and plants are bundled together into living forms, and instances of each, like worms and bacteria being clustered together as creepy-crawlies, whilst lions and tigers might form under the HOKS of the noble beast.

Two things about HOKS are clear. The first is that the semantic memory of such entities has structure, which at first sight seems to be hierarchical; furry and feathered animals are all vertebrates, and when you add in worms and insects to the cluster they are all animals which are different from plants and fungi. However, experiments point to a second feature, which is the extraordinary flexibility of cluster formation – there is nothing rigid about the concept of a dog which includes a domesticated wolf, a companion and friend, a guide for the visually impaired, and a danger to people who deliver the mail. Exactly how one understands the world and communicates with others about it depends on which cluster of dog or friend, that is, which HOKS one is using at any time, and which are always context-dependent.

The notion of HOKS owes much to the 1930s work of the British psychologist F.C. Bartlett, who did for the study of memory what the social scientists did for the science of culture – he de-atomized it. Prior to Bartlett, the psychology of memory was studied mostly through the remembering of discrete items, like lists of, usually, unrelated words. What Bartlett did was establish a kind of science of Chinese whispers; he studied what happened when whole stories were transmitted down a chain of individuals, one person telling a story to another, who then told it to another person, and so on down a chain of "rememberers". What Bartlett found was that memory is not some passive process of storing details, but is instead an active process of creative reconstruction. Memory *changes* as we actively restructure components of it, partly in response to emotional needs of want and desire, of how individuals want the past to be, and partly as a result of generic knowledge structures that form unconscious anchoring points for memory. He called these anchoring knowledge structures schemata, a notion subsequently and independently developed by Jean Piaget for whom schemata were inferred elements of cognitive structure that determine the recurrence of actions and thoughts into higher-order structures. However, the resurgence of schemata theory in recent decades owes more to Bartlett than to Piaget.

Schemata influence all aspects of semantic memory, and the important point of schemata is that they are partly culturally determined. I have previously used the metaphor from astronomy for Bartlettian schemata as centres of conceptual gravity shaped by the cultures within which a person lives, which then serve to attract to themselves the memories of particular experiences which are in turn then shaped according to the dominant culture. Tell one person a story set in a forest and what will be accentuated or added will be mythical animals and the spirits of the dead if that person comes from one culture, or details of deforestation and species close to extinction because of climate change if they come from a different culture. What Bartlett specifically found was that memories are systematically degraded for details from unfamiliar cultural settings by those who were creating them on the basis of inadequate cultural background because they lacked the appropriate schemata, the centres-of-memory-gravity; subsequent studies have demonstrated the positive effects of schemata if the material to be remembered chimes well with the cultural background of the person doing the remembering.

For some years the importance of Bartlett's work was drowned out by the roar of atomized memory research. This changed in the 1970s with the rise in cognitive science, the accompanying decline in the influence of associationist schools of thought, and with the rise in the study of artificial intelligence. Some of the leaders of work on artificial intelligence believed that the intelligence of machines should be modelled upon that of the cleverest creatures on the planet, that is, humans. Marvin Minsky believed that Bartlett's work of some four decades previously, based on the notion of generic, culturally shaped, knowledge is the most characteristic form of human intelligence. He adopted Bartlett's conception of schemata, that he called frames, which he developed within computer programmes having the features of Bartlett's schemata. The frame for schools, for example, would be inclined to give rise to particular clusters of features, such as the presence of a small number of instructors, larger numbers of learners, the division of the latter by age groups, all capable of being influenced by specific values depending upon experience.

Cognitive psychology of the 1970s and 1980s was in turn influenced by the work of those in artificial intelligence. The psychologist David Rumelhart, for example, reworked the frame notion back into that of schemata with specific characteristics. They are networks of interrelations based on experience dependent on goals and actions: they "represent knowledge at all levels – from ideologies and cultural truths to knowledge about what constitutes an appropriate sentence in our language to knowledge about the meaning of a particular word". The most important point about schemata is that they are not passive receptacles of knowledge. They are active, generative and dynamic knowledge structures. Schank and Abelson went on to develop the notion of scripts, generic knowledge of how to act and what to expect in specific situations, for example when in a restaurant as opposed to a place of worship. Schank further developed the ideas of memory and thematic knowledge organizational packets – MOPS and TOPS.

Schemata theory has been applied to real-life situations such as the acquisition of knowledge by children in school settings, and also by David Rubens amongst others on memory for oral traditions in cultures that have no written script – which, of course, until the invention of writing, a very recent event in human evolutionary history, was the only means of passing traditions down across generations. The telling of stories with specific meanings, and the passing of such tales down generations, may have been an important part of human evolution.

The significant point about schemata theory is that one of the most important features of cultures are the HOKS that characterize it: the cultures of shops, schools, and restaurants comprise HOKS that bear little relationships to those of spirit worlds, clan loyalty, and the habits and behaviours of animals. Cultures as processes may bear common features, but the contents of cultures may be very different from one another.

Possible mechanisms of cultural transmission

Just how such HOKS are acquired involves mechanisms quite different from those responsible for the imitation of actions of the kind seen in our nearest relatives. Thorndike, whose work on instrumental learning was described in the previous chapter, defined imitation as "learning to do an act from seeing it done". Human culture, however, is never adequately encompassed by the sharing of acts, no matter how complex those acts might be such as writing, driving a vehicle, or using a tool. There is no way of knowing what role imitation played in the evolution of culture, and as already commented, it likely did have a part but we can never know what it was. What is certain, though, from observing culture as it now exists is that what defines culture is a rich conceptual fabric of shared meanings and values. Whatever the psychological mechanisms that underpin culture and drive cultural change they certainly go far beyond those necessary for the sharing of acts. There is near-universal agreement that one of these mechanisms is language, yet remarkably there are no signs of general agreement as to how language itself works, or even whether it is a uniquely human capacity built upon a specifically evolved organ of mind. It is one of the odd facts of the human sciences that language is one of its most contentious subjects. As noted at the start of this chapter, a few years ago

Chomsky, Hauser, and Fitch provided a nicely reasoned argument for understanding language within a comparative-evolutionary approach that distinguishes between the faculty of language in the broad sense which includes particular sensory-motor and conceptual-intentional systems which we may indeed share with some other species, and a faculty of language in a narrow sense, a truly uniquely human property and which is defined by the existence of recursion, which is a device or system that is able to invoke itself and hence which gives it the capacity for an "infinite array of discrete expressions" from a finite set of elements. Even this moderate, almost conciliatory, argument by the founding-father of the conception of a universal grammar has not found wide acceptance. A very recent paper by Christiansen and Chater, for instance, argues against the Chomskian notion of any form of evolved universal grammar underpinned by specific genetic selection for particular mental organs. Instead they claim that language is indeed a product of evolution, but not that which is a product of genetic change (amongst others, such as epigenetic mechanisms), but that "language itself (is) a complex and interdependent 'organism' which evolves under selectional pressures from human learning and processing mechanisms. That is, languages themselves are shaped by severe selectional pressure from each generation of language users and learners". Thus are they arguing for language as being the product of selection processes, but processes operating at a different, a cognitive, level as opposed to the selection of conventional evolutionary theory. This, of course, is just another form of evolutionary epistemology that hinges upon the notion of selection processes operating at different levels, akin to the kind of general theoretical conception of Campbell described in the previous chapter.

Whatever language is, how it evolved and continues to evolve, no serious scientist would deny its place as one of the essential mechanisms of culture; and no one who knows this literature could claim that language comprises imitation and nothing else. However crucial language might be, though, it is unlikely to be the sole mechanism of human culture. In 1978 Premack and Woodruff published a seminal paper on a psychological mechanism that later came almost to overshadow the study of language. Their concern was with what they called a theory of mind mechanism, by which they meant "that the individual imputes mental states to himself and to others ... a system of inference of this kind is properly viewed as a theory, first, because such states are not directly observable, and second, because the system can be used to make predictions, specifically about the behaviour of other organisms". As with language, the possibility of the existence of the attribution of intentional mental states to others in apes has been considered, the consensus currently being that if it does exist in creatures like chimpanzees it takes a very limited form. What is without doubt now is the importance of theory of mind to cognitive development in humans. Over the last quarter of a century there has been a steady accumulation of evidence about a relatively invariant ontogenetic sequence in the development of theory of mind. Neonates show a marked sensitivity to the eyes of carers, and by 9 months of age there is good evidence for the existence of shared visual attention. Protodeclarative pointing, which involves the use of an extended index finger combined with checking on the direction of the gaze of the individual the child is interacting with and its congruence with the direction of the child's pointing, appears around 13–14 months with an accompanying shift from dyadic to triadic representation (I see X, you see X, we both see X); and by 18–24 months pretend play manifests itself, indicating an understanding of the presence of mental states in others. At this age children also begin to use the language of mental states, like knowing and wanting, yet until the age of about 4 years, children think that what the child knows is what others know. As Simon Baron-Cohen and others have documented, it is only from about the age of 4 years that children become cognizant that others have intentional mental states, and that these might be different from their own and might also be false. Thus was it inferred by Gopnick that children do some complex mental work in establishing for themselves the theory of mind by which they infer the intentional mental states of others and how these relate to their own mental states. There is now widespread agreement amongst cognitive psychologists that inferring the intentional mental states of others is closely wrapped up with language in establishing communication that extends beyond the referential semantics of language alone. Sharing the meaning of HOKS rests upon the joint action of both language and theory of mind, but there is likely a third ingredient that acts as a kind of psychological adhesive in the sharing of cultural knowledge that is probably a uniquely human psychological mechanism, and this is the mechanism of social force.

In 1936 Sherif described a classic series of studies on how we influence each other's thoughts and decisions. Sherif used an optical illusion called the autokinetic effect, a phenomenon that occurs when a stationary point of light in a darkened room is fixated upon, and after a period of time the light appears to move – though in fact the light remains in a fixed position and the apparent movement is an illusion. The illusion of movement is sufficient for people to provide an estimate of distance when they are tested alone. When tested in a group and sharing their experience of the illusion, which they do not know is an illusion, the judgement of distance is quickly settled upon as some shared standard or norm. The establishment of shared norms is, argued Sherif, a fundamental feature of social life and exists across a wide range of beliefs and judgements.

Almost 30 years later, Jacobs and Campbell (the same Campbell who became the father of evolutionary epistemology though here in the role of social psychologist) extended Sherif's work by putting together groups in which the estimates of the distance the stationary light seemed to have moved was shared between individuals, all but one of whom were "plants" who had been instructed to greatly exaggerate the claims for distance moved. Only one person in the group was a genuinely naïve subject, and the judgement of that naïve individual was significantly skewed in the direction of the claims of the planted subjects. Then, one at a time, the phoney subjects were removed and replaced with genuinely naïve subjects during repeated trials of exposure to the stationary light until eventually the group was made up entirely of naïve subjects. Yet for some five "generations" after the removal of all the planted subjects, the cultural tradition of overstating the amount of perceived movement was maintained. What was so striking about the results of this experiment is that the beliefs that were being so distorted by the social force of combined judgement concerned an illusion – the light never actually moved.

An even more impressive, and startling, demonstration of social force has its beginnings in the 1950s in the work of Solomon Asch, another American social psychologist. What is important about Asch's work is that it gave rise to scores of replication studies and showed identical results in many different cultures. The experiment was simple. He brought together a group of people, showed them a vertical line on a card, and then asked them one at a time which of three lines on another card matched in length the line initially seen. The match was easy to make, but the situation was not what it seemed to the naïve subjects because only one of them was just that, the others being "plants" or stooges, confederates of the experimenter instructed to give erroneous answers on 12 of the 18 trials (of those 12, six were answers that selected a line longer than the original, and in the remaining six, a shorter line was chosen. The situation was also rigged such that the incorrect answers generally were given before the naïve subject was asked to give an answer). What Asch found was that although about a quarter of the true subjects maintained their own view, more than half capitulated to the staged answer, which to anyone with normal vision was clearly the wrong answer. When Asch asked his true subjects why they had given in to the majority view, even when it was so clearly wrong, most said that they knew they were giving the incorrect answer but had felt varying degrees of anxiety and uncertainty, and that they feared some obscure sense of disapproval by the majority.

Asch and others subsequently ran many variations on the original experiment, varying the numbers of stooges, the degree of familiarity between the stooges and true subjects, and the cultures from which the subjects were drawn. By the 1990s the data indicated that conformity to the norm does indeed alter slightly depending upon cultural background – cultures that value individuality and independence of judgement do show somewhat reduced levels of conformity than those in which the group is esteemed above all else. Nonetheless, the tendency to conform is significantly present in the majority of people, irrespective of the culture from which they are drawn.

An even more extraordinary, and disturbing, series of studies was carried out at Yale University in the 1960s by Stanley Milgram and his associates and described in stark detail in his 1974 book. Milgram's work was driven by the horrors of the Holocaust, and by what Hannah Arendt called the "banality of evil"; how it was that seemingly ordinary people who had lived ordinary lives were able to commit unspeakably evil acts against others provided that their behaviour was sanctioned by authority and meshed into the ordinariness of their unremarkable lives, as documented in Christopher Browning's "Ordinary Men", a terrifying account of how middle-aged German men from a variety of civilian backgrounds were turned into ruthless killers in Poland in the 1940s. In Milgram's experiments, subjects were drawn from a wide spectrum of the population of New Haven, and taken to a laboratory on the Yale campus believing that they were taking part in an experiment on learning and memory. The experiments were staged as if they were being conducted under the guidance of a senior academic scientist, who provided the sense of authority to the proceedings. Designated "the teacher", each subject was directed to administer electric shocks of increasing severity to "the learner", who was restrained in a chair with electrodes attached to an arm, each time "the learner" was declared to have made an error. What the subjects believed was that the electric shocks originated in a device that clearly indicated the strength of the shock as ranging from slight, to strong and severe, and on to "danger at 450 volts". What the subjects did not know was that the slight, amicable and harmless figure of "the learner" was actually an actor who never received any shocks at all, but who did grunt, shout, and scream as the strength of the supposed shocks were increased.

Prior to the start of the experiment Milgram consulted with "experts", many of them psychiatrists, as to what they thought the results would be. Almost all believed that none of the subjects would administer anything more than mild electric shocks and would defy "the experimenter's" authority when ordered to deliver higher levels of punishment, the supposed power of the experimenter lying in his representing the practice of science within a famous and respected university. What Milgram found was that over 65% of his subjects, his ordinary people, completed the experiment by administering the maximum punishment. The figure included men as well as women, and frequently were obtained within circumstances of apparent brutality. The subject often protested vehemently at what they were being told to do, but they did what they were told when nothing would have stopped them from refusing and simply walking away from the situation, which they knew they could do.

In one significant variation on the experiment, stooges placed with the sub-jects, "the teachers", refused to do what they were told and went and sat in a distant part of the room. In these circumstances, obedience from the subjects fell to just 10% – an instance of conforming not to be conforming.

The results of Milgram's studies were, and remain, shocking despite the continuing evidence of what people will do to one another, as shown by massacres in different parts of the world from the Balkans to Rwanda commit-ted by "ordinary" people. Considered by some to be the most important experiments ever carried out by psychologists – work which subsequently introduced ethical considerations into psychological experimentation makes it impossible to take further or even replicate the study, though the main find-ings were repeatedly replicated at the time – they are stark pointers to the power of social force. Milgram was himself careful to point out that his exper-iments were on "obedience", which he believed arises in circumstances of hierarchical systems of power and authority, whereas the work of Asch and Sherif were instances of conformity which occurs in the absence of such social structure. While the difference is clear, it nonetheless is the case that both are variations on the same social force that emanates from the presence of groups of individuals, which is the normal environment of the majority of human beings. It is likely that both obedience and conformity are variants of the same mechanism that is rooted in the presence of others.

Social constructions: another feature unique to human culture

More space has been devoted here to social force than to theory of mind and language not because it is the more important of the psychological mecha-nisms that underlie the processes of human culture and cultural change – we don't know how to weight the relative importance of the various mechanisms of the human mind with regard to culture – but partly because we understand much less about the psychological mechanisms and the neurological basis of social force than we do about those of language and theory of mind, and partly because most biologists who have written about culture from a biological perspective have largely simply omitted any consideration of the crucial impor-tance of social force in establishing cultural values and beliefs. But there is another reason for the emphasis on social force. This is that it is likely a crucial ingredient of the second component of human culture that marks it off as quite different from the culture of non-humans, this being social construc-tions and social reality.

Humans enter into culture at birth and become enculturated through a mix of formal tuition and a less formal and structured immersion in culture which results in a kind of "soaking up" of beliefs and values. We are social-cultural sponges, and a part of that absorption is driven by the human propensity for obeying and conforming, which if it were possible to give any form of precise quantification, is likely the greater cause of cultural transmission than formal tuition. As important and unique as HOKS are in human culture, they are likely outweighed in importance by social constructions, the acquisition of which is rooted in social force.

HOKS have abstract qualities but are firmly based upon specific physical entities. A school is a place, usually a structure within which particular kinds of people interact in specific ways with other people in order to achieve an explicit goal; a restaurant is somewhere people go and where, in exchange for something called money, they are served food and do not have to wash up the dishes after they have eaten. Both are material things or aggregates of material things. Social constructions are less rooted in the material world and, while they may and often do acquire material appendages, they are a product of some shared set of ideas and beliefs whose most important material form are the neural networks of the minds of those sharing those beliefs. Patriotism is a social construction and so too is religious belief. They may have material expression, like the building of places of worship and printing of texts, or the fighting of wars, but their existence seems to go beyond the material world. They have an invented quality that supersedes material existence and the world of our senses. They are "things" that we imagine, and when we share the imagined qualities with others and collectively subscribe to them, they become extraordinarily potent forms of human culture that determine how we live, and often how we die. They are what truly mark us out as different from all other animals. Social constructions are imagined worlds which we make real by sharing with others. The following paragraphs are owed largely to the philosopher John Searle, whose *The Construction of Social Reality* is the most important work yet written on social constructions.

Searle's analysis rests on the distinction he makes between two forms of reality which is essential to an understanding of the world we live in, and of ourselves. One form of reality is the stuff of Rutherford's physics, the atomic theory of reality. Everything is made up of particles, or aggregates of particles which would include the strings and superstrings of contemporary physics, or the electrons, neutrinos, quarks, force particles like photons or bosons, and their aggregates in the form of elements like hydrogen, compounds such as water, and compounds of compounds like oceans and giraffes. The second form of reality is what this book is about; it is what is encompassed by evolution, by how selection and niche construction have given rise to cellular and organ structures, and organisms, including ourselves with our evolved brains which cause and maintain consciousness. It is consciousness that gives rise to intentionality, which Searle defines as "the capacity of the mind to represent objects and states of affairs in the world" apart from itself, including the intentional states of knowing, believing and wanting, states that exist within ourselves as well as others.

Now consciousness is a physical, biological, property of human beings – and perhaps of other animals, but that cannot be known with any certainty – and its intentional properties give rise to a further fundamental distinction. This is the distinction between "brute" facts and "institutional" or "social" facts. Brute facts are the presence of snow and ice at the summit of Mount Everest or the presence of gravel in the soil of flood plains. They are facts whose existence is independent of conscious, intentional, humans. Institutional facts, like marriage or ownership of property, only came into existence with the evolution of human consciousness and its accompanying intentional states. Being married is an institutional fact, a fact that arose only when certain forms of human culture arose, which is a socially constructed reality based on a collection of agreements between people regarding a set of matters ranging from a formal contract of relationship, the meanings of the rituals marking that contract, the ensuing rights and privileges concerning things like property, income, and access to and authority over children, and inheritance rights amongst other forms of agreement. The crucial point is that snow and ice would exist on high mountains and gravel accumulates on flood plains without regard to the existence of humans. Brute facts are intrinsic to nature and owe nothing to human consciousness. Institutional facts, however, are wholly dependent upon human intentionality and human agreement. If we humans did not exist and, crucially, if we did not agree on the state and consequences of marriage, the social reality of marriage would not exist – to state the obvious, there is no equivalence to the state of human marriage in other species.

Distinguishing brute facts from institutional facts is central to Searle's analysis, and he derives from it another important distinction, which he labels intrinsic and observer-relative features of the world. Take an object which is made of some mixture of materials, steel and wood, with a specific form. The wood and metal are the object's intrinsic features. However, it is also to a human observer a hammer because its construction was driven by the notion of its having a specific function relative to a human observer. The brute facts of its being made of metal and wood are unchanged, but the hammer has an added epistemic feature relative to its purpose for the human observer, which is its function as a hammer. This epistemic addition is, of course, the result of the intrinsic qualities of the hammer's observers and users, these intrinsic features being the psychological processes and mechanisms that are expressions of the structure and function of the observers' and users' brains.

We need a conceptual framework, though, as to how observer-relative features give rise to the institutional facts of social reality. Searle does this by arguing for three essential elements. The assignment of function, which Searle considers likely to be a uniquely human property of intentionality, is the first of these. We assign functions to all sorts of things, including natural objects like lakes (which are for swimming in) or trees (which give shelter), as well as constructed objects, such as hammers and houses. Unlike the rest of nature, which is just an endless chain of cause-effect relations, human intentionality invents functions that are not necessarily intrinsic to features of the world. We may assert that adults are role models, when, in brute fact, they are simply humans of a certain age. Furthermore, there is another distinction to be drawn, between agentive functions (functions of specific purpose, such as this is a hammer and its function is to strike objects) and non-agentive functions (functions that humans impose upon the naturally occurring objects of the world, such as the function of the heart is to pump blood). A very important category of agentive functions is a special form whose function is to represent or "stand for" other things, which may be maps, numbers or, most familiarly, words. These are the intentional functions of symbolism and meaning, language in its many forms, whether it is meaning imposed upon the brute facts of sounds caused by vocal tracts or successive movements of limbs as occurs in signed language and gesture.

If the assignment of function is primarily an aspect of human cognition, Searle's second essential element for the construction of the social reality of institutional facts has a significant emotional component, and this is what he, and other social philosophers like Bratman, and Tuomela and Miller, refer to as collective intentionality or "we intentionality". Collective intentionality is the shared intentional state of a social group. That group might be the shareholders in a company, all of whom may want to resist a hostile takeover of the company they have an interest in, or the members of a political party seeking to win power for their candidate. What is shared is knowledge of the circumstances of their interest, and what they want the future to hold for their interest. They may also share other characteristics of group membership such as ethnicity, or identification with the place they live. Searle believes that collective intentionality may give rise to individual intentionality, but crucially it is a form of intentionality that may exist prior to that of the individual; when people vote for the same political party they do so because of a shared desire, and knowledge of, the social values of the candidate that they support and the intentional knowledge that they do indeed share certain values with others. The collective intentionality of shared political values is different from the individual intentionality that each person has as they go about their daily lives. The "we-intention" of voting in an election is different from the individual intentional state that drives social interaction at a dinner party. The collective intentionality of both the supporters of a sports club and the players on the team is different from the individual intentionality each person has as they contemplate their bank balance.

Collective intentionality lies at the heart of Searle's analysis and is, he argues, absolutely central to the psychological and sociological understanding of human culture. It is the source of that social force that provides the extraordinary social glue that binds cultures together. It is not the sum of individual intentions and it is not reducible to them. It stands apart from the individual and takes the form of "we intend" or "we are doing this" or "we believe that" and the force of the collective intentionality fuels individual intentionality and individual action. It is Searle's view that every institutional social fact rests on collective intentionality.

One cannot overstate the importance of collective intentionality to Searle's analysis. It is at the heart of all of the human sciences, and indeed its existence is what makes us human. There is also pleasure in collective intentionality, and this is the emotional component that drives social force. We do many things in order to enter into collective intentionality. We join others in social groups, be it at the water fountain at work, or in clubs or pubs outside of work because there is an emotional pleasure to be gained from the shift of functioning in terms of I-intentionality to we-intentionality. There is an inextricable link between the social and the emotional, and that link is we-intentionality. It is probable that social force and theory of mind are amongst the essential psychological mechanisms of collective intentionality.

Searle's third essential element for the existence of observer-relative conditions that give rise to social reality are constitutive rules and how these differ from regulative rules. Regulative rules, Searle argues, are low-level conditions by which complex human life is governed. The pathways of vehicles, be they cars, boats or aeroplanes, are governed by simple rules, such as driving on the right in most countries and observing signals like traffic lights, which reduces accidents and facilitates the flow of traffic. They are mere conventions of convenience. By contrast, constitutive rules create the conditions that govern our lives by giving us a sense of identity and meaning.

All institutional facts exist within the framework of the constitutive rules that govern them. When I go shopping for a book and pay by means of a credit card, this occurs within a specific complex of constitutive rules. The credit card stands for money, and money in turn stands for a capacity to acquire goods based on my past history of providing some form of service to others in my society who have rewarded me accordingly by transferring money into my bank account, the money shifts from my ownership to that of the book seller, and the ownership of the book is reversed; and the transaction occurs within a sea of deeper constitutive rules, such as my then owning the book as a physical entity but not its contents, the copyright of which remains with the author and publisher, and my money is in the care of an organization which is itself owned by some of my fellow citizens who have given their money to buy shares in the bank. All of this, and much else, comprises the complex set of constitutive rules that govern the lives of each and every one of us.

According to Searle's analysis, social reality is based on social constructions that are formed out of the assignment of function, like ownership or citizenship, the collective intentionality that comes from shared intentional states regarding these functions, and the constitutive rules that govern their workings. Furthermore, all of social reality and its institutional facts rests on a specific structure of "X counts as Y in C". Thus does a particular document (a passport, X) count as proof of citizenship (Y) of a specific country (C); as does a certain ceremony performed by a special functionary (X) counts as a marriage contract (Y) in at least some countries (C). The basic structure of X counts as Y in C can be, and often is, repeated with variations across different cultures. Thus the individual officiating in a marriage must have specific training and study (X) thus conferring religious and/or civic status (Y) on that individual which in turn confers further obligations and duties on those entering into marriage under the direction of that individual (C). Other Xs and Ys in different Cs, be these religious affiliations, specific national attachments, membership of a sports club or subscribers to a belief in unidentified flying objects, and many besides, exist which may be linked in concatenations of the structure "X counts as Y in C", or independently of one another.

Citizenship, religion, ownership, the existence of countries with national boundaries, money, patriotism, national socialism – all are social constructions that conform to the structure of X counts as Y in C: "The central span on the bridge from physics to society is collective intentionality, and the decisive movement on that bridge in the creation of social reality is the collective intentional imposition of function on entities that cannot perform those functions without that imposition" writes Searle. The physical substance of money as paper with printed dyes is the same as a set of brute facts as snow and ice on a mountain, but the brute facts of a fifty pound note is not what gives that piece of paper power to move people. The literal value of a banknote is trivial and much the same as a handful of snow; but a banknote can be exchanged for food or shelter, whereas no one will give anything in exchange for snow. The difference between brute facts and social reality is pervasive and takes many forms: thus standing on a piece of land does not confer ownership, whereas inheriting it does and inheritance takes different forms in different cultures; and an island off the northwest coast of a landmass called Europe does not make it Britain but international agreement does.

Two very important points need to be made about social reality and social constructions. The first is their power. There are no human beings whose lives are not ruled by the social constructions which they enter into and which rule the beliefs and values which guide their behaviour. These range from religion, attitudes to money, treatment of other people, considerations about environmental issues, how we rule and are ruled, and a veritable host of others that make up human life. And that is what social constructions are – they are the things that make up our lives. They also often determine our deaths. The International Committee of the Red Cross claims that the vast majority of wars in recorded human history have been driven by social constructions like national identities, ideologies, religious and ethnic differences, and political, financial and resource advantages. In just the last few centuries, hundreds of millions of people have died because of such social constructions, and many millions more have been affected in other ways by such conflicts.

Yet, contrasting with their power is the fragility of social constructions. Central to Searle's analysis is what he refers to as the metaphysical giddiness that arises when we think carefully about institutional facts and social reality that never ever occurs when we ponder upon hammers or the ice and snow on mountains. No one experiences conceptual dizziness when thinking that "this is a bed and I can lie on it". But the statement "this is money and I can feed myself with it" involves a non-physical and non-causal relationship between the X and Y terms in the structure "this piece of paper or metal (X) has value as money (Y). Well, does it? In some places in the last 100 years money has ceased to have value and has been replaced with things like cigarettes or direct exchange of goods and services. National socialism that drove appalling events in Europe in the 1930s and 1940s simply ceased to exist after 1945, as did apartheid in South Africa in the 1990s. One does not get giddy contemplating ice and snow on a mountain, but it is not difficult to question just what citizenship means, or whether the United Kingdom really is united. All social reality can bring on bouts of giddiness and a sense of wonder as to whether they really exist, because they do so solely as a result of the sustained agreement of the individuals making up a social group.

This does not mean that social constructions have no physical substance; they are not ethereal entities that float above our heads and between ourselves. They have specific structure and mechanism within our neural network states and within the psychological mechanisms of theory of mind, collective intentionality, higher-order knowledge structures, social force, and our capacity to communicate. They are simply the most complicated material things that we know about in the world, the products of mechanisms we yet know little about in detail.

HOKS and social constructions are the most potent forms of human culture, and they are what is unique about human culture. Therefore any analysis of human culture as being driven by selection processes and expressed within some general process theory must deal adequately with HOKS and social constructions as human culture's most important components.

The science of memetics

Alfred Kroeber, disciple of Franz Boas, the founder of cultural anthropology, and inheritor of his mantle, in a review of 1953 declared that human culture "not only is *in* nature, but is *wholly* part of nature" (italics in the original). Whilst there are, and were, different interpretations of what Kroeber might have meant, one of the most obvious is that a science of culture should be causally integrated into the other natural sciences. We should be able to understand culture using the same explanatory and conceptual tools that we use to describe and analyse other biological phenomena. Three years later, George Murdock suggested that cultural change must be understood within the context of selection theory, but it was to take another 20 years before this notion rose to any prominence with the writings of Richard Dawkins, one of the founders of universal Darwinism. In the final chapter of his book *The Selfish Gene* Dawkins pondering upon culture, cultural change and cultural transmission, and in the context of the writings of the like of P.F. Jenkins on birdsong, Popper on science, and the anthropologist Cavalla-Sforza (see next chapter), suggested that we should think of culture and cultural change in terms of replicator theory, and in the final sentence of that very influential book, raised the idea that by way of our cultural replicators, memes as he termed them, "we, alone on earth, can rebel against the tyranny of the selfish replicators", the genes.

As described in Chapter 3 of this book, replicator theory had its origins in the theoretical work of Hamilton and G.C. Williams as they attempted to explain altruistic behaviour within the context of a Darwinian theory of evolution in which genes, specifically DNA, are the only units of selection because unlike gametes, or whole organisms, the structure of DNA allows for a high degree of copying accuracy. Opponents of selfish gene theory, replicator theory in its original form, like Stephen Gould, had opposed it precisely because they wanted a theory of evolution that is expanded to take in other levels of selection. And that is what Dawkins was offering, if in a limited form, at an early stage in this often ferocious controversy. That Dawkins and Gould were actually singing from the same hymn sheet is a small and usually unremarked aspect of the history of theoretical biology; what really matters is that Dawkins had a specific framework within which an expanded evolutionary theory was offered: "For more than three thousand million years, DNA has been the only replicator worth talking about in the world. But it does not necessarily hold these monopoly rights for all time. Whenever conditions arise in which a new kind of replicator *can* make copies of itself, the new replicators *will* tend to take over, and start a new kind of evolution of their own. Once this new evolution begins, it will in no necessary sense be subservient to the old. ... Once self-copying memes had arisen, their own, much faster, kind of evolution took off" wrote Dawkins (italics in the original), and it is imitation "in the broad sense" which is the means by which memes replicate themselves.

A curious feature of the history of biology's slow march towards a truly general theory of the kind that Rutherford believed made physics unique was the seeming reluctance of both biologists and social scientists to take up Dawkins' notion of memes and cultural evolution; some 20 years were to pass before the likes of Susan Blackmore and Robert Aunger began to run with the idea. There are two possible reasons for this: the first is that selfish gene theory, with the emphasis on genes and hence its capacity to generate fierce disagreement, was centre-stage for so long in the story of the development of a possible unified theory of biology that it overshadowed its expansion to culture by way of replicator theory; the second is that memetics as a form of universal Darwinism was considered flawed, some of the problems being noted by Dawkins himself in his 1976 book.

In *The Selfish Gene* Dawkins had specified three characteristics of replicators: longevity, fecundity and copying-fidelity. Considered in the light of memes as qualifying for the status of replicators alongside of genes, Dawkins in that final chapter significantly diluted the importance of these criteria. Longevity, correctly, was described as "relatively unimportant". In any general application of selection theory, longevity is indeed a characteristic relative to the unit that is being selected and the essential nature of the change that is being driven by the processes of evolution. Longevity may be important to the phenomenon of speciation but not to other forms of the selection process. Fecundity he granted much more importance to in the context of memes and cultural evolution, but without any basis in evidence. Some cultural values and beliefs, especially those relating to identity and religion, are indeed fecund; others concerned with, say, fashion and unidentified flying objects are much more restricted and rare, but still are clearly instances of memes by Dawkins' own definition. As to copying-fidelity, Dawkins admitted to being on "shaky ground". Memetic transmission, he wrote, "looks quite unlike the particulate, all-or-none quality of gene transmission. It looks as though meme transmission is subject to continuous mutation and also to blending".

Memes as particulate units of culture and cultural evolution may not conform to a universal Darwinism framed within the, perhaps, excessively regimented requirements of longevity, fecundity and copying fidelity, but do they survive any examination within a less restricted approach to a universal selection theory of the kind that Lewontin advocated; that is, one based on variation, differential selection, and the transmission of selected variants which is not tied to the restricted conditions of replicator theory as applied to speciation? In an earlier analysis of just what the basic unit of selection is than Dawkins' 1976 book, G.C. Williams in 1966 provided an abstract definition of a gene as an "entity that must have a high degree of permanence and a low rate of endogenous change, relative to the degree of bias". More than 30 years later, at a 1999 conference at Cambridge University that specifically set out to examine the notion of the meme and the viability of a science of culture based on memetics, David Hull, in a clear reference to G.C. Williams' classic work, defined a meme as "the least unit of sociocultural information relative to a selection process that has favourable or unfavourable selection bias that exceeds its endogenous tendency to change". Hull's point was that Williams' work, one of the most influential 20th century accounts of evolution, was based upon a highly abstract definition of the basic unit of selection; memetics too should be able to bear the burden of a similar level of abstraction if it is to provide the basis of a natural science of culture.

However, whilst it is correct to assert that a substrate-neutral formulation is essential for any general theory in biology that provides a theoretical account of change across a wide range of phenomena, including speciation, immune system function, and at least certain forms of knowledge, it is not correct to assert that we can model a theory of culture upon an assumption that the mechanisms that instantiate the physical basis of the process of change are irrelevant. This is not a contradiction. Darwin did not know anything of genetics, but he clearly understood that there is a physical basis for transmission of information between parents and their offspring that stood outside of the conceptions of wish-fulfilment or prayer. One should not assume absurd possibilities for underlying mechanisms, no matter how attractive a substrate-neutral stance is for the formulation of a general theory. Well, in exactly the same way, a science of culture must be built upon a notion of mechanism that is compatible with what we know about what constitutes culture, especially human culture, and most discussion and writings on memetics fail this test.

In his 1976 book, Dawkins gave as examples of memes "tunes, ideas, catchphrases, clothes fashions, ways of making pots, or of building arches". This is a list strong on the range and richness of human culture, but it does ignore what is really important about human culture. "Ideas" is sufficiently broad and vague to take in HOKS and social constructions but are these on a par in terms of their relative importance with tunes and the making of pots? A science of human culture based on simple motor acts just will not do. And even with regard to the simplest items in Dawkins listing, does a substrate-neutral account of something like a tune provide a convincing basis for a science in the 21st century? One of the strong features of replicator theory was the formulation of the difference between replicators and vehicles or interactors. Ignoring modern technological innovations like CDs, I-pods and computer hard-discs, when a tune is sung is it the pattern of sound waves or the brain state of the singer that is the meme, and which is the replicator and which the interactor? The transience of the sound waves suggests that that is what is the interactor, transient in the same way as a phenotype is a transient entity compared to the structure of the genes as replicator. But if the sound waves generated by a singer's vocal cords is the interactor, then the replicator of a tune must be the brain states of the singer. But it is doubtful as to whether the neural network states of the singer are identical each time the tune is sung. Modern neuroscience tells us that at any time the brain is a mass of interacting activity patterns. Also, one of the lessons taught to us by Bartlett is that memory is a complex process of re-membering, in which the memory is often altered as it is re-structured through its interaction with intervening brain states, the schemata. Simple tunes may not present too great a problem in terms of complexity, but a complicated symphony will do so, as will a story like Hamlet, or indeed the story of each one of us as we re-structure and re-define our own life stories – in fact, the differences between the dynamics of episodic memory (the memory each of us has of our own experiences) and semantic memory it itself a further complication.

Complexity should never serve as a criterion in judging science, but its avoidance may signal a lack of conceptual clarity, and that is what memetics has aplenty. Consider two other aspects of the notion of memes as cultural analogues of genes. The claims of some epigeneticists apart (see Chapter 1), we know with certainty that the inheritance of acquired chararcters does not and cannot occur by way of genes. However, a commonplace assumption about cultural change and inheritance is that that is precisely how culture differs from biological inheritance – we pass on to others the experiences that each of us acquires by experience. In his essay "The Naked Meme" David Hull argued strongly for this being a wholly incorrect conception, in part because we cannot yet identify the cultural equivalents of memetic replicators and interactors – we just do not know which are the replicators and which the interactors. His arguments are correct, but our inability to know exactly what we mean when the basic terms of replicator theory are applied to memes suggests that if memetics is science of some kind, it remains a very immature and uncertain science.

The second feature of memetic complexity is the notion, still advanced by those arguing for the viability of memetics as the basis for a science of culture, that imitation is the means of transmission with the accompanying imagery of memes leaping from brain to brain and effecting cultural change on a time-scale orders of magnitude faster than the transformation of species. However, it takes little thought to realize that this is an absurd view of cultural transmission and cultural change. As with so much else, the history of the evolution of culture is unknowable and always will be. From what we know of non-human culture, it is plausible that "learning to do an act from seeing it done" played a part in the evolution of human culture, but science is not based upon the notion of what is plausible. There is simply no evidence to support the idea. And the conception of imitation as the basis for understanding what a school is, or what is an ancestral spirit, much less that the meaning of national socialism or money being transmitted by imitation, is risible. So too is the notion that cultural evolution is so much faster than biological evolution. HOKS and social constructions come to be understood, transmitted if one likes, over a long period of cognitive and emotional development. What this means is that much of human culture is transmitted over a single, prolonged, period of enculturation within the lifetime of each individual; both biological and cultural transmission are "one shot" processes that occur over roughly the same time period. And while there are instances of rapid change in popular culture, like fashions in clothes or music, cultural entities, be they HOKS relating to schools or social constructions concerning omniscient beings, are mostly thousands of years old and hence reasonably stable.

None of this detracts from arguments for the power of substrate neutrality and the possibility that the processes of cultural change in humans provide strong support for the existence of truly general theory in biology. But to insist that motor imitation, language learning and the acquisition of abstract forms of knowledge or belief are all instances of some single mechanism of imitation, and hence for that reason memetics is an important component of a universal Darwinism, is an instance of psychological illiteracy.

A more inclusive approach to culture and cultural change as conforming to a process theory

There are a number of people working and writing within this field who have largely set memetics aside, or who consider it a small part of a much larger picture, and who continue to assert that cultural evolution occurs by way of selection processes that are the same that biologists ascribe to species change, and these certainly deserve serious attention. A good example is to be found in the writings of Alex Mesoudi, Andrew Whiten, and Kevin Laland. Mesoudi and his colleagues argue that cultural change, specifically that of *humans*, has key Darwinian properties and hence that the "same tools, methods, and approaches that are used to study biological evolution may productively be applied to the study of human culture, and furthermore, that the structure of a science of cultural evolution should broadly resemble the structure of evolutionary biology". They take two slightly different approaches to make their point. One is to look at culture and cultural change through the perspective of Darwin's arguments in *The Origin of Species*; the other is to take the widely accepted divisions of modern evolutionary biology in terms of macroevolution (in turn divided into systematics, palaeobiology and biogeography) and microevolution (with its divisions of population genetics, evolutionary ecology and molecular genetics) and show how the study and knowledge of culture maps onto each of these evolutionary disciplines. A summary of their case will use the first of these approaches because Mesoudi et al. make the potent point that "many contemporary commentators … appear to be rejecting Darwinian cultural evolution on grounds that might have led them to reject the fundamental case made for evolution through natural selection in *The Origin*". Since no scientist of virtually any stature now rejects evolution in Darwin's sense, rejecting the case for cultural evolution would, now in the 21st century, therefore place them in the camp of creationists and those advocating intelligent design.

Mesoudi, Whiten and Laland thus present their argument close to the kind of headings that Darwin himself might have done, the first of these being variation, because, in Darwin's own words, variation provides the "material for natural selection". Cultural variation exists in massive abundance and takes many different forms. From the 6000 extant languages of the world, through the 4.7 million patents issued in the United States in the last two centuries to the 500 different types of hammer manufactured in Birmingham in 1867, the range and magnitude of cultural variation that they point to is simply astonishing. Mesoudi et al. make no mention of social constructions, but it should be noted that these elements of culture likewise are rich in potential for variation. The structure "X counts as Y in C" provides the basis for as many forms of variation as there are forms of social reality. "Pounds count as money the United Kingdom" whereas "cigarettes counted as currency in post-war Germany"; "marriage means separate ownership of assets in Britain" but "marriage in France means co-ownership"; "Micky Mouse is emperor in Fantasia" but "the king rules in Nepal". The possibilities are almost endless because while X, Y and C may not be able to vary entirely independently of one another, social constructions can take as many forms overall as there is human imagination and inventiveness in the attempt to understand human existence and how we should live our lives. Here, then, are evolutionary worlds without end.

Mesoudi et al. note that the sources of variation are of many different kinds. Many relate to prior variants, as Basalla has documented for technological variation (see next chapter), though this is not a necessary feature of the process of generating cultural variation. Even when it is, this does not make cultural variation significantly different from evolution as a process as documented by biologists. Biological evolution is itself always constrained insofar as the potential for variation is dependent upon genes present within gene pools and how these are expressed as phenotypes. The word "blind" is of doubtful accuracy in any evolutionary process, and this is certainly the case for culture, based as it is on cognitive mechanisms which, as documented in an earlier chapter, are heavily dependent on cognitive biases that constrain cognition – what elsewhere this author has referred to as "necessary knowledge" if cognition is to work at all. Yet, as Hull et al. stated in their 2001 essay on selection theory, "we see no reason to put any adjective before variation in our definition of selection". A recent report in *Science* by Wuchty and others noted that teams of researchers increasingly dominate individual scientists in generating knowledge, reinforcing earlier studies by K. Dunbar on how variation in the detailed knowledge-base of the individuals making up research groups determines the productivity of each group, despite the cognition of each individual being constrained and all being driven in their thinking by broad-based shared knowledge. Cultural variation may be cognitively constrained, or constrained by the circumstances within which variation is generated. But it is not constrained by human imagination, which is boundless.

Competition is the second heading in Mesoudi's analysis, based on Darwin's recognition that "a struggle for existence follows from the high rate at which all organic beings tend to increase". Cultural competition, and the resultant reduction or even extinction of some variants and the dominance of others, have been recorded by archaeologists and anthropologists studying artefacts like pottery and weaponry, by linguists recording changes in languages, and historians studying adherence to ideologies such as national socialism and Marxism. The competition between various religions, all social constructions, have fuelled massive causal effects on millions of people in the last two millennia. Even the competition between scientific ideas like evolution and the big bang on the one hand and fundamentalist religious beliefs on the other bear witness to the competitive phenomenon of culture and cultural change. And just as in Darwin's observation that competition is most severe between "closely allied forms", so it is the case for cultural evolution: the social construction of money itself competes only weakly with conceptions of how it should be distributed, whereas the family of ideas on how wealth should be shared are in fierce and constant competition.

Inheritance is Mesoudi et al.'s next heading. "Any variation which is not inherited is unimportant for us" wrote Darwin, even though the detailed mechanisms of inheritance only began to be understood decades after his death. Classic studies by Cavalli-Sforza and others in the 1980s showed how inheritance in the form of cultural transmission is shared between vertical transmission (from parents to offspring) and horizontal transmission (between individuals who are not a parent and offspring, but who may be genetically related, as is the case of siblings). Cultures vary as to what is more likely to be transmitted vertically, and what horizontally, but the existence of horizontal transmission raises the possibility of general principles of horizontal cultural transmission quite different from those of genetic transmission. Boyd and Richerson's frequency-dependent conformist bias is one such candidate for a transmission mechanism that draws on the social forces considered earlier in this chapter with regard to the transmission of HOKS and social constructions, and which turns cultural transmission into a different form and dynamic from that which governs genetic transmission.

Other features of Darwin's evolution that are demonstrated by cultural change include the accumulation of modifications, geographical distributions that accord with the means of transmission, convergent evolution, changes of function, and the existence of lineages. Of course there are disanalogies between biological evolution and cultural change, like the existence of horizontal transmission and the fragility that the necessity of agreed belief brings to culture, which are the result of entirely different mechanisms that the selection processes are based on. There is an undoubted quality of fluidity to cultural change, even if in important respects the rates of change in the evolutionary process of culture is not that great relative to species change. But in one respect, cultural evolution presents an equivocal quality that Darwin's evolution does not have, or does not have with quite the same potency, and this relates to the issue of adaptation. The following few pages repeat many of the points made in this and previous chapters, but all revolve around an issue of sufficient importance that justify the repetition.

The problem of adaptation as applied to cultural evolution

Adaptation is the one concept in evolutionary biology that troubles some scientist, including those like Lewontin and Gould who have been significant figures in the recent history of the biological sciences. Mesoudi and his colleagues mirror this frailty that attaches to the notion of adaptation in that it is a characteristic almost absent from the parallels that they draw between biological and cultural evolution in terms of the disciplines of microevolution and macroevolution; and in the first of their papers that draws on Darwin's *Origin* they quote the great man's observation that "natural selection will not produce absolute perfection". They are correct in this, but there is no question but that the concept of adaptation, of design, was central to Darwin's 1859 book, selection acting on variation to result in "better adapting individuals to their altered conditions, (which) would tend to be preserved". In excluding adaptation from the parallels that Mesoudi et al. draw between biological and cultural evolution, they highlight the difficulties that the notion of adaptation presents to understanding cultural change as being driven by the same processes that drive species change. Put rather crudely, there is, in more than one way, an "ify" quality to the concept of adaptation and that raises serious concerns for some biologists; and that "ify" quality is the greater when applied to cultural evolution.

The notion of adaptation as features of living organisms that have the appearance of design for specific function first appears in the fourth of Aristotle's scheme of four causes – final cause. For Aristotle, final cause refers to what an entity exists for, what its ends or goals are. He did not restrict final cause to living things, the whole universe and everything in it, he argued, is subject to a form-giving, finalistic force, a force of causation, that drives everything towards a state of perfection. The supposed harmony and perfection of the living world was subsequently adopted into religious thought as evidence for a divine being who created all of life in accordance with the conditions of the world in which they exist. Whether it be in the version of Aristotelian finalism or its theological form, such thinking places the causation for good design as some instance of knowledge of how the world will be before the forces of final cause have acted – *a priori* causation, in other words - and hence is counter to cause-effect relations as the likes of Descartes and Bacon developed thinking about causation. Theological finalism achieved its most famous form in William Paley's *Natural Theology* of 1802, in which he ascribed the design of living forms to the omniscience of a divine creator. Apart from the argument for, and evidence of, species change, the most potent feature of Darwin's 1859 book was the conception of design in living things, adaptations, as products of mechanical processes operating within a scientifically acceptable *a posteriori* scheme of historical causation: a history of selection pressures acting on variant forms. As so many have noted, Darwin's theory solved the problem of teleology for all time.

The potency and correctness of Darwin's explanation of design in living forms, in its most general terms, are doubted now only by creationists and peddlers of intelligent design. Nonetheless, a science of adaptations is fraught with difficulties. Adaptations are usually understood to be phenotypic features, but not all phenotypic attributes are adaptations – the colour of blood, for example, is a by-product of the light-absorbing properties of the molecules of haemoglobin and of no adaptive significance. Nor are phenotypic features that are undoubted adaptations perfect in their design for the functions that they carry out, Darwin himself, as noted earlier, acknowledging this. In a famous paper of 30 years ago, Gould and Lewontin cited the random fixation of alleles, pleiotrophy (the multiple effects of genes on phenotypic characters) and allometry as reasons to be cautious about the concept of adaptations as the products of only a history of selection pressures. In general, all genetic and developmental events are constrained by cascades of interactions that may detract from perfect design. H.A. Simon's neologism *satisficing* captures very well the notion of adaptations not as optimal solutions but of satisfactory, practical, design to adaptational problems. And despite theoretical approaches like optimization, there remains uncertainty as how to measure adaptations relative to one another. But even if we could do this with any certainty, three problems remain, which have special force when considered in the light of cultural change as being a form of evolution driven by the same processes that lead to the transformation of species.

The first of these relates to the work of Lewontin, as outlined in previous chapters. Not unlike William James' objections to Spencer's adoption of a Lamarckian stand on evolution, Lewontin developed an increasing antagonism in his writings to the seemingly "passive" role of the organism in evolutionary theory. The organism had become a kind of second-class citizen in the causal forces of evolution when compared to the primacy of selection forces. This, he argued applied as much to selection theory when considered in terms of knowledge gain, that is evolutionary epistemology of the Donald Campbell type, as it does to mainstream evolutionary theory. Thus did Lewontin write that "the fundamental error of evolutionary epistemologies as they now exist is their failure to understand how much of what is 'out there' is the product of what is 'in here'. Organism and environment are co-determined". And the error of evolutionary epistemology applies to evolutionary theory in general, and in all its forms, including its application to culture. For Lewontin, as the philosopher of biology Godfrey-Smith put it, adaptation is a "bad organizing concept" for theory in biology.

As noted earlier in this book, the work of Odling-Smee and his colleagues on niche construction has always been an explicit attempt to correct for this "passive" conception of the organism: "In the presence of niche construction, adaptation ceases to be a one-way process, exclusively a response to environmentally imposed problems; it becomes instead a two-way process, with populations of organisms setting as well as solving problems", as they note in their 2000 review in *The Behavioural and Brain Sciences*. This applies as much to evolutionary theories of cultural change as it does to any other application of evolutionary theory. The invention of written script was a causal force in the invention of the printing press, of libraries and of the internet and the downloading of e-books. And social groups, be they of genetic kin or peers, create the ideas and values, the cultural niches, that each individual has to adapt to. Niche construction goes a long way to correcting for the "bad organizing concept" that is adaptation in its conventional form. But there is another, the second, problem and this relates to Goulds notion of exaptation.

In a classic account on the "onerous" concept of adaptation, G.C. Willimas defined adaptation in terms of the necessity to attribute "the origin and perfection of (this) design to a long period of selection for effectiveness in this particular role". However, evolutionists, including Darwin himself, long ago recognized that some phenotypic features of organisms have a current utility of function which is not consistent with its original function, or even with any function at all. "Preadaptations" was the word commonly used to refer to such traits; in his various writings, Gould used the word "exaptations" for phenotypic features co-opted for new adaptive usage and argued that exaptation should be predominant as an adaptational concept when considering the evolution of the human brain and mind.

Staying with the example from cultural niche construction, writing and reading are obvious instances of exaptive function given that script was invented just 5000 or so years ago and widespread literacy is a cultural phenomenon of just the last few centuries. The evolution of reading and writing as "biological" adaptations could not have occurred. When any person writes or reads they are using previously evolved adaptive mechanisms and structures, like visual pattern recognition and fine motor control, co-opted to new functions. And the reach of exaptations extends far beyond writing and reading. Spoken language itself co-opts to the function of communication a whole range of previously evolved functions such as working memory and the capacity to discriminate between certain sounds, both of which almost certainly pre-date in evolutionary terms the appearance of language. Suggestions by Corballis and by Frank Wilson that hand gesture may have been incorporated into the language mechanisms, or that certain cognitive mechanisms for dealing with social organization, as speculated upon by Calvin and Bickerton, as necessary precursors for the appearance of language, are other examples. If just some of such suggestions are correct, then language itself is an exaptation. The same kinds of arguments apply to theory of mind and social force. Applying the concept of adaptation to human culture means that the essential component mechanisms of culture are exaptations, and culture itself is an exaptation of exaptations. Here is complexity of a kind that evolutionary theory has never had to deal with before.

The significance of the notion of exaptation remains controversial, even if its existence cannot be denied. Dennett is inclined to the view that it is merely an insignificant play on words and dismisses the whole idea with the comment that "no function is eternal". In this he is surely correct. However, for those like Pinker for whom reverse engineering, which builds a picture of how a trait has come to be shaped to the form that it now has by building a history of past selection pressures, is important, exaptations of exaptations makes this a hazardous, if not an impossible, form of analysis.

But even if niche construction addresses Lewontin's general criticism, and one simply dismisses the concept of exaptation as a trivial aspect of evolutionary theory, there remains the third difficulty regarding the notion of adaptation when applied to culture. The arguments of Murdock, Mesoudi, Dennett, Dawkins, and others that cultural change conforms to a selection process are persuasive and seem difficult to deny. But as Darden and Cain asserted in their classic analysis on selection type theories, "selection theories solve adaptation problems by specifying a process through which one thing comes to be adapted to another thing". If the theory based on general processes of evolution is clearly applicable to cultural change just as it is to species change, then just what are the adaptive advantages that are driving the processes of such change, and to whom or what do the advantages accrue? What is the "one thing" and what "the other thing" of Darden and Cain's analysis? The problem is that human culture presents the possibility of multiple forms of replicators in the form of shared neural networks but of very different kinds relating to a multiplicity of acts, beliefs, knowledge, and truth claims; and the the interactors are not always the individual humans who are members of a culture.

It is not difficult to dream up adaptive advantages for individual humans acquiring specific motor skills such as the fashioning of stone tools or the shaping of weapons like spears or arrows through cultural transmission. Nor is it beyond imagining that HOKS, as products of the particular features of human conceptual functioning, aid social communication and raise levels of social interaction. In such cases the fitness gains are individuals and the adaptive advantages of such cultural exchange are no different from the fitness advantages of other cognitive phenotypic traits, the only difference being direct transmission between individuals which adds to the complexity of evolution by adding in additional levels in the selection process. The advantages to individuals of specific conceptual subcultures, such as medicine and engineering, are also obvious and supported by data such as population trends and increases that correlate with advances of such knowledge. That three quarters of children with leukaemia now survive when compared with just half a century ago is powerful, if indirect, evidence of the adaptive significance of some forms of culture for individuals.

What, though, of social reality and social constructions which long pre-date advances in medicine? What is driving the process of cultural change as Marxism, apartheid, or particular forms of religious fundamentalism evolve and increase within specific cultures? Who or what gained in fitness from the rise of national socialism in Europe in the 1930s which resulted in the deaths of millions of people, some in the death camps and others on the battlefields? A general theory of the biological and social sciences must be able to supply a causal explanation for evolutionary worlds without end that encompasses **all** forms of social reality as well as the emergence of living forms on dry land or the appearance of bipedal gait. That is the challenge for any theory of selection that claims generality. There may be room to doubt that selection theories always solve adaptation problems, or at any rate adaptation problems that relate to individual humans. It may be that the adaptive advantages accrue to the collectives of individuals that share certain values or beliefs, that is to the *groups* of individuals that share particular cultural beliefs and values. That introduces the still controversial issue of group selection, which we will return to in the final chapter.

Chapter 6

Further applications of selection theory to aspects of human culture

The ideal form of a truly general theory of transformation of biological systems framed within a causal process account of change extending from speciation to culture, and taking in individual development, learning and immune system function, would, when applied to human culture, have a single section or chapter that encompassed all aspects of human culture and cultural change. However, we do not yet have a sufficient understanding of culture to know just how to carve it at its natural joints and hence how to provide a single and integrated account, if there be such a thing, of all aspects of the culture of our own species. Partly for that reason, and partly because I have attempted some semblance of an historical account of how Darwin's theory has been expanded to take in other forms of biological change, culture has already appeared in Chapter 3 in the specific form of science, and in Chapter 5 in its most pervasive presence as the shared knowledge, beliefs and values that are the mark of all human social groups. But, there are yet other aspects of human culture that have been considered within some form of evolutionary account that warrant discussion. These are economics, technology, and gene-culture coevolutionary theory. That they are dealt with here in a separate chapter should not, as will become clear, be taken to mean that they are cultural phenomena different from other forms of culture, both human and non-human.

Evolutionary approaches to economics

Economics is that branch of the human sciences that studies the production, consumption, and distribution of resources within social groups, such groups comprising individuals within economic institutions (such as banks, shops, or construction companies, to name but a few), these institutions themselves being embedded both within wider nation state groupings (for example "blue-collar workers", or the "middle-classes") and across national boundaries (such as "developed economies" and "third world countries"). All such groupings, of course, are products of the social reality described in the previous chapter. They exist only because there is agreement that they exist.

One of the core issues that has occupied economists and economic philosophers has been the concept of "economic man" – the question as to whether all humans approach the distribution of scarce and necessary goods by way of specific psychological propensities that are themselves the products of evolution, and which maximize individual gain or advantage through an "unbounded" rationality, or whether humans approach economic issues with a "bounded" or limited capacity for thinking and acting within an economic context. Herbert A. Simon phrased it thus: "Scarcity is a central fact of life. Because resources – land, money, fuel, time, attention – are scarce in relation to our uses for them, it is a task of rationality to allocate them. The discipline of economics has taken the performance of that task as its focal concern". But how rational is rationality? In the 19th century, the social scientist and philosopher Augustin Cournot assumed limited cleverness, a constrained rationality similar to the constrained learning described in Chapter 4 on evolutionary epistemology. Almost a century later, the mathematician John von Neumann and the economist Oskar Morgenstern developed a form of analysis and empirical study, which has come to be known as game theory, of how decision-making agents whose concern is to maximize their own utilities (that is, each of whom tries to do the best they can for themselves) should interact with other individuals also determined to maximize their own utilities. The agents do not necessarily have to be individual people. They could be groups making up companies, military groupings, or even whole countries – raising the issue of the levels of selection, which will be dealt with in the next chapter.

Whatever the constitution of the agents, a variety of different kinds of "game" have been developed, one of which, the ultimatum game, has thrown strong light on the extent to which human rationality is indeed bounded or constrained. First described in a study published in 1982 by Guth, Schmittberger, and Schwarze, the ultimatum game is a situation where two individuals must make a decision on how to share some resource, usually taken to be a sum of money. The proposer or allocator makes a take-it-or-leave-it offer on how to split a sum of money with another person, sometimes referred to as the recipient. If the proposer's offer is turned down by the recipient, then neither proposer nor recipient receives any money at all. It is one of the oddities of this game that when told of the conditions, people who are not players make an initial judgement that the recipient should accept whatever the proposer offers because any amount is better than nothing. In effect, the recipient is getting something for nothing. But that is not what those actually playing the game think or do. Experiments with the ultimatum game in studies carried out in a variety of European countries, as well as in north America and Japan have consistently shown that if the proposer offers any amount less than 20% of the total to be split, the offer is almost always rejected, and usually only offers of twice that amount, close, that is to a 50/50 split, are consistently accepted. As Heinrich and others noted, these findings suggest that the "selfishness axiom", the notion that all humans act to maximize their own material gains at the expense of others, and expect everyone else to do the same, is simply wrong as a fundamental assumption for the human, and specifically, the economic, sciences.

Critics, however, have questioned whether these results really do hold across different cultures; are people in Germany, say, really different in cultural attitudes towards money or other material goods than they are in Japan? The doubts were strengthened by those pointing to the near universality in these studies of the use of undergraduate students as subjects. In order to answer this question Heinrich and his colleagues embarked on a large study in 15 small-scale societies in Africa, South America, central Asia, and the Far East, whose ways of life encompassed pastoralism, foraging, and small-scale farming amongst others, most of whom operated within "economic systems" devoid of money in which what was shared or bartered varied with the basic forms of subsistence. It is difficult to sustain the criticism of social and cultural uniformity amongst the peoples studied by Heinrich et al., yet what they found was a remarkable consistency across all 15 societies when tested with the ultimatum game: this was a failure to find a prevalence of self-interest. "In every experiment" recorded Heinrich et al., "the vast majority of proposers violated the prediction of the selfishness axiom". The previous findings from studies mostly using student subjects in industrialized societies had shown mean offers of between 40 and 50%, whereas in the Heinrich studies, there was greater variation within a range of 26% to 58%, and some evidence of sex-differences in the "generosity" of the offers. Nonetheless, what they concluded is that in societies that included slash-and-burn horticulturalists, nomadic herders, and small scale agriculturalists, no behaviour within the ultimatum game situation is consistent with the selfishness axiom.

It is important to note that it is not just the tendency of the proposers to be fair and sharing in their offers; the recipients were also minded to reject easy small gains which would have left them as "losers" when compared to the disproportionately larger gains of selfish proposers. Here, then, is an indication that just as it is certain that learners have evolved predispositions to acquire certain kinds of knowledge and not other forms of information, as described in Chapter 4 – that we and other animals that acquire knowledge about the world are not epistemologically unbounded – so too are humans not possessed of unbounded economical rationality. It does seem to be the case that we have universal tendencies to make judgements and to behave in particular ways with regard to the distribution of goods.

Whether the results from the ultimatum game really do violate a "selfishness axiom" is arguable, given that the rule of the game is such that the proposers welfare is threatened by small offers to the recipient as much as is that of the recipient – both parties may lose out when the recipient rejects selfish and unfair offers by the proposer. Reasoning and a theory of mind that projects for the proposer the consequences of offers for the recipients may explain the results just as well as some form of "innate fairness propensity". Nonetheless, Herbert Gintis is correct to assert that "evolutionary biology underlies all behavioural disciplines because *Homo sapiens* is an evolved species whose characteristics are the products of its evolutionary history", and this is as true for understanding economic man as it is for any other aspect of human cognition and behaviour. Predispositions to behave in particular ways when interacting with others within an economic context are products of human evolution. So too are the capacities for reasoning and understanding the intentional mental states of others.

But does that mean that human economic activity follows a Darwinian form of change? Hodgson and Knudsen assert that many social scientists have argued that "socio-economic evolution" is Lamarckian in form. Simon, for example, in his essay on economic rationality describes Darwinian evolution as "completely myopic", proceeding by "incremental step-by-step improvement from one situation to another". And while it is realistic, he argued, to consider economies to evolve "by some kind of generator-and-test process" with each "business firm ... adapting to an environment of business firms and consumers which is changing and evolving at the same time", which seems to be a position entirely at one with the notion of change and adaptation within the same general conception that Darwin put forward, but, and it is a big but, "in contrast to biological evolution, successful algorithms may be borrowed by one firm from another. Thus the hypothesized system is Lamarckian, because any new idea can be incorporated in operating procedures as soon as its success is observed and successful mutations can be transferred from one firm to another".

Hodgson and Knudsen, on the other hand, argue that while the acknowledgement of evolution as a force driving change within social groups is a positive advance within the social sciences, including economics, of recent decades, the appeal to a Lamarckian evolutionary explanation, they insist, is an error. They are probably correct in this because it lacks conceptual force and arises principally from a failure to understand the essential differences between the processes advanced by Lamarck and Darwin. It may also be interpreted, within the framework of this book, as an insouciant denial of the possibility of a general theory in biology.

The claim that economic change is driven by a process of Lamarckian evolution is based on two misconceptions of Lamarck's theory and a failure to understand neo-Darwinism within the framework of replicator theory. The first misconception, and one pointed to by a number of eminent evolutionists like Ernst Mayr and Robert Richards, is the result of a widespread failure to understand the French 'besoin' as meaning 'need' and not 'want'. For Lamarck the primary engine of change in organisms was change in the world which altered the *needs* of organisms, *not* their wants as an intentional state; the intentional state of 'wanting' was wholly absent from Lamarck's writings. Curiously, Darwin himself committed the same error, as Richards notes, when Darwin wrote in the margin of his copy of Lamarck's *Histoire naturelle* "Because use improves an organ, wishing for it, or its use, produces it!!! Oh—". However, contrary to Darwin's and others error in this regard, intentional states were simply not accorded any causal role in Lamarck's theory. And in any event, as Hodgson and Knudsen point out, intentional states are themselves products of evolution; they are themselves caused.

The second error made by those who claim that economic change is Lamarckian is to place the emphasis on Lamarck's second law, that of the inheritance of acquired characters (a belief deriving from a form of folk biology that, as noted in Chapter 2, many have pointed out long pre-dates Lamarck's writings), whilst virtually ignoring his first law, the law of use and disuse which stated that "frequent and continuous use of any organ gradually strengthens, develops, and enlarges that organ and gives it a power proportional to the length of time it has been so used; while the permanent disuse of any organ imperceptibly weakens and deteriorates it, and progressively diminishes its functional capacity, until it finally disappears". The heart of Lamarck's theory is given in the title to Chapter 7 of his *Philosophie Zoologique*: "Of the influence of the environment on the activities and habits of animals, and the influence of the activities and habits of these living bodies in modifying their organization and structure". Any approach to economic change built upon Lamarck's conceptions should pay at least as much attention to his first law as the second. But above all, such theoretical approaches should attempt to identify the entities that are the economic equivalents of organisms, their organ systems that are used or disused, and as well as what constitutes their inheritance systems, and this has almost never been done.

As noted in Chapter 5 in the discussion of memetics, any claim for transmutation in culture equivalent to, or based upon the same processes as those driving the transmutation of species, has to be able to identify the replicators and interactors to substantiate any claims to the evolution in question conforming to Lamarckian or Darwinian characteristics. It was David Hull in his

"The Naked Meme" essay who argued that without such identification, any claims for evolution being instructional (Lamarckian) as opposed to selectional (Darwinian) are futile. "Not until memes become translated into non-memetic action do we reach the phenotypic level. The conceptual phenotype is the *application* of theorems" (italics in the original). In the sphere of economics, something like the idea that interest rates affect inflation levels would be a replicator, and the actual changing of interest rates to control inflation would be the interactor or phenotype: but is it the action of a central bank in altering interest rates that is the interactor, or the bank itself whatever its collective decisions or actions, or the consequences in terms of change in inflation levels as a result of the bank's decisions? Until such identities are established, it is doubtful that any strong claims can be made for economics conforming to any form of evolutionary process, Lamarckian or Darwinian, beyond the vague evidence of change itself in economic systems.

In a separate paper on a generalized Darwinism as applied within economics, Hodgson and Knudsen argue that "while Darwinian principles are always necessary to explain complex evolving population systems they are never sufficient on their own". What they meant, in the language of the distinction drawn in Chapter 1 of this book, is that the processes driving economic change are selectional in the Darwinian sense, but that the mechanisms subserving such selection processes are entirely different in the social-economic sphere from those that subserve the transmutation of species. They are likely also different from those subserving selectional processes in individual learning. But whether or what they share in terms of mechanism with other forms of cultural change is unclear. Again, it turns on identifying which are the replicators and which the interactors. For Hodgson and Knudsen "they include human institutions, as long as institutions may be regarded as cohesive entities having some capacity for the retention and replication of problem solutions. Such institutions would include business firms." This raises the issue of group selection, which will be considered in the next chapter.

As with most forms of cultural transformation involving agreement between individuals creating social constructions, there is a fearsome problem of complexity and instability, which is well brought out in the analysis of Coriat and Dosi with regard to what they term "the institutional embeddedness of economic change". Whilst committed to an evolutionary analysis of economic change in which "adaptation and discovery generate variety" and "collective interactions within and outside markets perform as selection mechanisms yielding differential growth (and possibly also disappearance) of different entities which are, so to speak, 'carriers' of diverse technologies, routines, strategies, and so on", such change must be seen within the wider context of the historical processes "by which technical change is generated, ranging from the microeconomic level all the way to national systems of innovation". The development of trade routes and navigational aids, the harnessing of carbon-based fuels to drive industrial production, enhanced trading interactions resulting from more rapid exchanges over longer distances, information technology, the development of other forms of energy capture and exploitation, and changes in the dimensions of industrial technologies, all based on the activities of individuals and their implementation within economic groupings ranging from localized business firms to global industries and national regulation; all of these have to be understood within some kind of embeddedness framework. Nothing in the economic sphere can be understood in isolation, and they offer five levels of analysis by which this is to be done. These range from nanoeconomics through microeconomics, aggregate dynamics, "co-evolution" between technologies and corporate organizations, and on to "grand history" based on "general interpretative conjectures on long-term historical patterns".

Long on vision if short on the application of any kind of detailed evolutionary analysis, Coriat and Dosi's essay lays out just how much ground has to be covered, how many layers of embeddedness must be uncovered, in any evolutionary analysis of economics and economic change. A similar case for a broad evolutionary approach is made in a recent review by Richard Nelson, one of the founders of the recent emergence of evolutionary approaches to economics.

Nelson argues that an evolutionary theory is necessary for an understanding of how industrial structures and business firms, and their supporting institutions, change in time. Indeed he makes the case for such an approach long predating Darwin's theory, claiming that evolutionary social science has an intellectual standing in its own right; that the writings of Bernard Mandeville, David Hume, and Adam Smith had described changes in technological, social and economic structures and ideas over time in ways that did not show overall design a century and more before the *Origin of Species* was published. He concedes, though, that it was Darwin who provided the first account of change driven by specific processes. Nelson is inclined, unfortunately, to use the words process and mechanism interchangeably, and thus loses some clarity in his argument, but he correctly homes in on variation and selective retention as the heart of the relevant processes. And like Coriat and Dosi, his emphasis is on the multiplicity of co-evolving processes and entities. Technology he sees as an essential part of economic change, itself an evolving body of practice, more of which in the next section of this chapter. Business organization and practice, however, provides a less coherent picture of evolutionary change because of the complexity that is involved, a complexity deriving from the co-evolution "not of genes and memes, but of technology and business organization".

As with other theorists of economic change who attempt any form of analysis within evolutionary perspective, part of the problem lies in identifying the relevant units. Within firms, individual managers compete with one another, but there "are also companies that compete". In addition, different aspects of economic activity have different dynamics of change and selection. Innovations in business practice, Nelson argues, "tend to be more 'blind', more random, less sharply focussed by research, than technological innovation". Replicability is difficult to measure, with strict replication of practice being impossible. "In recent years, a rather extensive literature has developed on the difficulties of replicating business practices. Among other things, it is clear that the broad understanding that underlies business practice is far weaker than the understanding that underlies many modern technologies, and this makes both reliable imitation and successful innovation much more difficult for business practices than for technologies". Nonetheless, Nelson insists, there is the possibility of a universal Darwinism being applied to economics provided it takes into account certain intertwined characteristics of economic change.

The first of these is the role of "human purpose, understanding, and intellectual interaction". Whilst not denying the evolution of the psychological basis for entering into complex cultural interactions like economic activity, Nelson believes it a mistake to play down the importance of being able to think "off-line", which he suggests is a uniquely human trait. For Nelson, a "good proportion" of the variation that is generated and selected is in "human minds, and explored through calculation, discussion, and argument, rather than in actual practice", and so "the actual variation at any time is a small portion of the contemplated variation, and an important part of the selection process involves the winnowing of alternative ideas for action before final action is taken". This is a standard evolutionary epistemological line in which he insists that "human purpose and intelligence often plays a major role in the evolution of culture does not mean that the process is not evolutionary".

The second characteristic of economic change as evolutionary transformation lies in the selection criteria and their mechanisms. Surprisingly, he asserts that there is no simple analogy in economic terms to the natural selection and inclusive fitness of organisms as posited by contemporary evolutionary theory. This is because "the survival of the individuals and the organizations simply is not at stake". Writing this book in 2009 during one of the worst financial crises of recent history with widespread job losses and business bankruptcies, this is difficult to take seriously. Nelson softens his position by stating that "the selection mechanism in a market setting may involve business judgement and decision making, and the shifting of what firms do, as much as it involves the birth and death of firms". He also notes that economics takes in many forms of non-profit, public, organizations like hospitals and schools where the selection criteria are different from those operating in the private sector.

The third characteristic of economics as an evolutionary process of change is that it is an error to view economic culture solely in the context of individual attributes: "… elements of culture have a life that transcends the individuals that identify with those elements at any time". There is some form of collective process that has to be taken into any account of cultural change such as that in the economic sphere. As argued in the previous chapter, there is indeed some form of collective or social force operating in all forms of culture, and it is perhaps not uniquely human, as will be argued in the next chapter. Nonetheless, economic culture surely does have some characteristics that make it different from some other cultural beliefs and values. This is a focus, an intentionality, regarding resources and their usage which is closer to individual survival and the physical qualities of peoples' lives, and which is absent from stamp collecting clubs and, dare one say it, art, and even religious beliefs and values.

Nelson concludes his review by warning "against attempts to force the details of cultural evolution into a framework that works in biological evolution", specifically not to assume that entities like genes and processes such as inclusive fitness exist in the cultural sphere. Yet Nelson, and others such as Hodgson and Knudsen, argue that economic change proceeds through "processes involving variation, systematic selection, (and) renewed variation". If the latter claim is correct, then evolutionary economists must identify what entities are showing variation, how they can be tracked and measured, and how variations are selected and transmitted. Until such entities are identified with reasonable certainty, claims for economic change being driven by the same processes responsible for the transmutation of species, are, in Noam Chomsky's words, simply vague analogies without any serious scientific basis.

Technological evolution

Richard Nelson defines technology as "on the one hand, a collection of artefacts or operating procedures that are operative at any time, say aircraft being produced by particular companies and used by particular airlines, and on the other hand, a body of understanding, including but transcending design concepts that is possessed by members of a technological community. In the evolution of technology, the two aspects co-evolve". In addition to these three elements, the artefacts themselves, operating procedures, and the body of understanding pertaining to the physical objects, Nelson binds technology tightly to economic evolution in the form of competition between business organizations.

A contrasting approach is taken by George Basalla in his wonderfully lucid and interesting *The Evolution of Technology*. Basalla, a historian of technology and unlikely ever to describe himself as an evolutionist in the biological, or

even wider, sense of that word, set out some 20 years ago to document technological change within the confines of what he describes as an "evolutionary
metaphor", which he pursues with caution "because there are vast differences
between the world of the made and the world of the born. One is the result of
purposeful activity, the other the outcome of random natural process". Less
conversant with the wider application of evolutionary theory to areas such as
individual knowledge gain, and science as a form of communal knowledge,
than the evolutionary economists of the previous section of this chapter,
Basalla has one advantage over other writers in this field in the form of a simple
focus on artefacts as the principal objects of analysis – for Basalla the artefact is
the fundamental unit in the study of technology and technological change, and
all else, such as the supposed necessity of technological change as it relates to
human survival or its close linkage to economic growth, are, he argues, either
overstated or simply erroneous. Much of what follows in the next few pages is
owed to his monograph, in which diversity, continuity, and selection are the
principal themes.

Basalla uses the fabled wheel to make his main points. The wheel probably
first appeared around 4000 years B.C. in Mesopotamia, and was likely developed from the placing of cylindrical rollers under sledges for moving heavy
objects. They appear to have spread rapidly into north-western Europe as solid
discs used to facilitate the movement of vehicles employed in ritualistic and
ceremonial events. Only later was the wheel adopted for use in warfare, and
subsequently for general transport purposes, and then only in restricted areas
of the world. Whether independently invented or copied, the wheel appeared
in India and China within a thousand or so years of its first use in the Middle
East. However, in large swathes of the world, including all of the Americas,
sub-Saharan Africa, southeast Asia, Australasia, and Polynesia, the use of
rotary motion for any form of transport purposes simply did not exist – though
there is indisputable evidence in the form of preserved figurines that were
wheeled which show that the principle of rotary motion was well understood
in central America, even if not put to practical use. Basalla's point is simple.
We live now largely in a wheel-centred culture, but the notion of the wheel as
essential to technological advance is a myth. A particularly interesting event
occurred in the Middle East and north Africa between the third and seventh
centuries when wheeled transportation was abandoned in favour of the more
efficient and speedier method of moving goods and people using the camel –
and still is. The wheel is simply not a uniquely effective mechanical contriv-
ance necessary or useful to all peoples at all times. Like all of technology, the
wheel must be seen within a wider cultural, historical, and geographical perspective. We generate artefacts, Basalla avows, to meet locally perceived needs,
and not to accomplish some universal functional requirements thrust upon us

by nature: "The artefacts that constitute the made world are not a series of narrow solutions to problems generated in satisfying basic needs but are material manifestations of the various ways men and women throughout time have chosen to define and pursue existence". For Basalla, artefacts are as old, indeed, older, than modern humans, and are an essential part of human nature.

Basalla notes the line of thought developed by Samuel Butler in his essay "Darwin among the machines", and reviewed recently in a book of the same title by George Dyson, in which Butler mused upon the notion that machines evolve in a manner so similar to Darwin's transmutation theory that their rapid evolution may eventually surpass that of humans and lead to a form of machine domination over ourselves. This led to a fashion for evolutionary inspired science fiction novels in the late 19th and early 20th century. However, unless the computer age proves different, machines are not yet able to reproduce themselves with appropriate variation. They do not evolve autonomously. But technology certainly does display features that suggest that through human agency it does display characteristics suggesting a comparable process to Darwin's transmutation of species. Basalla pursues his analysis through a consideration of certain basic properties: diversity, continuity, and selection.

Basalla is adamant that science does not dominate technological evolution in broad historical terms. From stone tools, through the remarkable achievements of ancient Chinese technology and even on to the advances of the English industrial revolution, technological change owed nothing to scientific knowledge – indeed largely predates the existence of science. The artefact, he declares, is the primary unit for the study of its evolution, which owes little to scientific knowledge, and equally little to social and economic factors. He bases his argument on wide-ranging examples, from stone tools to the cotton gin, and to steam and internal combustion engines, all of the evidence from which makes the case that the importance of variation is dependent upon two principal factors, which revolve around a culture choosing to place high value upon a particular artefactual variation rather than some property intrinsic to it, and to continuity with pre-existing artefacts and practices. An invented artefact is only as important as that accorded to it by the culture within which it appears, and every "new" artefact owes its existence to already known objects or practices. He bolsters his analysis with a myriad of examples, ranging from barbed wire to the transistor and argues for specific factors, including the culture-bound notion of the inventor-as-hero and mistaken ideas of material progress and nationalism, for the error of failing to see the importance of continuity in the evolution of artefacts. "Any new thing that appears in the made world is based on some object already in existence"; in the famous case of Eli Whitney's cotton gin, these include ancient roller gins and the structure of the human hand.

Continuity, however, does not rule out the importance of novelty as a source of diversity. Artefacts change, and that change is multiply caused. Some of it is random, what he terms universal artefactual diversity, and some is guided by reasoning in response to specific environmental demands, and others in recent times by scientific innovation. An example of the former were the changes wrought upon the form of the axe in the American new world. The early settlers in the American colonies brought with them European-style axes, suitable for cutting and shaping logs. But they were not well suited to the task of felling trees, and trees of different sorts that were cleared to make way for agricultural space. The result was a diversification of axe forms such that by the 1860s, one American axe manufacturer listed some 15 different forms of axe, most named after the states in which they were best suited for specific forest forms (Kentucky, Ohio, Michigan etc), and by the early 20th century the number of different axe forms manufactured in the United States exceeded one hundred. This is an instance of design resulting in adaptation to specific environmental conditions, and is thus a good example of design of artefacts conforming to Darden and Cain's teleonomic principle. But it is hardly science.

In recent centuries, of course, artefactual change has indeed been strongly influenced by scientific knowledge. In the 17th and 18th centuries the French scientist Denis Papin conducted experiments with heated water in tightly confined spaces to generate movement of pistons caused by the expansive force of steam. But it was a non-scientist, one Thomas Newcomen of England, an ironmonger, who developed Papin's work to invent pumps that would drain water from the Cornish and Devon mines. In a similar fashion, the science of James Clerk Maxwell and Heinrich Hertz on electromagnetic waves was developed by a non-scientist, Guglielmo Marconi, to invent wireless transmission that would eventually result in trans-Atlantic radio communication. Basalla's point is not that science has not played a prominent role in recent centuries in the evolution of technology, which it manifestly has done, witness transistors and nuclear power both as weapons and generators of electricity, but that the technological advances based on the findings of scientists has often been the result of the work of non-scientists.

Many social conditions are picked out by Basalla as generators of diversity in technology. These include conflict between workers and the owners of resources like mines and factories; heightened commercial competition; labour scarcity; the increasing costs of natural resources; market demand; and in the world of today, one might add climate change and the need for renewable energy sources. He also notes the existence of a curious conservative force in technology, which is sufficiently prevalent for archaeologists to coin a new word to describe the tendency for new materials to be handled and worked quite unnecessarily like older materials, a phenomenon called skeuomorphism, equivalent to the constraints on learning described in Chapter 4.

Pursuing his "evolutionary metaphor", Basalla devotes two chapters to the selection forces that operate in technological evolution. Here, like many evolutionary economists, he draws what he considers to be a strong disanalogy between evolution that leads to the transmutation of species, and that which results in technological transformation. Unlike evolution by natural selection which has "no preordained goal, purpose, or direction", technological evolution is more like artificial selection by plant and animal breeders and "is the result of a conscious process in which human judgement and taste are exercised in the pursuit of some biological, technological, psychological, social, economic, or cultural goal". He does recognize that slow changes in artefacts over time, as in stone tool history, may conform more closely to the transformation of species or organism, but argues that, at least in the last ten or twelve millennia, humans have used intelligence to fashion new artefacts.

However, as argued earlier in this book, and as will be repeated in the final chapter, if aspects of intelligence, of the capacity to acquire knowledge, or to generate different forms of social reality, *occurs by way of the same processes that cause the transmutation of species,* then there simply is no disanalogy. The intentional use of intelligence to narrow the range of variation is, in kind and in consequence, no different from the genetic and developmental constraints on variant generation long recognized as existing in the evolution of species.

Another disanalogy was, Basalla, points out, noted by the anthropologist Alfred Kroeber over a half century ago. Kroeber, in a broad ranging review of his discipline, drew up for comparison two family trees, one of biological species, and the other of cultural artefacts. The former looked like any biological tree ever observed, with separate branches splitting to represent transmutation, but the various branches then remaining separate and isolated, never curving back and joining with other separated branches to form new life forms. This does not apply to the tree of cultural artefacts whose branches merge with other branches to produce hybridized entities like the automobile which was a fusion of the internal combustion engine and the horse-drawn carriage. But again one needs to be cautious in pointing to supposed disanalogies. As noted in an earlier chapter of this book, it is now accepted that hybridization is far more common in plant evolution than was thought even just a decade or two ago. One should also note the way in which the epigenetic approaches to evolution considered in Chapter 1 have widened the theoretical approaches to the processes that are causal in evolution. Disanalogies based on outmoded thinking are not disanalogies at all.

Basalla is especially interesting in pointing to the vagaries and uncertainties that relate to the selection of artefacts. When Thomas Edison first invented the phonograph he specified ten ways in which the invention might be used and further developed. Musical reproduction was not high on his list, but, of course, it was precisely recorded music that saw the greatest development and usage of the phonograph. It is equally difficult to establish selection forces within a historical perspective. The use of water power in the form of water mills extends back to the first century B.C., but it took some 500 years before the waterwheel transformed European food production, with medieval water power technology, Basalla avows, laying the foundations for the industrial age of the late 18th century. Why the history of the use of water technology was so prolonged, given the, with hindsight, understanding of the huge advantages of waterpower over that of human or animal labour, is unclear. Basalla also points to the uncertainties regarding economic selection factors of relatively recent technological change. He points to questions that have been raised regarding the widely accepted views that the railways were a crucial factor in the 19th and 20th century advances in the technology and economic growth of the United States, and notes that questions have been raised as to whether the development of canal systems might not have achieved the same results at lower costs. Exactly why railways were selected over canals is unclear.

Deeply based cultural selectors also have a part to play in the story of technological change. European firearms were introduced into Japan by Portuguese travellers in the 1540s. They were quickly selected by Japanese craftsmen because of their obvious advantages in combat over the sword, spear, and bow and arrow, and within 150 years there were more guns in Japan than anywhere else in the world. Then at the height of their production and usage, the Japanese renounced the gun in favour of traditional weapons because the elite warrior class, the samurai, preferred to fight with swords and spears. Guns simply did not accord with traditional symbols, artistry, and cultural values. They failed to match ancient ideals of heroism and courage, and failed to link with aesthetic notions of the use of the human body. By the late 18th century firearms were an antiquated and unused technology until the collapse of Japanese resistance to the intrusion of western ideas. Within a few decades Japan had re-established itself as a major military power based on modern technology. Yet for a significant period "the Japanese proved that deep cultural values can overcome practical considerations" in the selection of technology.

Basalla concludes that "a workable theory of technological evolution requires there be no technological progress in the traditional sense of the term" but accepts that limited progress may be observed within very restricted frameworks, and at certain periods of human history. In this sense too, technological evolution appears to resemble the change of species in time.

Attempts to analyse technological change within an evolutionary framework have one advantage over the application of evolutionary theory within the wider cultural sphere, including economics. This is in the clarity with which one of the basic evolutionary units can be identified. The artefact, whether a hand-held tool or a waterwheel, is the operator or interactor, to use the phrases of C.H. Waddington and David Hull. It is what acts on the world with specific consequences for their selection. However, what are the replicators is much harder to resolve, a problem in common with the wider issue of analysing cultural change within the context of the fundamental process of evolution. Replicators exist within the complex of neural network states of the inventors, their written works and calculations by which they are preserved in time, the very neural network states of the craftsmen who make the artefacts, and also the forms of the technological entities, the artefacts that manufacture the artefacts.

The notion that technological change can be understood, and should be understood, within the context of evolutionary theory, is, however, a point that continues to be debated. Brian Loasby's work is a good example of the doubts expressed by what might be called "the-devil-is-in-the-detail" school of thought, in which the details reveal too many differences for any strong claim for identity of process. The basic difficulty for Loasby is the old problem that humans think, and thought takes technological evolution to a quite different realm from that which occurs in the transmutation of species. The difference between the latter and the former is that technological change hinges on a process in which "selection takes place before the event" – the event being, presumably, the construction and use of an artefact – and "there is thus no room for any kind of process that might be reasonably be called 'evolutionary'". Furthermore, "human action is often the result of human design; but human design is inherently fallible, however secure its logic, since it is based on knowledge that is usually incomplete or erroneous". Another difficulty for Loasby is that "neo-Darwinian explanations of human activity. … ignores human purpose".

Once again it must be pointed out that thought, purpose, and fallibility in no way rule out the operation of general selection processes. Loasby does recognize that such an approach cannot be built upon the notion of a single unit of selection: "techniques, artefacts, and firms are all relevant, and so too are institutions, organizational arrangements, and bodies of knowledge, including know-that, know-why, know-how, and know-who. The essential requirement is to distinguish, at each stage of analysis, between the elements and connections that remain stable and the elements and connections that change. This combination varies according to time and circumstance; and there is no simple hierarchy". Loasby is correct here in pointing to the enormous complexity of all forms of cultural change and evolution. He also quotes in admiration someone as saying that innovation begins with "the imagined, deemed possible", a phrase not unlike that used by this author elsewhere in describing social reality of the Searle kind (see previous chapter) as "the imagined world made real". Indeed, hierarchies are never simple. But complexity does not rule out the existence of general processes; and for anyone familiar with the biological theories of evolution of living forms in their Darwinian and neo-Darwinian versions, complexity is not a stranger.

At the end of his book, Basalla notes that most biologists have avoided the notion of evolution as progressive and directed towards some predetermined goal. "In similar fashion I have resisted the tendency to make the advancement of humanity or biological necessity the end toward which all technological change is directed"; instead, Basalla writes, he has chosen to see technological evolution as the ways in which people throughout human history have chosen to define and pursue their existence. This places technological change firmly, and tangibly, within the reach of some general theory of cultural change.

Gene-culture coevolution

As noted in an earlier chapter, it is a wholly wrong conception of our species to see culture as anything other than a prominent, perhaps the most prominent, part of human nature. In a recent book, *Not by Genes Alone*, Richerson and Boyd, two of the pioneers of gene-culture coevolutionary theory, describe what they term the "big mistake" hypothesis, which is the idea that from the genes' point of view, a great deal of modern human behaviour is a horrible error in that it acts against the only thing that "matters" to genes, which is their perpetuation. What Richerson and Boyd argue, however, is that from the example of the most materially rich of people having, on average, the lowest numbers of children, through the overindulgence in obesity-causing fast foods, and on to the terrible destructiveness of warfare, "much human maladaptation is an unavoidable by-product of cumulative cultural adaptation". Culture and genes coevolve, and in so doing, the adaptive value of culture, an inherent part of human nature, across time leads to improved conditions for human life. However destructive some aspects of culture might be, culture, as a part of human nature, in general works to the benefit of humans, with changes in both culture and genes being indissolubly linked.

It may seem obvious to the casual observer, contemplating the availability of food for most people and the treatments for disease, that the conditions for survival and reproduction are much improved now than they were hundreds of years ago, and much the more so if comparisons are made with thousands of years in the past. But providing specific and quantifiable instances of how cultural change have positively affected human survival is less easy, and only recently have formal models been developed that capture the long-term interactions of culture and biological evolution. One of the best known instances of gene-culture coevolution, and one of the earliest to stimulate the development of gene-culture modelling, is that of lactose consumption and the cultural evolution of animal husbandry, as described by the anthropologist William Durham.

Lactose is the sugar found in mammalian milk, and whilst the enzymes for digesting lactose are present in the alimentary tracts of all people prior to weaning, the enzymes decline in level, and often disappear completely, from weaning onwards in some two thirds of all people rendering the majority of humans, post-weaning, lactose intolerant with illness caused by the consumption of lactose often being quite severe. There is now extensive evidence showing that lactose tolerance or intolerance is characteristic of whole populations. Some 95% of all Scandinavians are lactose tolerant, as are around 80% of central and western European peoples, whereas almost all African, southern and East Asian peoples are lactose intolerant. Furthermore, across Europe, extending from the north-west to the south-east there is a significant gradient in tolerance to lactose post-weaning with high levels in the north and west declining steadily as one samples peoples in the east and south; There is also a correlated gradient of milk and milk-product preparation and consumption with people in northern Europe routinely consuming unprocessed milk and its products like cream, whereas towards Africa and the Levant the consumption of milk products are largely processed such that lactose levels are much reduced as in yoghurt and kefir, amongst others.

Lactose tolerance is known to be the result of a genetic mutation, so what led to the fixation of the mutated gene in some populations and not others? There are two answers to this question. The consumption of milk from domesticated animal stocks, which has occurred over some thousands of years, is a significant solution to the energy demands of people living under conditions of severe malnourishment, provided that their genetic constitution was such as to allow the eating and drinking of lactose products after weaning, the mutated gene, of course, being heritable and hence increasing the fitness of the individuals in such populations. However, as Durham notes, the spatial distribution of lactose tolerant people is somewhat odd, with kinks in it that nutritional value of lactose alone cannot explain. One other factor must also be important in driving the mutated gene to fixation, and this, it is now thought, is the facilitating effect that lactose has on calcium absorption in the gut. Calcium is a crucial element for a number of essential bodily functions, including that of the nervous system, and this is especially the case in those deficient in vitamin D which facilitates calcium absorption. And vitamin D deficiency is itself an acute condition in those whose lives are spent in low levels of sunlight, because the production of vitamin D is an important by-product of ultraviolet radiation on the skin, the lack of which also has serious consequences for bone development, low levels of which result in illnesses such as rickets and osteo-malacia. The combined effects of the calorific values of milk, together with the importance of calcium and vitamin D is now generally held to have been the conditions of selection that have driven the mutated lactose-absorbing gene to fixation in populations living under circumstances of acute nutritional stress in climates with low levels of sunlight.

The important point, however, is that the ready availability of lactose long after weaning of infants comes from animals, and is the direct result of specific cultural practices that derive from animal husbandry. The latter, and its accom-panying dairying activities such as the conversion of milk products into cheeses and yoghurt, are specific instances of agricultural invention and food prepara-tion that date back about ten thousand years, and were the crucial factors that created the conditions for the genetic fixation of lactose-tolerance in a minor-ity of human populations. Had the cultural activities of agriculture not been invented and propagated within human populations, then the mutant gene in question would not have been driven to fixation. Here is a specific instance of gene-culture coevolution that does not depend upon generalized and merely intuited statements as to the beneficial effects of culture on humans. It also points to the causal power of culture. In 1981, Lumsden and Wilson wrote a book that included the phrase "coevolutionary process" in its title. The general tenor of the work, however, was not for some equality of causation for genetic and cultural processes, but of the supremacy of "genetically determined epige-netic rules"; culture, they avowed, certainly does have causal powers, but these are always subject to a kind of "genetic leash". At about the same time, Cavalli-Sforza and Feldman, and another collaboration between Boyd and Richerson developed mathematical models of gene-culture coevolution in which the causal powers of genetic evolution and cultural evolution are considered to be on a par with one another. It requires little scholarship to know that Lumsden and Wilson's conception barely survived birth, whereas that of Cavalli-Sforza and Feldman, and Boyd and Richerson, has thrived. Laland and Brown describe gene-culture coevolutionary theory as "a hybrid cross between memetics and evolutionary psychology, with a little mathematical rigour thrown into the pot. Like memeticists, gene-culture enthusiasts treat culture as an evolving pool of ideas, beliefs, values, and knowledge that is learned and socially trans-mitted between individuals". But for the descendents of both pairs of theorists, the "leash that ties culture to genes tugs both ways" as Laland and Brown put it. Gene-culture coevolutionary theory, in essence, describes two parallel tracks of evolving processes, each, of course, resting upon entirely different mecha-nisms, but neither is independent of the other, and these interactions are medi-ated by way of the neural networks that give rise to human intelligence.

Gene-culture coevolutionary theory is one of the quintessentially multidisciplinary corners of modern science. In their 1985 book, Boyd and Richerson recognized this by devoting a significant amount of several chapters to what are the essentially *psychological* issues of social learning, which they consider to be the kingpin of cultural transmission. They rejected the notion of culture as embodied in discrete particles such as memes (as Dawkins would have it) or culturgens (the version of Lumsden and Wilson), but strongly embraced the notion that social learning, that is the acquisition of information from others, is different from individual learning in which other people play no role at all: "social learning and individual learning are *alternative* ways of acquiring a particular behavioural variant" (italics in the original). A child that learns particular dietary preferences by observing what other eat, for example, is mediated by different mechanisms from those which determine eating behaviour as a result of individual experience that does not involve the behaviour of others. At the time of writing this, Boyd and Richerson could have known of nothing to support this conjecture, but recent work on the involvement of particular parts of the brains of humans and some other primates, and of the role of specific so-called mirror cells in these brain regions thought to be involved in both imitation and the inferring of intentional mental states in others, suggests that it is possible that Boyd and Richerson may have built into their modelling assumptions about underlying mechanisms that may yet prove to be correct. The point of their distinction is they needed to make the assumption of differences in operating costs and differences in error rates arising from different mechanisms operating in environments in which change is occurring at different rates. Individual learning may be a more adaptive form of learning in environments that are constantly altering, whereas social learning may have greater fitness benefits in more stable environments. These are, however, details about assumed mechanisms which may or may not be correct, but which do not detract from the main point of such modelling, which is of a mutual dependence and constant interaction between biological and cultural evolution mediated by selection within both spheres.

Boyd and Richerson also make important distinctions between gene-based evolution and cultural evolution in terms of the degree of randomness operating within each, and the forces that constrain change. The transmission between individuals in cultural evolution need not be wholly "vertical" between parents and offspring, as is the case for the genetic evolution in all animals that exhibit culture, but may involve transmission between individuals that are not strongly genetically related. Another difference, and one of the most important for Boyd and Richerson, is that in cultural evolution there is a frequency-dependent bias: "The tendency of an individual to acquire a particular cultural variant may be influenced by the commonness or rarity of the trait among that individual's cultural parents". In particular, a frequency-dependent bias that predisposes people to accept the views of the majority provides an immediate link between gene-culture coevolution and the social force discussed in Chapter 5 of this book. The greater the number of people adhering to a particular belief or practise, the more likely it is that that belief or practise will be adopted by others. This was not a novel idea. Published in the last years of the 19th century, the French sociologist Emile Durkheim in his *Sociology and Philosophy* wrote of the influence of the views of others thus: "It … subsumes the variable under the permanent and the individual under the social". It is no contradiction that the propensity of humans to enter into culture and to be so dominated by it is a result of a simple predisposition of the human mind to be significantly influenced by the social force exerted by the views and beliefs of others. But what was novel in Boyd and Richerson's thinking was to place social force at the heart of gene-culture coevolution. This is as powerful an example as can be found of the extent to which nurture and nature are one, providing that nature furnishes nurture with specific mechanisms. It is one of the distinctive features of Boyd and Richerson's modelling and it is one of the central features of their theory.

A recent review by Kevin Laland on gene-culture interactions pays particular attention to and the way in which such coevolution should be married to the concept of niche construction and ecological inheritance. Laland's conclusion, which one can deduce was really the starting point to his analysis, is that given the overwhelming force of culture in our species when compared to that of other animals, if gene-culture coevolution does occur, then such coevolution is likely to be one of the dominant sources of evolutionary adaptation for our species. He notes at the start of his review that geneticists are showing that a significant proportion of genes in the human genome have been relatively recently selected – usually estimated to have occurred in the last 100,000 years – and that a substantial proportion of these, something in the region of 20% of newly selected genes, though some give a figure closer to 40%, are expressed in brain function. Given that a significant proportion of human genes find expression in the nervous system, and that it is the human brain that is the substrate, the hardware, of culture, this is, perhaps, not surprising. Laland's second and related point which he makes at the outset of his analysis that "among the challenges, in the last 100,000 years, humans have spread from East Africa around the globe, experienced an ice age, begun to exploit agriculture, witnessed rapid increases in densities, and, by keeping animals, experienced a new proximity to animal pathogens … what is immediately striking about these major challenges is that all except one (the ice age) have been self-imposed; that is, human activities have modified selection pressures, for instance by dispersing into new environments with different climatic regimes, devising agricultural practices or domesticating livestock", and in all of these, cultural innovation and cultural transmission have played a major role. It is not possible now, and perhaps never will be possible, to put a date on the appearance of culture. As already indicated, the evidence for the existence of mirror neurons in other primates suggests that at least some of the basic mechanisms have been present for millions of years. But just when culture of the kind that we accept as human-specific first appeared cannot be known with any certainty, though most palaeoanthropologists put it at somewhere in the last one to two hundred thousand years. If the gene-culture coevolutionary theorists are correct, then the appearance of culture in our species would have become a powerful additional force in human evolution. This is the argument central to Laland's analysis, together with the additional case being made for the importance of niche construction and ecological inheritance.

The potential scope for gene-culture coevolution is immense, animal husbandry and lactose tolerance being just one example. Another is yam cultivation through slash-and-burn agriculture by some of the peoples of west Africa and the increased frequency of the sickle-cell S allele, the agricultural practise giving rise to increased breeding pools for mosquitoes and hence the increase numbers of people suffering from malaria. A third example, which Laland and his colleagues analysed within the framework of coevolutionary theory, was sex-biased infanticide and its effects on sex-ratios in human populations. In his 2008 review, Laland considers two other instances of possible coevolution. One is the intriguing case of handedness in humans. There is evidence for a weak tendency towards a predominance of right handedness in chimpanzees, indicating that handedness is an ancient trait in human evolution. Archaeological and anatomical indicators demonstrate an increasing bias towards right handedness in lower and middle Pleistocene hominids and in Neanderthals. In modern humans, some 90% are right handed. Yet there are puzzles with regard to claims that handedness is solely genetically caused. Some 30 years ago, Morgan and Corballis noted that knowing a person's handedness tells us "virtually nothing of the handedness of that person's twin or sibling", which remarkable fact Laland notes is as true on the basis of most recent data in 2008 as it was in 1978. Equally odd is the fact that identical and fraternal twins have identical concordance rates for handedness, leaving the conclusion that handedness in humans does not show strong heritability.

There are other data that support the notion that other, experiential and cultural, factors affect handedness. Children in China and Taiwan exhibit left-handedness in 3.5 and 0.7% of cases respectively for handwriting, which is itself a significant difference; and children of oriental ancestry but raised in the United States show left handedness for writing in some 6.5% of cases. Laland also notes claims that over the last century there has been a decreasing trend for right handedness in both the United States and Australia. Developing a model based on both genetic and cultural determination of handedness, Laland shows that in the absence of cultural factors, of which the handedness of parents are the principal component, humans would be 78% right handed. However, we are a species in which culture is a significant determiner of many of our traits, especially behavioural characteristics. Children with two right handed parents are likely to be right handed themselves in 92% of cases, whilst two left handed parents decrease the likelihood of being right handed by an equal amount to 64%. Children with parents of mixed handedness have the effects of parental handedness cancelled out. Exactly how parents determine the handedness of their children through cultural means is unclear – presumably some mix of inadvertent influence through imitation, but perhaps some specific instruction as well. In any event, whilst there is clearly a general pattern of inheritance in handedness, not all of that inheritance is genetic with "patterns of variation in handedness within families and across societies (being) ... the product of a cultural influence". If Laland is correct, and he surely is, handedness is a clear example of gene-culture coevolution.

Laland's second example is the controversial area of sexual selection in humans. Insofar as a field as relatively new as evolutionary psychology can be described as having traditional approaches, one such is mate selection for which the majority of evolutionary psychologists have claimed a predominance of genetic causation in which women are attracted by potential mates who will provide adequate resources for child rearing, whilst men are predisposed to seek out mating opportunities with as many women as possible who display physical characteristics indicating high levels of fertility. Evidence of the importance of cultural transmission in mate preference, however, was laid out in the early writings of Cavalli-Sforza and Feldman and of Boyd and Richerson, the founders of gene-culture coevolutionary theory; and there are now data available of how learning influences mate choice in non-human species and the rapid shifts that occur amongst humans regarding sexual attractiveness. Sexual selection will, by definition, play a central role in the evolution of any species, and evidence for a cultural causal force in such selection, the evidence for which is strong, provides a very powerful case for gene-culture coevolution as providing the potential for a potent combinatorial force in determining evolutionary change that would be less pronounced were the cultural element lacking.

As one of the principal contributors to the literature on niche construction, it is this aspect of coevolution upon which Laland lays most emphasis. As noted in Chapter 1, the sources of niche construction are organisms, whereas natural selection includes not only other organisms but also abiotic environmental events. Moreover, in contrast to natural selection, niche construction must be informed and directed by what Odling-Smee at al term "semantic information". "By semantic information we mean information that relates to the fitness of specific organisms, about their requirements, about their local environments, and about how to operate in their local environments in ways that satisfy their requirements, and that is, in this sense, 'meaningful' to organisms in their local environments" wrote Odling-Smee et al. in their 2003 monograph. Natural selection, on the other hand, is blind, and "need only obey the laws of chemistry and physics". If Odling-Smee et al. are correct, niche construction is what makes biology, and that includes the social sciences, different from physics and chemistry, and hence provides the basis for a unified science in its own right whose general laws must include the causation relating to "semantic information". It is not a pun to assert that semantic information, "knowing" how to operate in local environments, is more obviously present in cognition than in any other area of biology; and that for humans, enculturation and acting upon culturally transmitted knowledge is the most potent form of cognition. Culture is at once a phenomenon, an entity, that both creates local environments and allows for adaptation to them.

If Odling-Smee et al. are correct, then culture is not just some curious phenomenon unique to humans and a small number of other species. Culture is something a proper understanding of which may show the way to generating general evolutionary laws that incorporate the notion of semantic information in its most prominent form. It is therefore unsurprising, then, that Laland should lay stress upon niche construction in his analysis of gene-culture coevolution. Niche construction, in a manner quite unlike that put forward by Jablonka and Lamb (see Chapter 1), provides a non-Lamarckian means by which acquired characteristics can influence the process of evolution: "While the information acquired by individuals through ontogenetic processes cannot be inherited because it is lost when they die, processes such as learning can nonetheless still be of considerable importance to subsequent generations because learned knowledge can guide niche construction in ways that do modify natural selection" writes Laland, a phenomenon that is significantly enhanced by social learning which results in novel learned traits, behavioural traits, to sweep through populations and thus expose individuals within those populations to novel selection pressures. This, he argues, is amplified by the effects of stable trans-generational culture which at once provides the basis for the transmission of learned behaviours, knowledge, beliefs, and values, but also is a source for the shift in niche constructions that, in the context of this book, are so characteristic of the fragility of social reality and social constructions. The invention of written script provided a whole new form of niche construction; what information is transmitted by script, and today via the internet, has a richness and a capacity for change that is awesome.

Laland does not extend his arguments to culture in the form of the social reality and social constructions of the previous chapter, but in principal they must also apply. He develops a coevolutionary model that incorporates niche construction based on three key assumptions. The first is that a population's capacity for niche construction is influenced by the frequency of a particular cultural trait; second, that some resource in the environment is dependent upon such niche construction; and third, that the resource in question influences the strength and pattern of selection on alleles at a genetic locus. In the case of West African yam cultivation, for example, the agricultural practise stands for the cultural practise that has the potential for affecting the environment, the niche construction activity; the resource is the effect on standing water and hence the presence of mosquitoes; and the relevant allele is the sickle-cell S. His analysis demonstrates that cultural niche construction is a plausible cause of human genetic evolution, and that biased cultural transmission will increase the range over which niche construction will have an effect.

The main point of Laland's analysis is that unbiased cultural transmission will have a similar effect to gene-based niche construction; but biased transmission favours particular cultural traits that may, and almost certainly will, increase the range over which niche construction has an impact. The ease with which in many parts of the contemporary world there is now easy access to high-energy foods, and the cultural forces that push people to their consumption, is leading to changes in selection for people with particular genetic constitutions. Culture-specific changes in attitudes to obesity, for example, will further complicate the interactions between human biology and the cultures that are the product of that biology. Here, then, is one of the evolutionarily-based powers of culture: "… cultural transmission biases favouring particular cultural traits may increase the range of parameter space over which niche construction has an impact" and hence has had a profound impact on the evolution of our species.

Other forms of coevolution?

Laland has no doubt that gene-culture coevolution and cultural niche construction have played a significant role in hominid evolution. The richness of variation thrown up by biological evolution has, in humans, been supplemented by the incredible fertility of cultural variation. The increase in brain size in hominids over the last two million years has been greater and more rapid than any other known change in brain size within a lineage. The interaction of biological and cultural variation has led to evolutionary worlds truly without end. However, there is a further possibility to consider. Gene-culture coevolution is what happens when two different forms of evolutionary change, instantiated in different mechanisms, genetic and cultural, interact with one another. Is it possible that there is a further set of evolutionary interactions that should be considered, interactions between individual cognition which is also based on evolutionary selection processes of the kind described in a previous chapter on evolutionary epistemology, and cultural evolution? Let us call this cognition-culture coevolution. This may not be as fanciful as might first seem to be the case, nor even a novel idea.

The notion that human cognition may be dependent upon external conditions and entities, and hence the extent to which the human mind is or is not bounded within the physical limits of each human mind and brain, is a well recognized issue within the philosophy of mind. In one sense the argument embraces the rationalist-empiricist divide and goes back to ancient Greek philosophy. Empiricists like David Hume were pivotal in bringing into the debate about the principal causes of action and belief the world outside of the mind. Psychological science has always been inclined to a form of externalism in its inclination towards empiricism, and never more so than the behaviourists. However, externalism in recent decades has taken a rather different form beginning with the writings of the like of the philosopher Hilary Putnam and the polymathic Herbert Simon. The latter in particular believed that extrasomatic storage of information was a significant extension of human cognition, and hence of the human mind. In 1998, the philosophers Clark and Chalmers argued for an "active externalism" based on the role of the environment in driving and supporting cognitive processes. "Epistemic action, we suggest, demands spread of *epistemic credit*. If, as we confront some task, a part of the world functions as a process which, *were it done in the head*, we would have no hesitation in recognizing as part of the cognitive process, then that part of the world *is* (so we claim) part of the cognitive process. Cognitive processes ain't (all) in the head" (italics in the original). Thus, they argued, are cognitive processes extended into the world just as the world is drawn into the mind by cognitive processes. Language they singled out as particularly important in this regard, being "a central means by which cognitive processes are extended into the world. Think of a group of people brainstorming around a table, or a philosopher who thinks best by writing, developing her ideas as she goes. It may be that language evolved, in part, to enable such extensions of our cognitive resources within actively coupled systems".

Clark has expanded upon these ideas in a recent book entitled "Supersizing the Mind". Epistemic credit is extended to parts of our bodies outside of our brains, notably our limbs and the ways our limbs impact upon the physical environment outside of our bodies; and also to artefacts such as maps and to tools. Many of his examples, like tools and tool use as well as language, are products, at least in part, of human culture. And this brings us back to the issue of coevolution and of niche construction. The coevolution of genes and culture is not, in principle, limited only to the interaction of genetic and cultural evolution. If coevolution does occur, and there is no reason at all to doubt that it does, then it should occur when any two evolutionary processes interact, whatever their physical instantiation on mechanisms might be. Genetic-cognitive coevolution, whilst not given that name, is nonetheless widely acknowledged. As noted in the earlier chapter on evolutionary epistemology, cognition is a product of genetic evolution and bears the marks of predispositions to acquire specific forms of knowledge. Learning is fast and frugal because the demands of Waddington's uncertain futures problem make it so; predispositions to acquire certain forms of knowledge and not others, the pointing of learning towards specific features of the environment, are the products of genetic evolution which has determined specific features of learning in all animals that can learn. That such cognitive predispositions are effective in solving Waddington's uncertain futures problem is the other term in the genetic-cognitive coevolution interaction in which each exerts some causal force upon the other. Cognition has positive fitness value.

In similar fashion, if cognition and culture are both driven by the same evolutionary processes, but instantiated in different mechanisms, then cognitive-cultural coevolution should also occur. There is good evidence to support the notion that cognition is affected by the culture within which individuals develop their cognitive capacities. The attribution of intentional mental states to others, so-called theory of mind, is present in all normal humans. However, as Angeline Lillard has documented, the form that it takes is culture-specific. What Lillard calls the European-American (EA) theory of mind is the understanding of intentional mental states within a framework in which what are central are individual needs and desires. This is different from the theories of mind in which the individual has reduced importance or is even quite absent. There are numerous well described cultures like the Illongot of the Philippines and the Tallensi of Africa, where what matters is the group, the individual being subsumed within more complex entities such as the spirit world and the collective notion of ancestry. A striking cultural difference lies also in sensory sphere within which knowledge is couched. Vision and hearing dominate the EA theory of mind ("do you hear what I am saying" or "do you see that?"), whereas the Ongee of the south Pacific, for example, place olfaction as the central form of common knowledge. Theory of mind is central to human cognition argues Lillard, but the forms that it takes varies according to specific cultural influence.

Perhaps even more fundamental are the findings on reasoning and thought within different cultures. Richard Nisbett and his colleagues have described how cultures determine holistic as opposed to analytical thought. Reviewing a wide body of evidence, from the writings of ancient Chinese and Greek philosophers to contemporary empirical studies, Nisbett et al. "find East Asians to be holistic (in their thinking), attending to the entire field and assigning causality to it, making relatively little use of categories and formal logic, and relying on 'dialectical' reasoning, whereas Westerners are more analytic, paying attention primarily to the object and the categories to which it belongs and using rules, including formal logic, to understand its behaviour". These are quite fundamental differences in reasoning that are "embedded in different naïve metaphysical systems and tacit epistemologies". Nisbett et al. conclude their 2001 review hoping they have persuaded readers that "cognitive processes may not be so universal as generally supposed, or so divorced from content, or so independent of the particular character of thought that distinguishes one human group from another".

Equally fundamental to human cognition is reasoning with numbers. Beller and Bender reported in *Science* in 2008 on differences in languages relating to number words that significantly affect mathematical reasoning. Based on studies of reasoning with numbers in different cultures, each of course with different languages, from Melanesia and Polynesia they concluded that "there may be no other domain in the field of cognitive sciences where it is so obvious that language (i.e. the verbal numeration system) affects cognition (i.e. mental arithmetic)", and language varies widely in this regard across different cultures. But perhaps most startling of all, because it showed both psychological and neurological differences caused by differences in cultures, was a report by Siok and others in *Nature* a few years ago. Using functional imaging techniques with reading-impaired Chinese speaking children, they were able to demonstrate "functional disruption of the left middle frontal gyrus" which is not found in English speaking children with developmental dyslexia. Because the Chinese language is logographic it makes different cognitive processing demands than does the reading of English script. Here, then, is a stark example of cultural differences imposing differences in cognitive processing embodied in different neurological substrates. Other example of cognition-culture linkage can be found in the work of Medin and Atran on categorization of living forms and in Michael Cole's more general 2006 review.

There is little doubt that different cultures impose differences on a range of cognitive processes. But can it be considered a form of coevolution, cognition-culture coevolution, similar to gene-culture coevolution? There is no easy answer to this question. It turns upon the nature of cognition of different kinds and whether they conform to the same causal processes as cultural evolution. To repeat the point made earlier, central to coevolutionary modelling of any sort is the idea of general evolutionary processes instantiated in different mechanisms causally affecting change in each system, though not necessarily in equal amount though almost certainly always as a two-way process, and often mediated by niche construction. Nobody working in this corner of science doubts gene-culture coevolution. The evolved constraints on individual learning are now widely accepted, as are the fitness benefits of individual learning; thus do we have gene-cognitive coevolution in principle, though how far it extends depends on how many cognitive processes operate through universal evolutionary processes of variation and selection.

Culture remains a less disciplined and more diffuse conception; language, tools, and the social constructions that provide the cognitive and emotional embodiment of beliefs and values are all instances of culture. All are niche constructing, and all are subject to change, and at least some of that change is likely explicable within an evolutionary framework. All may be causal in altering the cognition of the individuals sharing in those cultures. And it is certainly the case that the capacity for entering into culture is itself the product of specific cognitive processes, some of which are themselves changing by way of the evolutionary processes of variation and selection.

The difficulties of extending coevolutionary theory in this way lies in the uncertainty of just which forms of change, cognitive and cultural, are evolutionary; and of identifying and quantifying those entities within each evolutionary sphere that are subject to variation and conserved by selection; and of just how they effect niche construction forces. These are formidable problems. But establishing a truly general theory of biology of the kind Rutherford thought holds in physics was never going to be easy. Coevolution in general must be part of the answer; just how these different evolutionary spheres are held together is the final part of the puzzle to which we now turn.

Chapter 7

Levels of selection

Levi-Strauss argued in 1969 that the use of fire was the defining feature of humans. So too did the sociologist Johan Goudsblom in his 1992 book on the use of fire in human history when he wrote that "learning to control fire was, and is, a form of civilization. Because humans have tamed fire and incorporated it into their own societies, these societies have become more complex and they themselves have become more civilized". Goudsblom accepted that the word "civilization" has unpleasant evaluative and ethnocentric overtones, and that the notion of culture as shared knowledge should be substituted for the word civilization; thus should it be said that all modern humans enter into culture, and a universal characteristic of all cultures is the use of fire. The geological evidence points to the presence of fire on our planet that goes back at least 350 million years to the existence of forestation, and likely much earlier than that, natural fires caused by lightning and volcanic eruptions acting on flammable organic material present in most parts of the Earth, excepting polar regions, extreme desert environments, and high mountain peaks. Human evolution over the last few million years occurred against a constant backdrop of such naturally occurring fires which would likely have been experienced by most humans several times in their lives. There have been numerous claims by palaeontologists of the controlled use of fire by Hominids. In the 1940s Raymond Dart in South Africa argued for evidence of controlled use of fire by *Homo habilis* or *Homo ergaster* as long as one and a half million years ago, but the claim was much disputed. Better evidence indicates controlled use of fire by *Homo erectus* in the region of 400,000 to 500,000 years ago. The use of fire would have required the evolution of specific cognitive features relating to the understanding of the basic advantages of fire control and its maintenance; this would have been followed by technical advances in how to maintain or instigate its occurrence. Exactly how, when and in what sequence such cognitive mechanisms evolved will never be known. What is reasonably certain is that our own species evolved with the constant use of fire. Why is this of any significance?

In 1995 Leslie Aiello and Peter Wheeler put forward the expensive-tissue hypothesis. The hypothesis is that both brain tissue and the splanchnic organs (the liver and gastro-intestinal tract) are metabolically expensive organs, the most metabolically expensive of all organ systems apart from the heart and to a lesser extent the kidney. How, asked Aiello and Wheeler, can we afford to provide the energy requirements of all of these organs, given that modern humans stand at the current end of a lineage which over the last two million years has exhibited the largest increase in brain size in the history of life on Earth. There are several formulae for calculating encephalization depending on whether total brain size is used, or some more specific brain region such as cerebral cortex, and with which groups of animals comparisons are being made. Using total brain mass and restricting the comparison to all other members of the class Mammalia, modern humans have an encephalization quotient of 4.6. This means that modern humans have a brain size 4.6 times larger than would be expected from their body size when compared with the average brain size of all other mammals; using more selective brain areas and calculating encephalization across all vertebrates, human encephalization may be as great as 7 times that which would be expected from human body size.

The second factor that needs to be considered is the metabolic cost of the brain. Maintaining the distribution of ions across neuronal membranes such that action potentials (nerve impulses) can be generated at very high frequencies, requires a great deal of energy. The mass-specific metabolic rate of the brain is nine times greater than the average mass-specific metabolic rate of the human body as a whole, and that means that a large amount of energy-containing substrate and oxygen must be delivered to the brain to keep it functioning normally. One way of solving the problem of the energy requirements of increasing encephalization in the evolution of humans would be to evolve an equivalent increase in basal metabolic rate. However, there is no correlation between relative basal metabolic rate and relative brain size in humans, nor indeed in other significantly encephalized mammals: "the mean BMRs of mature men and women straddle the values predicted by both primate and eutherian equations for mammals of comparable body mass. Consequently, there is no evidence of an increase in basal metabolism sufficient to account for the additional metabolic expenditure of the enlarged brain. Where does the energy come from to fuel the encephalized brain?" asked Aiello and Wheeler.

The answer they gave was that the energetic requirements of the massively enlarged human brain comes from a reduction of the energy requirements of the rest of the body, notably that of the splanchnic organs. On the basis of a survey of organ mass in many species of primate, as well as other mammals, and taking into consideration data drawn from measurements of organ mass in 65 kg human males, Aiello and Wheeler find that while the average human is virtually identical in the total mass of metabolically expensive tissue to that expected or observed in a 65 kg primate, the mass of the splanchnic organs is almost half that of the expected amount, with a correspondingly greatly increased mass of the human brain. This is of significance in the light of gut being energy expensive during the assimilation of nutrients. As Aiello and Wheeler note, the picture is made complex and somewhat uncertain because just how expensive gut is relative to other organ systems including skeletal muscles, depends both on diet and bodily activity such as running or carrying heavy objects. There can be no certainty as to how much physical activity was necessary for our early ancestors. But what is clear is that increased energy expenditure, however it is incurred, involves additional metabolic energy by the gut itself in order to meet such energy costs. And what is not uncertain is that the measurements taken of existing mammals, including our own species, shows a large decrease in gut size and a massive increase in brain size. This change over in specific expensive tissue mass occurred sometime during the last 4 million years.

Aiello and Wheeler provide an extended analysis on the relationship between gut size, foraging strategies, and social interactions, and the energy yields from different kinds of diet (contrasting, for example diets of low energy grasses and leaves as opposed to those of high energy fruits or the flesh of animals that are hunted down). But the evolution of gut and brain size in human evolution is a fact, however complex the interactions between possible causal factors. And one of the causes may have been the introduction of the cooking of food some-time in the last few hundred thousand years: "Cooking is a technological way of externalizing part of the digestive process. It not only reduces toxins in food but also increases its digestibility. This would be expected to make digestion a metabolically less expensive activity for modern humans than for non-human primates or earlier hominids". Cooking food, of course, involves the control-led use of fire.

The expensive tissue hypothesis has been, on the one hand, criticized by Hladik, Chivers, and Pasquet, and on the other greatly expanded upon by Richard Wrangham and his colleagues in their 1999 paper on cooking and human origins in which they wove together the claims for the use of fire in cooking together with a diversity of human characteristics including decreased body-size sex-determined dimorphism, dental reduction, pair-bonding, and enhanced female sexual receptivity amongst other human features. No matter how complex the story of human evolution, and often impossible to prove in detail, one thing is certain. The use of fire for cooking would have spread between humans by means of cultural transmission of con-trolled fire technology. Thus is the cultural transmission of fire use in cooking the most likely explanation for the change in relative gut and brain size in recent human evolution, which, with increasing brain size, likely resulting in further gains in the evolution of the cognitive foundations of human culture.

It is a wonderful example of gene-culture coevolution, even if the precise steps and interactions for its occurrence remaining always unknown.

The coevolution of brain and gut size mediated by way of culturally transmitted food technology, with possible consequences for further anatomical evolution such as effects on sexual dimorphism and patterns of bonding and sexual behaviour, all speak of one issue; the complexity of evolution when selection is acting on more than one form of interactor and their underlying replicators. There are many other examples which either do not involve our own species or in which cultural causation is not pivotal. Recent reports in *Science* by Robinson, Fernald, and Clayton on genes and social behaviour, and by Donaldson and Young on the neurogenetics of sociality make the point.

Robinson et al. reviewed studies showing how genes and their regulatory sequences in a range of insect, fish, and bird species contribute to neural circuits in the brains of these animals that lead to specific forms of social behaviour which behaviours themselves lead to further changes in genetic and other molecular changes. For example, the transcription factor-encoding gene *egr1* is present in many species of songbird and hearing the song of another bird induces *egr1* expression in specific subregions of the zebra finch auditory forebrain, such effects not occurring to other sounds, the molecular consequences leading to changes in social behaviour. The same genes are present in cichlid fish which display elaborate social dominance hierarchies that rule the behaviour of males. Changes in position in such hierarchies induce specific behavioural changes which in turn induce changes in *egr1* induction in restricted regions of the hypothalamus which result in the release of hormones critical to the expression of reproductive behaviours. The results all show how specific forms of social information lead to changes in social behaviours mediated by molecular effects which are crucial to reproductive behaviours, and hence which may effect evolutionary change. Social signals have also been shown to trigger long-lasing epigenetic modifications of the genome in rats. The mothering style of female rats, for example, alters the responsiveness of the pups to stress, which stem from changes in DNA methylation not attributable to alterations in DNA structure (see Chapter 1 on the work of Jablonka and Lamb). In all such examples, and many others, social behaviour "adds an additional tier of complexity" that drives changes in complex molecular events, which in turn effect further changes in social behaviour.

The Donaldson and Young review considers the growing evidence of how the neuropeptides oxytocin and vasopressin modulate complex social behaviours in humans and other mammals, "social interactions (that) affect every aspect of our lives, from wooing a mate and caring for our children to determining our success in the workplace". Needless to say, in our species such social interactions have cultural consequences, which adds another layer of causation. Yet culture itself is genetically constrained, as shown experimentally by Olga Feher and her colleagues in a recent paper in *Nature* on the establishment of wild-type song cultures in zebra finches. "Culture is typically viewed as consisting of traits inherited epigenetically, through social learning. However, cultural diversity has species-specific constraints, presumably of genetic origin". What Feher and her colleagues showed was that isolated finches with song characteristics specific to the isolates, and significantly different from that found in natural colonies, over several generations drifted back to normal wild-type song characteristics of the species.

Human language, that organ of mind so crucial to human culture, has been shown to be similarly constrained. For example, it has long been known through the work of linguists like Derek Bickerton that when people who speak different languages are thrown together as adults, they communicate with one another by a great deal gesturing and miming, but they also develop a highly restricted spoken protolanguage, a pidgin. Pidgins are structurally very restricted, drawing basic semantic features from the original languages, and are without grammatical rules. But when the children of pidgin speakers grow up within the language environment of pidgin, at the age when language is normally developed, these children spontaneously transform the pidgin into a creole, a grammatically complex "real" language, and they do so without any formal instruction, just as children acquire other languages without formal instruction. This can only be understood as inherited neural network states imposing structural restrictions on the acquisition of language; an instance of genetics imposing constraints on human language. Remarkable instances of such structural constraints on language have been published in recent decades on deaf children acquiring sign language. Goldin-Meadow and Mylander demonstrated the existence of identical features of sign systems in deaf children of American and Chinese children reared in cultures that differed in child rearing practices and the manner in which gesture is related to the spoken languages of their parents. Perhaps the most extraordinary example of how the human genome constrains language in people is documented in the study by Ann Senghas and her colleagues of the creation of a novel language in deaf Nicaraguan children. Sociopolitical changes in Nicaragua in the 1980s and 1990s resulted in the coming together of previously isolated communities of such children. The result was a signed protolanguage, a pidgin of the deaf. Children who were then exposed to this signed pidgin through their infancy then transformed the signed pidgin into a signed creole with specific structural features similar to those found in the sign language of other deaf children raised in other linguistic environments. Thus is the evidence overwhelming that human language is constrained both by our genes, as well as the language cultures in which we develop.

So, whether it be cooking in human evolution, social hierarchies and repro-ductive behaviours in cichlid fish or songbirds, or the transformation of sign-ing pidgins into signing creoles in deaf children, all such examples point to a complexity of causal sequences and structures. How to make sense of such complexity? "The architecture of complexity" was the wonderfully apt title Herbert Simon gave to a paper of 1962 in which he surveyed "adaptive systems (by way) of the concepts of feedback and homeostasis … in terms of the theory of selective information" with specific reference to "complex systems encoun-tered in the behavioural sciences". It does not, of course, require any consid-eration of behaviour for complexity to be invoked in almost any analysis of living systems; as noted in the first chapter of this book, complexity in biology may be what stands in the way of any truly general theory in biology of the kind that marks off physics as different from most of the other sciences. So perva-sive is complexity in the biological and social sciences, however, that it may be that anything approaching a general theory in biology must be built upon some notion of what that "architecture of complexity" is that binds together possible general processes into complex causal networks.

Complexity and the levels of selection problem

As noted in the first chapter of this book, and then repeated in almost all later chapters, every biologist and social scientist works and thinks within an implicit, occasionally explicit, framework of levels of organization. Whether one is working or reading about molecular biology or an organ system such as the gut or brain, there is always an awareness that the level of organization being invoked is different in each case; the same awareness of level of organiza-tion attaches to the notion of ecological succession, as it does to the behaviour of a single animal, interactions within genetically related families of individu-als, or changes in the shared beliefs of a culture. The "levels" concept, and the way in which different levels relate to one another is fundamental to theo-retical biology. But what defines a "level" and differentiates it from other levels?

The word "level" covers more than two pages in the *Oxford English Dictionary*. It has two general, and related, meanings. The first concerns elevation within a horizontal plane, relative height in other words. The second refers to position or status within some scale. The latter is closest to what biologists mean when they use the word, because "level" always has two features. The one is some element of functional or structural coherence that binds the entities together within a level. A subcellular level refers to all things contained within cellular membranes; a whole organism level refers to all entities that constitute indi-vidual living creatures; an ecosystem is a level that embraces populations of interacting and interdependent species of organisms. The second feature of the "levels" concept is the relationship that each level bears to other levels. By relationship is meant that each level must be able, in some way, to have an effect on any other level. Both coherence and relationship assume meaning within the general framework of selection theory and niche construction, specifically within the framework of the essential units of variation and their propagation and maintenance in time.

Darwin, it will be remembered from Chapter 3 of this book, had in his *Origins* pondered upon the problem of sterile insect casts and how such wonderfully adapted creatures could have evolved by selection given that they cannot themselves reproduce. The answer he gave was that their adaptive features are "profitable to the community", as opposed to the individual, and had thus unwittingly drifted from the central conception that the individual organism is the unit of selection to an acceptance that, at least on some occasions, a group of organisms might be the unit of selection. At the time, and for decades after, little regard was paid to the differences or similarities between selection acting to propagate features, variations, of individual organisms, and that which acts to conserve the properties of groups of organisms functioning as some kind of whole. Explicit recognition of the importance of providing a conceptual framework for explicating the similarities and differences between individual and group selection came in the 1960s with the work of Hamilton and G.C. Williams. The puzzle of altruistic behaviours and how such behaviours could have evolved was solved, supposedly, by the understanding that the recipients of such behaviours are more frequently than not close genetic kin, and hence the notion of individual fitness was married to the wider idea of inclusive fitness because it is the survival of genes that is crucial, not the survival of individual organisms. Subsequently, Williams and Dawkins developed replicator theory as a more neutral theoretical stance on how to understand evolution by selection. Replicators, exemplified by genes in the form of DNA, are able to make copies of themselves with a high degree of accuracy and may compete with other replicators in order to do so. They may also evolve additional chemical assemblages to assist them in replicating themselves, phenotypes in the language of classical evolutionary biology, or interactors, which may not be the passive vehicles for containing replicators as initially formulated, but may themselves have causal powers in assisting the conservation of replicators.

The replicator-interactor conception of evolution was an attempt to formulate a simple but powerful abstraction of the evolutionary process by advocating possible multiple levels of selection acting by way of multiple forms of possible interactors, all of which serve in the non-intentional competition of replicators to make copies of themselves. This attempt to reduce evolution to the copying of molecules and the preservation of their molecular structure over time by way of complex interactions between auxiliary chemical structures, the interactors, and the environments in which these auxiliary structures exist, ran into two problems. The one, conceded early on by Richard Dawkins, one of the original formulators of replicator theory, was that if evolution as a process or set of processes is to be applied to change other than that relating to species transformation, specifically to cultural change, then one of the strict requirements of replicator theory, the accuracy by which replicators must make copies of themselves, immediately becomes suspect. Memes, if they exist in the context of selection theory, display much less fidelity to the copying process than do DNA molecules (see Chapter 5). This reduces significantly the power of the replicator-interactor conception of evolution as a general set of processes leading to adaptive change. The second problem concerns group selection, the issue of whether groups as a whole can have characteristics that can be selected for, even if such selection is at the cost of selecting for certain characteristics of the individuals making up the group.

Chapter 3 considered how Darwin slid easily between individual and group selection because he simply failed to see any difference of importance or theoretical significance between them. The founders of the synthesis of Darwin's theory of evolution by joining selection to population genetics, Fisher, Haldane, and Sewall Wright, had all briefly considered the possibility of selection acting at multiple levels, including that of groups of organisms, and did not dismiss the possibility of group selection. In 1970 Margulis published an important book proposing that nucleated cells evolved from prokaryotic bacterial cells whose integration as a single organism occurred because of the selective advantages such concerted structure and its associated activity bestowed upon the nucleated cell as a group structure. A decade earlier the likes of Wynne Edwards (again see Chapter 3 of this book) had formulated the importance of group selection for social and reproductive behaviour in what came to be subsequently labelled as "naïve" group selectionism. Yet in the twenty or so years that followed, mostly through the influence of the analysis and writings of William Hamilton, G.C. Williams, and Richard Dawkins, the notion of group selection had become nothing less than a heresy within much of evolutionary biology. One of the reasons for this has something to do with the seeming analytical power of reductionism that had come to be seen by some, witness Williams' 1985 paper, to be an important goal of evolutionary theory. Rutherford would have approved. But it would take a thorough sociological and historical study to uncover exactly what led to the branding of group selection as a theoretical nonsense. One possible, and likely, reason for this is because the whole question of group selection became caught up in the controversial issue of sociobiology and the extension of evolutionary explanation to human social behaviour with overtones of the racial theories and eugenics of a previous era. The writings of a small group of mainly American biologists, notably D.S.Wilson and Michael Wade starting in the 1970s, however, kept the idea of group selection alive and in recent years there has been a resurgence of support for the notion, even from those like Maynard Smith who had been dismissive of the idea in the 1960s and 1970s. It should be noted that even today, with strong support for group selection coming from the work of Elliott Sober, E.O.Wilson, and D.S. Wilson, this continues to be a highly controversial issue. For example, in June 2009 the journal *Nature* published a paper by Wild and others claiming that the whole issue of parasitic virulence can be adequately explained by inclusive fitness theory without there having to be any recourse to group selection explanations.

The evolution of virulence is relevant because in his classic paper on the units of selection, Richard Lewontin pointed to virulence as an important test for the idea of group selection. If individual and gene selection are the dominant forces, then organisms like bacteria and viruses should evolve to maximum virulence. This is because the survival and reproduction of the individual is the principal means by which genes are replicated, and so the organisms that infect their hosts, and which display genetic variability on which natural selection acts, should as infectious agents compete against one another within their hosts such that the most successful reproduce at the highest rates with consequentially the most damaging effects on the host. The death of the host is the extreme result which, unless this is an essential part of the life-cycle of the infectious agent, results in the death of those most "successful" infectious agents, which is actually a cataclysmic evolutionary outcome for all those agents. A much better outcome for the infectious agents is a reduced virulence which ensures the survival of the host and hence the continued survival of the agents. In effect, the good of the individual agents needs to be reined back to ensure the good of the whole group. This, of course, is the altruism problem described in Chapter 3 but in a slightly different guise from that considered by Wynne-Edwards. The reduced virulence of some, perhaps all, agents means that the host survives and hence so too do the infectious agents.

It should be noted that whatever the explanation for the reduced virulence of infectious agents, there is data aplenty to support its occurrence. The best known was the introduction of the virus *Myxoma* into the rabbit population of Australia in an attempt to control the explosion in the numbers of these animals over a relatively short time. The resulting myxomatosis at first proved devastatingly effective in curbing the numbers of these animals by killing them in huge numbers. But after some years this ceased to be the case, and this was for two reasons. One was the evolution of a degree of resistance to the virus by the rabbits. The other was the demonstrable reduction in virulence of the virus. The evolution of group selection where the structure of the group has become a unit of selection, is one possible explanation, but group selection occurs only under specific conditions. If the benefits of individual selection within the group far outweigh the benefits to the individuals of group selection, then the latter will not occur. In such circumstances, individual selection will win out. For group selection to occur the benefits of group selection must be sufficiently great when compared to individual selection and, as in the models developed by D.S. Wilson and his colleagues show, the ratio of individual to group fitness benefits must be balanced by the periodic dispersal of individual members of each group and the reconstitution of new groups with the right balance of individual and group fitness benefits. This is because what matters is the numbers of each type of agent in the population of groups as a whole and not just what is happening within any one group. In the latter case, individual fitness would always triumph in the end as selfish individuals win out inevitably against the less selfish individuals contributing to group fitness; but if the groups are periodically reconstituted, the less selfish individuals will eventually come to dominate all groups. As Sober and Wilson put it, "the differential fitness of groups … must be strong enough to counter the differential fitness of individuals within groups".

When the question of the units of selection became central to evolutionary theory in the 1960s, even the strongest of doubters of group selection, like G.C. Williams and John Maynard Smith, conceded that group selection is always a possible outcome of evolution but the arguments went that whilst possible, group selection will always eventually lose out to individual selection. Group selection can never be stable. But this is simply not the case, as D.S. Wilson and E.O. Wilson show in their 2007 review of group selection. Social groups from many diverse species, be they insects, birds or humans, display group-level adaptations which potentially reduce individual fitness but increase that of the group: "Two related themes give these examples conceptual unity. First, single traits can evolve despite being locally disadvantageous wherever they occur. For this to happen, an advantage at a larger scale (between groups) must exist to counteract the disadvantages at a smaller scale (within groups). Second, a higher-level unit (such as a social insect colony) can become endowed with the same adaptive properties that we associate with single organisms. There can be such a thing as a superorganism" wrote Wilson and Wilson.

This, of course, was Margulis' point almost 40 years ago. Eukaryotic cells are a form of superorganism, as are all multicellular forms of life. Energy supplies are always limited for one reason or another and multicellular organisms have to share those supplies across all organ systems. If the kidneys extract too much energy at the expense of some other organ, such as the liver, the successful functioning of the organism as a whole is threatened. As Wilson and Wilson wrote, "there is usually a tradeoff between *all* adaptations" (italics in the original), that tradeoff being, in effect, a form of cooperation. In a manner not dissimilar to Buss's theory of the history of life as the elaboration of successive self-replicating entities (see Chapter 1) but with the addition of a central role for the tradeoffs that cooperation represents, another American evolutionist, Richard Michod, wrote that "cooperation is a critical factor in the emergence of new units of selection precisely because it trades fitness at the lower level (its costs) for increased fitness at the group level (its benefits). In this way, cooperation can create new levels of fitness". A recent book by Samir Okasha on evolution and the levels of selection provides a scholarly account of the arguments and opposing, sometimes contradictory, positions taken over recent decades.

The Michod/D.S. Wilson conception of levels of selection driven by the tradeoffs of cooperation is closely related to the Szathmary and Maynard Smith scheme of the evolution of life being a history of major transitions in which self-replicating molecules have coalesced into higher-order levels such as chromosomes, eukaryotes, multicellular organisms, and social groups. For Szathmary and Maynard Smith, social group formation comprises two major transitions. One was dependent upon the evolution of language and the emergence of human culture in the evolutionarily recent timescale of just a few hundred thousand, or perhaps one or two million, years at most. The other, which occurred some 100 million years ago, was the emergence of what the entomologist William Morton Wheeler was the first to describe almost a century ago as superorganisms, in the form of intensely cooperative social insects like ants and the honey bee. Thomas Seeley provides vivid descriptions of the latter which are striking in terms of the degree of functional integration that they reveal.

Some 20,000 workers and a single mother queen that has mated with about ten males make up a typical honey bee colony. The ten or so patrilines in a colony means that workers are less genetically related than is often assumed. Nonetheless, because it is very rare for other workers to lay eggs, the queen forms a reproductive bottleneck through which the genes of almost all members of the colony must pass. Thus is the reproductive success and general welfare of the queen of vital importance to the whole colony. The workers in an astonishing concert of activity and effort shape the cells in which the queen's eggs are laid, the cells are regularly inspected and cleaned, the internal temperature of the hive is maintained, the nectar that foragers bring to the hive is stored, and food sources and new nest sites are sought, and the safety and integrity of the colony are ensured against intruders, all through the coordinated group action of the hive as a whole. None of these functions could be achieved by the actions of a single animal. The concerted activity is coordinated by a multiplicity of cues and signals diffused between groups of individuals and not coordinated by any single bee. There is no single centralized control. The structural integrity of any single member of a colony may yet exceed the structural and functional integrity of the colony, but it is no great exaggeration to claim that the hive, as a group entity, has a functional integrity and complexity that does not fall too far short of that of each of its individual members.

The greater functional coordination of each animal when compared to that of the colony is none too surprising given that multicellularity has been evolving for some five hundred million or more years than the existence of superorganisms such as ants and bees. Each single multicellular organism is a miracle of part-whole functional organization of individual cells. The tracheal system of any single bee which serves the combined functions of the lungs and blood of vertebrates, is an intricate structure comprising tens of thousands of cells, the tracheal system as a whole not, of course, being present in any one cell from which the system as a whole is composed. This applies to all organ systems, none more so than the nervous system and its cognitive functions. Each neuron, of course, has its own evolved specialist structures and functions which results in unequal ion concentrations across its membranes that form the basis for action potentials, and their transmission down the length of the axon and transmission by way of synapses to influence the activities of other neurons. Honey bees demonstrate a capacity for classical conditioning which is remarkably similar to that of humans. But conditioning, and indeed all forms of learning, are the product of the concerted activities of circuits of multiple nerve cells. Cognition is a product of neurons acting as groups. In the same way, the ventilation and temperature control of a hive, or the tracking of rapidly shifting nectar sources, are properties of the collective activity of many individual bees, not of some single animal. In each and every case we are looking at adaptations that are the outcome of multiple units acting at different levels of selection. Group selection is pervasive; what are different are the entities making up the groups, and the periods of time during which selection has consistently acted at different levels.

Just as the superorganisms of the social insects have been shaped by significantly shorter evolutionary time than that of multicellular organisms, so too has human culture been shaped by evolution for a small fraction of the time that social insects have been evolving. If evolutionary time is the determinant, at least in part, of the degree of adaptive coherence of the units of selection, be they of replicating molecules, compartmentalized molecules, whole organisms comprising groups, or any other of the major transitions singled out by Szathmary and Maynard Smith, then it is to be expected that the teleonomic quality of cultural adaptations, be they actions, or values and ideas embodied in higher order knowledge structures, or social constructions, may be relatively poor and short-lived when compared to other units of selection at other levels because of the comparatively brief period of time within which the evolution by selection of cultural entities has occurred. If culture is an expression of the outcome of group selection, and by definition of culture as shared values and knowledge it can be no other, then this may account for the rather fluid and fragile nature of social reality referred to in Chapter 5 – what Searle refers to as the "metaphysical giddiness" that comes with thinking about social reality. The temperature control of a bee colony may seem to be a "giddy" quality of adaptation when compared to the functional integrity of each individual bee; the "giddiness" of social reality, such as the cultural values of religious precepts or notions of patriotism, is something even greater.

A not wholly unrelated set of ideas is to be found in a very recent issue of the journal *Nature*, where Marc Hauser explores a novel approach to the possible parallels that might exist between the transformation of species in time and the changes that might occur within cultures. Hauser considers the "possibility of impossible cultures" in a manner similar to how "new molecular approaches have now sharpened our understanding of the sources of variation and of how developmental programs interact with and constrain evolutionary processes, leading to a restricted range of adaptations". There are, Hauser argues, demonstrable constraints arising from "developmental factors, physics, history, and ecology" that have restricted the possible forms that evolution has led to amongst the Animalia, and there are likely psychological constraints that restrict the possible forms of cultural variations that might evolve. Until we know much more than we presently do about the psychological mechanisms that give rise to culture, and the possibility that within culture itself there are different levels of selection, then the puzzles that certain kinds of social constructions such as National Socialism and apartheid, destructive to so many people, may remain. It may be that the means by which culture as a form of human group selection results in forms of social reality, specific cultural entities like National Socialism, which seem to flout the Darden and Cain condition of selection theory by which "one thing comes to be adapted to another thing" (see Chapter 3), is because we just do not yet know enough about the human mind and the constraints that lead to "impossible" cultures.

In short, human culture is, within the context of evolutionary and geological time, a very recent phenomenon – the most recent form of selected entities to have evolved within the Szathmary and Maynard Smith scheme. Some forms of contemporary, or near-contemporary, culture may be "experiments" in what Hauser refers to as "impossible cultures", cultures that are inherently unstable and cannot be sustained. Hence the appearance of cultural phenomena that appear to be damaging and fitness-reducing both to those outside of the social group defined by the cultural entities, and to the groups defined by those cultural beliefs and values as well as the individuals that comprise the groups that created the social constructions. In time, National Socialism was a social construction destructive both to those who subscribed to that set of beliefs, as well as to the victims of it. If Hauser is correct, then such cultures will gradually diminish and ultimately disappear. Many years into the future, if our species survives the consequences of "early" human social reality, such unsustainable cultures will have been eradicated and human culture will not present as evolved entities that do not conform to the Darden and Cain requirements of adaptive entities. This may seem to be a form of evolutionary idealism, in which what evolution ultimately gives rise to, even in the case of human culture, will be "good" and adaptive. But what cannot be denied is that there is a vast time difference over which evolution has been acting at these different levels; and human culture, if it is the outcome of selection processes, is still in its evolutionary infancy.

Hierachy as a possible connection between levels

Why is the issue of group selection of importance, and why do we keep returning to Darden and Cain's classic account of what selection theory must achieve? One answer is to point to the extraordinary range of life forms that evolution has given rise to extending from single-cell life forms to the superorganism of the social insects, and to consider whether selection theory can indeed provide a single explanatory framework for such astonishing diversity. The other is to ponder upon a single species, *Homo sapiens*, and to ask whether the characteristics of that one species can be accounted for within selection theory. A human being preparing a meal by way of the controlled use of fire is indisputably a product of natural selection and niche construction acting on the transformation over at least 600 million years of multicellular organisms, as well as cultural evolution and cultural niche construction, one component of which is the cooking of food, and another result of which is living within social groups whose cohesive properties can only be explained by currently poorly understood forms of social reality, whose cognitive and social properties are caused by complex chains of cognitive exaptations, a basic element of which is a form of trial-and-error learning that conforms to selection processes, and whose immune system function also can only be understood as working according to selection theory. Whether it be aimed at all organisms that have ever been, or just that of our own species, a general theory, built upon a general selection theory, must be one that can encompass selection processes operating at many levels, within cells, between aggregates of cells comprising organ systems, between organisms, and within and between cultures. How these interact, what the architecture of that complexity is, may be as important a part of a general theory in biology, as the selection processes themselves.

Reviewing Okasha's book on levels of selection, David Jablonski wrote that "in the natural world, as in human societies, complexity is almost always organized hierarchically. From the nested structures of armies and corporations to the classical biological progression from molecules to cell to tissue to body to species, the 'particles' at each level tend to be grouped into ever more inclusive units". Herbert Simon himself, in his original 1962 essay on the architecture of complexity, had considered hierarchical structure as central to any consideration of the architecture of complexity. An especially strong plea for the importance of the notion of hierarchy in theoretical biology was made by one of the doyens of theoretical biology, H.H. Pattee, in the third volume of the Waddington symposia published in 1970:

> "*If there is to be any theory of general biology, it must explain the origin and operation (including the reliability and persistence) of the hierarchical constraints which harness matter to perform coherent functions.* This is not just the problem of why certain amino acids are strung together to catalyze a specific reaction. The problem is universal of all living matter. It occurs at every level of biological organization, from the molecule to the brain. It is the central problem of the origin of life, when aggregations of matter obeying only elementary physical laws first began to constrain individual molecules to a functional, collective behaviour. It is the central problem of development where collections of cells control the growth or genetic expression of individual cells. It is the central problem of biological evolution in which groups of cells form larger and larger organizations by generating hierarchical constraints on subgroups. It is the central problem of the brain where there appears to be an unlimited possibility for new hierarchical levels of description. These are all problems of hierarchical organization. Theoretical biology must face this problem as fundamental, since hierarchical control is the essential and distinguishing characteristic of life".

Pattee has not been alone in making a passionate case for hierarchy in theoretical biology. The philosopher Marjorie Grene had argued that hierarchy is a concept central to the attempts by biologists to introduce some formal notion "of causality" to their discipline; and it is evident as well in much of the writings of Stephen Jay Gould who considered that evolutionary theory should be "reformulated as a hierarchical structure" because "the same processes of variation and selection operate throughout the hierarchy". It was no surprise that the longest chapter in Gould's *magnum opus* of 2002 was devoted to the matter of hierarchies. If Simon, Pattee, Grene, and Gould are to be taken seriously, and they surely must be, then hierarchy may be as central to a general theory in biology as selection processes themselves. Selection plus hierarchy may be the nearest thing that biology can wield as truly general theory.

The problem with hierarchies is that they take different forms and exhibit different properties. In its most general sense, a hierarchy is some partial ordering of entities, the order being based upon degree of connectivity, energy levels, and size amongst other measures. In each case the complexity of the whole is reduced to a degree of order and an increase of stability. That was the essence of Simon's 1962 parable of two watchmakers, whom he called Hora and Tempus. Both were fine craftsmen and much in demand for the complex devices that they made. In each case, the timekeepers comprised about 1000 different components, but being fragile things they fell apart if laid down before construction was completed. This happened when the phone rang with customers submitting orders and construction had to begin all over again. Hora and Tempus could have solved the problem in two ways. The one would have been to employ a subordinate to run the office while they did the clever stuff. The other, which is what Hora did in Simon's version of events, was to break the watches down into subassemblies of parts, each comprising just a 100 components, each of which would fall apart when laid down for orders to be taken, but having to reconstruct a component of just a hundred parts meant that the entire device could be built, on average, 10 times faster than if the structure had not been so structurally subdivided. Hora thrived whilst Tempus did not.

Hierarchies take different forms, which makes the story of complexity complex. Some hierarchies, such as those found in classificatory systems as in taxonomic systems, are merely descriptive outcomes of causal hierarchies. The latter make up the choices that Hora and Tempus faced. Hora chose a structural solution to the problem; had he hired help, that would have been a control solution. Structural hierarchies are characterized by the property of containment, the simplest and classic example of which is the Russian doll which contains inside it another doll, which when opened reveals another doll, until a "level" is reached where no further dolls are contained within the fundamental levels. This is what Mayr referred to as a constitutive hierarchy: "In such a hierarchy the members of a lower level, let us say tissues, are combined into new units (organs) that have unitary functions and emergent properties. The formation of constitutive hierarchies is one of the most characteristic properties of living organisms. At each level there are different problems, different questions to be asked, and different theories to be formulated". Molecular elements are literally contained within subcellular organelles, that are in turn contained within cells, each contained within organs, then organ systems, whole organisms, demes, species, and finally ecosystems.

All living forms are made up of structural hierarchies. And some structural hierarchies combine functionally to form control hierarchies. The literal physical containment that characterizes structural hierarchies does not apply to control hierarchies, in which the main causal relationship is what Dawkins in his 1976 paper described as "boss of". The units analysed by economic evolutionists are all control hierarchies. Every company has a chief executive officer, or its equivalent. The CEO exerts control over other executives, who in turn control more junior executives, departmental heads, down to the "level" of the most junior members of staff who deal with customers on the shop floor or who work on the assembly lines of factories. The CEO is not "made up of" the other members of her/his company, and despite a difference in degree of influence wielded within a control hierarchy, the degree of influence, of control, exerted moves in all directions; someone on the shop floor thinks of a better way to organize what is done at that level, which is passed on to managers who in turn inform their "superior", who may decide that the reorganization should be applied more widely, whilst, of course, decisions made at the highest level are imparted to and carried out by members of the company at "lower" levels. All forms of human social organizations and governance are made up of control hierarchies, be they economic, military, educational, religious or political. What characterizes them is an asymmetry in causal power that results in events at one level differentially affecting events at another level, but with the property that the influence of causal power flows in all directions, even if that strength of influence is not equal; what Donald Campbell referred to as "downward" as well as upward causation. Thus are the causal powers of control hierarchies not rigidly fixed but characterized by a fluidity of influence, with the levels of interaction and causation being greatest within levels of organization, but also subject to control and causal influence between levels.

If selection processes do form the basis for a general theory in biology, and if Pattee was correct in pointing to "any theory of general biology" requiring "the hierarchical constraints which harness matter to perform coherent functions", then it is likely that the hierarchical relationship between selection operating at different levels of living systems is as central to any general theory in biology as the selection processes themselves. Let us return yet again to the example of the controlled use of fire in the cooking of food. Our species, like every other, is the product of natural selection operating through thousands of millions of years in the manner first described by Charles Darwin, and formalized in recent decades by the like of Darden and Cain, and by Hull, Campbell, and others. One of the characteristics of our, and a relatively small number of other species, is the capacity to acquire information about the world by selecting neural network states that form a relationship of fit to some limited circumstances of that world. Learning, however, is always constrained by the specific evolutionary history of each species that has evolved the capacity for acquiring individual knowledge. Thus is the evolution of cognition nested under, and constrained by, the evolution of each species of learner. Here is one instance of selection operating at different levels of a control hierarchy.

Now consider the example of a species like ours, the individual organisms of which are able to learn from one another, thus by-passing the need for information transmission between organisms by some kind of individual reproductive channel. The mechanisms of such non-genetic information transmission are the products of evolution involving, at least for the last 500 million years, genetic transmission of selected information. There are likely many such neural mechanisms involving the concerted activities of millions of neurons giving rise to specific cognitive mechanism including different forms of memory, attention, and communication. One such collective of psychological mechanisms involves attending to the behaviours of others and determining the circumstances under which one behaves like others in our social group. One such set of behaviours includes the controlled use of fire, specifically in food preparation, a selected adaptation built upon many other adaptations. Here, then, is another level of the control hierarchy; a level which arises from cognitive mechanisms that cause individual learning giving rise to cognitive mechanisms that result in forms of social learning by way of the learning of others. That is what culture is. It is at least the third level of a control hierarchy, each level nested within, and hence part-caused by the other levels. But the causal forces run downwards as well as upwards. The constraints on learning show how selection at the genetic and developmental levels determine specific characteristics of individual learning; and learning from the learning of others is itself constrained and hence part-determined by the selection of individual learning mechanisms. But the learning from others, culture, has causal powers in determining the selection forces that act at the genetic and developmental levels, resulting in the further evolution of organ size and other organ characteristics, as occurred in the evolution of the reduction of gut size and the increase in brain size in our own species. Similar cross-level control hierarchy causal interactions likely have applied in the evolution of many other species, neural and cultural characteristics involving adaptations such as bipedal gait, manual control, and vocalization in hominid species, as well as in the behaviours and other characteristics in the superorganisms of the social insects. All are instances of coevolution occurring at different levels of control hierarchies.

The extension of evolutionary theory by John Odling-Smee and his colleagues to include the Waddington-Lewontin conception of the active organism as niche constructor was, from its first publication presented within the framework of hierarchical structure of multiple coevolving entities: "The redescription of the coevolutionary game at a different level therefore introduces a hierarchy of embedment of 'Chinese boxes' … which when fully extended becomes the complete ecological hierarchy of life". In all subsequent writings on niche construction and ecological inheritance, Odling-Smee et al. have pointed to the problem of levels. In their monograph of 2003, for example, they put it as follows: "Genetic processes, ontogenetic processes, and cultural processes operate at three distinct but interconnected levels. Each level interacts with but is not completely determined by the others: that is, learning is informed, but only loosely, by genetic information, and cultural transmission may be informed, but not completely specified, by both genetic and developmental processes. Genes may affect information gain at the ontogenetic level, which in turn influences information acquisition at the cultural level. In addition, ontogenetic processes, particularly learning, may be affected by cultural processes while population-genetic processes may be affected by both ontogenetic processes and cultural processes when humans modify their selection pressures".

In short, any general theory in biology must be built upon the fundamental notions of multiple selection processes whose outcomes modify their niches and which coevolve at different levels within complex structural and control hierarchies.

Was Rutherford correct?

How close are we, then, to a general theory in the biological and social sciences? The transformation of species in time, and the descent of all living forms from a single source dating back to about 3.8 billion years ago is not doubted by any scientist. That the principal causal forces driving this species transmutation are encompassed by the constant repetitive action of a limited set of processes involving the generation of variation and the selection and conservation of a limited subset of such variants is, of course, the main reason why anyone advocates such selection forces as being a universal explanation within the biological sciences and hence the basis for a universal theory. Even those advocating the separation of microevolutionary forces from macroevolution do not doubt the causal role of selection, albeit at a species level. Surely, then, even Rutherford would have had to concede that the same processes acting over billions of years to result in the astonishing diversity of living forms, numbering some scores of millions of different species of organisms in geological time, constitutes the basis for a general theory.

Add to the causal explanation for evolution in the form of species transformation the reasonable certainty that a specific form of individual learning, instrumental learning, or operant conditioning, which occurs in a relatively large number vertebrate species and at least some invertebrate species such as cephalopod molluscs, driven by the same set of variation generating and selection processes, but occurring within the neural networks of single organisms and hence operating at a within-organism level as well as the between-organism level of speciation, and the claim for a general theory explaining the causes of change in living systems is reinforced. The mechanisms of species change and at least some behavioural change in vertebrates are instantiated in wholly different mechanisms, largely genetic and epigenetic in the case of species change, and neural networks for behavioural change; but the processes that cause them are the same.

If the neural mechanisms driving some forms of behavioural change are a generic adaptation to Waddington's uncertain futures problem, then so too are the mechanisms that drive immune system function. And there is widespread acceptance that immune system function is a form of "Darwin machine" based upon the same processes of generating variation and selecting and conserving a small subset of the variants. Thus is the case for some general causal explanation for change in biological systems further enhanced.

Then there is the case of a much more restricted form of human cultural knowledge gain and transmission, science and technology, restricted both in terms of it being confined to a single species and comprising a specific form of cultural change; yet it is driven by the same set of processes operating within a collective of humans by the generation of variant ideas and formal hypotheses, and their rigorous testing and selection by empirical observation and experimentation. Taken together, the range of types of transformation driven by the same processes, from genetic and epigenetic evolution, through some forms of individual learning and immune system function, and on to a specific form of cultural knowledge gain, is impressive, and does indeed look to be the possible basis for a general theory in the biological and social sciences.

There are, however, difficulties for claims of a truly general theory of biological transformation. Change is ubiquitous in living systems, and a process of change that cannot with certainty be attributed to so many other forms of transformation across time can only, at least in our current state of knowledge, make a weak claim for true generality. A lack of current knowledge is a is a rather frail and frustrating basis from which to deny the possibility of a general theory, but at some point ignorance fails as an argument of any persuasion and must itself become transmuted into a claim for a failure of generality for any form of entity or process. The assertions for brain development being a form of neural Darwinism by the likes of Gerald Edelman simply do not yet have sufficient supporting empirical evidence, and may never do so. Indeed, recent studies on the way in which sensory information is spatially encoded in the brain to form topographic maps that are fundamental to sense-guided cognition point to chemical-affinity axonal sorting that owes nothing directly to selection processes, even if axonal sorting itself is a product of genetic evolution. And whilst instrumental learning conforms to the classic selection processes of variation generation and the selective conservation and propagation of a small subset of the variants, there is no strong case yet to be made for the many, and indeed much greater number, of other forms of learning studied by psychologists – including habituation, classical conditioning (both of which are widespread in invertebrates including arthropods, molluscs, and some species of segmented and flat worms), the acquisition of language and other forms of communication, motor skills, object recognition, and reasoning itself, amongst others – as being accounted for by the operation of selection processes.

Then there is the problem of culture in our own species, culture outside of the collective knowledge that science yields and which is indeed driven by selection processes. A significant part of the difficulties arise from our failure to be able to carve culture at its natural roots. As argued in Chapter 5, culture is much more than shared motor skills and the hard-won truths of science. Culture embraces the beliefs and values that make up social reality; higher-order knowledge structures are intertwined with social constructions, prod-ucts of our imaginations, in ways that we don't begin to understand. We don't even know what the basic units are of relatively easily demarcated forms of culture, such as economics; nor do we begin to understand how complex social realities such as moral conceptions and religious beliefs affect the entities that comprise economic worlds – beyond the clear knowledge that they do, that diverse religious systems have sharp differences in the ways in which economic entities like money and interest rates, for instance, are dealt with. Thus we do not yet know what the principal entities of human culture are; nor do we know how to measure them, much less how they interact with one another, and how and why they change in time. Until such time that we have a better science of culture, we can make no strong claims as to whether selection processes apply to culture in its many different forms. This is not an anti-evolutionary stand. Human culture is undoubtedly a product of evolution, and at least some cul-tural change may be driven by selection processes. Science certainly is. But we just don't yet know enough about the main characteristics of human culture in it widest sense, just what exactly it is, to be able to make any strong claims as to the extent to which cultural change itself is driven by the same processes that drives genetic and epigenetic evolution.

Niche construction does not in any way detract from the explanatory power of selection theory. Indeed, it adds to it by reinforcing the notion that there are causal powers inherent within the interactors which should not be conceived of as mere passive vehicles for replicators, it adds an additional route for the conservation of evolutionary change in the form of ecological inheritance, and as noted in an earlier chapter, it adds a semantic dimension to evolutionary theory: "Hence, evolution depends on two selective processes rather than one: a blind process based on the natural selection of diverse organisms in populations exposed to environmental selection pressures, and a second process based on the semantically informed selection of diverse actions, relative to diverse environmental factors, at diverse times and places, by individual niche-constructing organisms" as Odling Smee and his colleagues wrote in their 2003 monograph. The addition of a "semantic" element provides a broader conceptual basis for selection theory and hence strengthens the potential for a synthesis between Darwinian selection theory and the evolutionary epistemology of the likes of Donald Campbell, but that is the subject of another monograph. The main point to be made is that the notion of niche construction increases the potential of selection theory as being a truly general theory in the biological and social sciences.

Then there is the issue that this chapter and the previous one bring to centre stage in any consideration of whether a general theory is possible, which is the complexity of structure of multiple, interacting selection processes. Coevolution is not something that is restricted to genetic evolution and cultural change. It is inherent in any conceptualization of multiple selection processes, instantiated in different mechanisms, interacting causally to effect alterations in many, even if not all, instances of biological and social change driven by selection. That structure, and the causal forces generated by it, may be as much a part of a general theory in biology as the selection processes themselves.

So, what is certain is that Rutherford was wrong. Science is not just physics and stamp collecting. Biology, and the social sciences nested within it, are sciences in their own right with the possibility of general theory that does not fall outside of physics but of necessity goes beyond it, and which explains the astonishing variety of living forms that have existed, and do exist, on our planet. If there is life in other parts of the universe, and there likely is, then it too will have evolved and be evolving. If that life is sentient, imaginative and collective in the distribution of its knowledge forms and beliefs, then the notion of evolutionary worlds without end is what may be truly universal, and some part of that universality may be the set of general processes that drive these worlds.

References

Chapter 1

On Rutherford

Bizony, P. (2007) *Atom*. Icon Books, Thriplow Cambridge.

Cathcart, B. (2005) *The Fly in the Cathedral: How a Small Group of Cambridge Scientists Won the Race to Split the Atom*. Penguin, London.

On reductionism

Harré, R. (1972) *The Philosophies of Science*. Oxford University Press, Oxford.

Hull, D. (1974) *Philosophy of Biological Science*. Prentice-Hall, Englewood Cliffs, New Jersey.

Plotkin, H. (1997) *Evolution in Mind*. Penguin, London.

Popper, K.R. (1959) *The Logic of Scientific Discovery (quotation from pp. 59)*. Hutchinson, London.

Sarkar, S. (1998) *Genetics and Reductionism*. Cambridge University Press, Cambridge.

Schaffner, K.F. (1967) *Approaches to reduction. Philosophy of Science*, **34**, 137–159.

Sober, E. (1993) *Philosophy of Biology*. Oxford University Press, Oxford.

Williams, G.C. (1985) A defence of reductionism in evolutionary biology. *Oxford Surveys in Evolutionary Biology*, 2, 1–27.

Wimsatt, W. (1974) Reductive explanation: a functional account. In: Cohen, R.S., ed. *Bienial Proceedings of the Philosophy of Science Association*, pp. 671–710. Reidel, Boston.

On instrumentalism, realism, and behaviourism

Baars, B.J. (1986) *The Cognitive Revolution in Psychology*. Guilford Press, New York.

Bem, S. and de Jong, H.L. (1997) *Theoretical Issues in Psychology*. Sage, London.

Dear, P. (2006) *The Intelligibility of Nature: How Science Makes Sense of the World*. University of Chicago Press, Chicago.

Leahey, T.H. (2002) *A History of Modern Psychology*. Prentice-Hall, Englewood Cliffs, New Jersey.

On laws in science

Beatty, J. (1981) What's wrong with the received view of evolutionary theory? In: Asquith, P. and Gierre, R., eds. *Philosophy of Science Association* **Vol. 2 1980**, 397–426.

Smart, J.J.C. (1963) *Philosophy and Scientific Realism*. Routledge, London.

Smart, J.J.C. (1968) *Between Science and Philosophy*. Random House, New York.

On theories in science

Harré, R. and Madden, E.H. (1975) *Causal Powers: A Theory of Natural Necessity*. Blackwell, Oxford.

Nagel, E. (1961) *The Structure of Science: Problems in the Logic of Scientific Explanation.* Routledge and Kegan Paul, London.

Popper, K.R. (1959) *The Logic of Scientific Discovery.* Hutchinson, London.

Russell, B. (1912-1913) On the notion of cause. *Proceedings of the Aristotelian Society,* **13**, 1–26.

Sober, E. (1984) *The Nature of Selection: Evolutionary Theory in Philosophical Focus.* MIT Press, Cambridge Mass.

On evolution and change

Darwin, C. (1859) *The Origin of Species by Means of Natural Selection or the Preservation of Favoured Races in the Struggle for Life.* John Murray, London.

Lamarck, J-B. (1809) *Philosophie Zoologique.* English translation by Hugh Elliott (1914). Macmillan, London.

Gould, S.J. (1989) *Wonderful Life: The Burgess Shale and the Nature of History.* Norton, New York.

On process and mechanism

Bohm, D. (1968) Some remarks on the notion of order. In: Waddington, C.H., ed. *Towards a Theoretical Biology,* Vol. 2, pp.18–60. Edinburgh University Press, Edinburgh.

Dennett, D.C. (1995) *Darwin's Dangerous Idea.* Penguin, London.

Waddington, C.H. (1968–1972) *Towards a Theoretical Biology, Volumes 1-4.* Edinburgh University Press, Edinburgh.

On general theory in biology

Buss, L.W. (1987) *The Evolution of Individuality.* Princeton University Press, Princeton.

Godfrey-Smith, P. (2007) Is it a revolution? *Biology and Philosophy,* **22**, 429–437.

Haig, D. (2007) Weismann rules, OK? Epigenetics and the Lamarckian temptation. *Biology and Philosophy,* **22**, 415–428.

Jablonka, E. and Lamb, M.J. (2005) *Evolution in Four Dimensions: Genetic, Epigenetic, Behavioural, and Symbolic Variation in the History of Life.* MIT Press, Cambridge Mass.

Jablonka, E. and Lamb, M.J. (2007) The expanded evolutionary synthesis – a response to Godfrey-Smith, Haig, and West-Eberhard. *Biology and Philosophy,* **22**, 453–472.

Maynard Smith, J. and Szathmary, E. (1995) *The Major Transitions in Evolution.* Freeman, Oxford.

Szathmary, E. and Maynard Smith, J. (1995) The major evolutionary transitions. *Nature,* **374**, 227–232.

West-Eberhard, M.J. (2007) Dancing with DNA and flirting with the ghost of Lamarck. *Biology and Philosophy,* **22**, 439–451.

On epigenetics

Waddington, C.H. (1942) The epigenotype. *Endeavour,* **1**, 18–20.

Waddington, C.H. (1953) *The Strategy of the Genes.* Allen and Unwin, London.

Waddington, C.H. (1975) *The Evolution of an Evolutionist.* Edinburgh University Press, Edinburgh.

West-Eberhard, M.J. (2003) *Developmental Plasticity and Evolution*. Oxford University Press, Oxford.

On Niche construction

Dawkins, R. (2004) Extended phenotype but not too extended. *Biology and Philosophy*, **19**, 377–396.

Hull, D. (1988) Interactors versus vehicles. In: Plotkin, H., ed. *The Role of Behaviour in Evolution* pp. 19–50. MIT Press, Cambridge Mass.

Laland, K.N. (2004) Extending the extended phenotype. *Biology and Philosophy*, **19**, 313–325.

Lewontin, R.C. (1983) Gene, organism, and environment. In: Bendall, D.S., ed. *Evolution from Molecules to Man*, pp. 273–285. Cambridge University Press, Cambridge.

Odling-Smee, F.J., Laland, K.N., and Feldman, M.W. (2003) *Niche Construction: The Neglected Process in Evolution*. Princeton University Press, Princeton.

Waddington, C.H. (1969) Paradigm for an evolutionary process. In: Waddington, C.H., ed. *Towards a Theoretical Biology*, Vol. 2. pp. 106–124. Edinburgh University Press, Edinburgh.

Chapter 2

On change and constancy

Ayer, A.J. (1980) *Hume*. Oxford University Press, Oxford.

Barnes, J. (1982) *Aristotle*. Oxford University Press, Oxford.

Cranston, M. (1961) *Locke*. Longmans, Green and Co., London.

Fodor, J. (1998) *In Critical Condition*. MIT Press, Cambridge Mass.

Hare, R.M. (1982) *Plato*. Oxford |University Press, Oxford.

Hume, D. (1739–1740) *A Treatise on Human Nature, Vols. 1 and 2*. Reprinted by Wildside Press.

Kenny, A. (2004) *Ancient Philosophy: Vol. 1 of a New History of Western Philosophy*. Oxford University Press, Oxford.

Lloyd, G.E.R. (1968) *Aristotle: The Growth and Structure of his Thought*. Cambridge University Press, Cambridge.

Nelson, R.R. (2007) Universal Darwinism and Evolutionary Social Science. *Biology and Philosophy*, **22**, 73–94.

Plotkin, H. (2007) *Necessary Knowledge*. Oxford University Press, Oxford.

Popper, K.R. (1972) *Objective Knowledge*. Oxford University Press, Oxford.

Russell, B. (1946) *History of Western Philosophy*. Routledge, London.

Smith, A. (1776) *An Inquiry into the Nature and Causes of the Wealth of Nations*. Reprinted in 1993 by Hackett Publishing Company, Indianapolis.

PreDarwinian theories

Darwin, C. (1887) An Autobiography. In: Darwin, F., (ed) *Life and Letters of Charles Darwin*. Reprinted in de Beer, G., ed. (1983) *Charles Darwin and Thomas Henry Huxley: Autobiographies*. Oxford University Press, Oxford.

Lamarck, J-B. (1809) *Philosophie Zoologique*. English translation by Hugh Elliott (1914). Macmillan, London.

Mayr, E. (1982) *The Growth of Biological Thought*. Harvard University Press, Cambridge Mass.

Spencer, H. (1855) *The Principles of Psychology*. Longman, Brown, Green and Longmans, London.

Spencer, H. (1904) *An Autobiography, Vols. 1 and 2*. Williams and Norgate, London.

Darwin and his immediate successors

Asma, S.T. (1996) Darwin's causal pluralism. *Biology and Philosophy*, **11**, 1–20.

Baldwin, J.M. (1895) *Mental Development in the Child and Race*. Macmillan, New York.

Baldwin, J.M. (1909) *Darwin and the Humanities*. Review Publishing, Baltimore.

Barrett, P.H., ed. (1974) *Darwin's Early and Unpublished Notebooks*. Wildwood House, London.

Barrett, P.H. ed. (1977) *The Collected Papers of Charles Darwin*. University of Chicago Press, Chicago.

Darwin, C. (1859) *The Origin of Species by Means of Natural Selection* John Murray, London.

Darwin, C. (1871) *The Descent of Man and Selection in Relation to Sex*. John Murray, London.

Darwin, C. (1983) *Autobiography*. In: de Beer, G. (ed) Oxford University Press, Oxford.

Desmond, A. and Moore, J. (1991) *Darwin*. Michael Joseph, London.

Fox Keller, E. (2007) A clash of two cultures. *Nature*, **445**, 603.

James, W. (1880) Great men, great thoughts, and the environment. *The Atlantic Monthly*, **vol. XLVI**, 441–459.

Oppenheim, R.W. (1982) Preformation and epigenesist in the origins of the nervous system and behaviour: issues, concepts, and their history. In: Bateson, P.P.G. and Klopfer, P.H. eds. *Perspectives in Ethology, Vol. 5: Ontogeny*, pps. 1–100. Plenim Press, New York.

Richards, R.J. (1987) *Darwin and the Emergence of Theories of Mind and Behaviour*. Chicago University Press, Chicago.

Richards, R.J. (1992) *The Meaning of Evolution*. Chicago University Press, Chicago.

Chapter 3

Evolution observed

Endler, J. (1986) *Natural Selection in the Wild*. Princeton University Press, Princeton N.J.

Grant, P.R. and Grant, B.R. (2002) Adaptive radiation of Darwin's finches. *American Scientist*, **90**, 130–139.

Grant, P.R. and Grant, B.R. (2006) Evolution in character displacement in Darwin's finches. *Science*, **313**, 224–226.

Grant, P.R. and Grant, B.R. (2008) *How and Why Species Multiply: The Radiation of Darwin's finches*. Princeton University Press, Princeton N.J.

Harper, G.R. and Pfenning, D.W. (2008) Selection overrides gene flow to break down maladaptive mimicry. *Nature*, **451**, 1103–1107.

Irwin, D.E., Bensch, S. and Price, T.D. (2001) Speciation in a ring. *Nature*, **409**, 333–337.

Irwin, D.E., Bensch, S., Irwin, J.H. and Price, T.D. (2005) Speciation by distance in a ring species. *Science*, **307**, 414–416.

Losos, J.B., Warheit, K.I. and Schoener, T.W. (1997) Adaptive differentiation following experimental island colonization in *Anolis* lizards. *Nature*, **387**, 70–73.

Padian, K. (2008) Darwin's enduring legacy. *Nature*, **451**, 632–634.

Wake, D.B. (2001) Speciation in the round. *Nature*, **409**, 299–300.

On the modern synthesis

Dobzhansky, T. (1970) *Genetics of the Evolutionary Process*. Columbia University Press, New York.

Huxley, J.S. (1942) *Evolution: The Modern Synthesis*. Allen and Unwin, London.

Mayr, E. and Provine, W., eds. (1980) *The Evolutionary Synthesis*. Harvard University Press, Cambridge Mass.

Simpson, G.G. (1953) *The Major Features of Evolution*. Columbia University Press, New York.

Post synthesis

Dawkins, R.(1976) *The Selfish Gene*. Oxford University Press, Oxford.

Dawkins, R.(1983) Universal Darwinism. In: Bendall, D.S., ed. *Evolution from Molecules to Man*, pp. 403–425. Cambridge University Press, Cambridge.

Dennett, D.C. (1995) *Darwin's Dangerous Idea: Evolution and the Meanings of Life*. Penguin Press, London.

Depew, D.J. and Weber, B.H. eds. (1985) *Evolution at a Crossroads: The New Biology and the New Philosophy*. MIT Press, Cambridge Mass.

Dover, G. (1982) Molecular drive: a cohesive mode of species evolution. *Nature*, **299**, 111–117.

Eldredge, N. and Gould, S.J. (1972) Punctuated equilibria: an alternative to phyletic gradualism. In: Schopf, T.J.M., ed. *Models in Palaeobiology*, pp. 82–115. Freeman, San Francisco.

Goodwin, B.C. (1984) Changing from an evolutionary to a generative paradigm in biology. In: Pollard, J.W., ed. *Evolutionary Theory: Paths into the Future*, pp. 99–120. Wiley, Chichester.

Gould, S.J. (1980) Is a new and general theory of evolution emerging? *Palaeobiology*, **6**, 119–130.

Gould, S.J. (1982) The meaning of punctuated equilibrium and its role in validating a hierarchical approach to macroevolution. In: Milkman, R., ed. *Perspectives on Evolution*, pp. 83–104. Sinauer Associates, Sunderland Mass.

Kauffman, S. (1995) *At Home in the Universe: The Search for Laws of Complexity*. Viking, London.

Kimura, M. (1983) *The Neutral Theory of Molecular Evolution*. Cambridge University Press, Cambridge.

Mayr, E. (1963) *Animal Species and Evolution*. Harvard University Press, Cambridge Mass.

Milkman, R. ed. (1982) *Perspectives on Evolution*. Sinauer Associates, Sunderland Mass.

Plotkin, H. ed. (1988) *The Role of Behaviour in Evolution*. MIT Press, Cambridge Mass.

Plotkin, H. (1988) Learning and Evolution. In: Plotkin, H., ed. *The Role of Behaviour in Evolution*, pp. 133–164, MIT Press, Cambridge Mass.

Prigogine, I. and Stengers, I. (1984) *Order out of Chaos*. Wiley, New York.

Reader, S.M. and Laland, K.N. (2002) Social intelligence, innovation, and enhanced brain size in primates. *Proceedings of the National Academy of Sciences*, **99**, 4436–4441.

Segerstralé, U. (2000) *Defenders of the Truth: The Sociobiology Debate*. Oxford University Press, Oxford.

Von Bertalanffy, L. (1952) *Problems of Life: An Evaluation of Modern Biological Tought*. Wiley, New York.

Waddington, C.H. (1975) *The Evolution of an Evolutionist*. Edinburgh University Press, Edinburgh.

Weber, B.H. and Depew, D.J. eds. (2003) *Evolution and Learning: The Baldwin Effect Reconsidered*. MIT Press, Cambridge Mass.

Williams, G.C. (1966) *Adaptation and Natural Selection*. Princeton University Press, Princeton N.J.

On the essence of selection theory

Darden, L. and Cain, J.R. (1989) Selection type theories. *Philosophy of Science*, **56**, 106–129.

Hull, D.L., Langman, R.E., and Glenn, S.S. (2001) A general account of selection: biology, immunology and behaviour. *Behavioural and Brain Sciences*, **24**, 511–573.

Lewontin, R.C. (1970) The units of selection. *The Annual Review of Ecology and Systematics*, **1**, 1–18.

Skinner, B.F. (1981) Selection by consequences. *Science*, **213**, 501–504.

Sober, E. (1984) *The Nature of Selection: Evolutionary Theory in Philosophical Focus*. MIT Press, Cambridge Mass.

The expansion of selection theory

Burnet, F.M. (1959) *The Clonal Selection Theory of Acquired Immunity*. Cambridge University Press, Cambridge.

Changeux, J-P. and Danchin, A. (1976) Selective stabilization of developing synapses as a mechanism for the specification of neuronal networks. *Nature*, **264**, 705–712.

Changeux, J-P. and Dehaene, S. (1984) Neuronal models of cognitive functions. *Cognition*, **33**, 63–109.

Edelman, G.M. (1987) *Neural Darwnism: The Theory of Neuronal Group Selection*. Basic Books, New York.

Hull, D.L. (1988a) *Science as a Process*. Chicago University Press, Chicago.

Hull, D.L. (1988b) A mechanism and its metaphysics: an evolutionary account of the social and conceptual development of science. *Biology and Philosophy*, **3**, 123–155.

Jerne, N.K. (1967) Antibodies and learning: Selection versus instruction. In: Quarton, G.C., Melnechuk, T. and Schmitt, F.O., eds. *The Neurosciences: A Study Program Vol. 1*. pp. 200–205. Rockefeller University Press, New York.

Mach, E. (1896) On the part played by accident in invention and discovery. *The Monist*, **vol. VI**, 161–175.

Popper, K.R. (1959) *The Logic of Scientific Discovery*. Hutchinson, London. (*First published in 1934 as Logic der Forschung*).

Popper, K.R. (1961) Evolution and the tree of knowledge. In: *Objective Knowledge: An Evolutionary Approach*, pp. 256–284. Oxford University Press, Oxford.

Rajewsky, K. (1996) Clonal selection theory and learning in the antibody system. *Nature*, **381**, 751–758.

Toulmin, S.E. (1966) The evolutionary development of natural science. *American Scientist*, **55**, 456–471.

Chapter 4

On evolutionary epistemology in general

Campbell, D.T. (1974) Evolutionary epistemology. In: Schillp, P.A., ed. *The Philosophy of Karl Popper*, pp. 413–463. The Open Court Publishing Company, La Salle Illinois.

Kornblith, H. ed. (1994) *Naturalizing Epistemology*. MIT Press, Cambridge Mass.

Popper, K.R. (1984) Evolutionary epistemology. In: Pollard, J.W., ed. *Evolutionary Theory: Paths into the Future*, pp. 239–255. Wiley, Chichester.

Quine, W.V.O. (1969) Epistemology naturalized. In: Quine, W.V.O., ed. *Ontological Relativity and Other Essays*, pp. 69–90. Columbia University Press, New York.

On learning as an adaptation

Clark, A. (1993) *Associative Engines: Connectionism, Concepts and Representational Change*. MIT Press, Cambridge Mass.

Garcia, J. (1991) Lorenz's impact on the psychology of learning. *Evolution and Cognition*, **1**, 31–41.

Lehrman, D.S. (1953) A critique of Konrad Lorenz's theory of instinctive behaviour. *Quarterly Journal of Biology*, **28**, 337–363.

Lorenz, K. (1941) Kant's Lehre vom apriorischgen im Lichte geganwartiger Biologie. *Blatter fur Deutsche Philosophie*, **15**, 94–125. (English translation as: Kant's doctrine of the a priori in the light of contemporary biology. In Plotkin. H. ed. (1982) Learning, Development and Culture: Essays in Evolutionary Epistemology, pp. 121–143. Wiley, Chichester).

Lorenz, K. (1965) *Evolution and Modification of Behaviour*. Methuen, London.

Lorenz, K. (1969) Innate bases of learning. In: Pribram, K. ed. *On the Biology of Learning*, pp. 13–92. Harcourt, Brace and Janonovich, New York.

Schneirla, T.C. (1956) The interrelationship of the 'innate' and the 'acquired' in instinctive behaviour. In: Grassé, P-P., ed. *Instinct dan les Comportement des Animaux et de l'Homme*, pp. 387–452. Masson, Paris.

Todd, P.M. and Gigerenzer, G. (2000) Simple heuristics that make us smart. *Behavioural and Brain Sciences*, **23**, 727–741.

On learning as a process of selection

Dennett, D.C. (1981) Why the law of effect will not go away. In Dennett, D.C., ed. *Brainstorms*, pp. 71-89. MIT Press, Cambridge Mass.

Han, J-H., Kushner, S.A., Yiu, A.P., Cole, C.J., Matynia, A., Brown, R.B., Neve, R.H., Guzowski, J.F., Silva, A.J., and Josselyn, S.A. (2007) Neuronal competation and selection during memory formation. *Science*, **316**, 457–460.

Nelson, D.A. and Marler, P. (1994) Selection-based learning in birdsong development. *Proceedings of the National Academy of Sciences*, **91**, 10498–10501.

Simon, H.A. (1981) *The Sciences of the Artificial 2nd edn.* MIT Press, Cambridge Mass.

Skinner, B.F. (1966) The phylogeny and ontogeny of behaviour. *Science*, **153**, 1205–1213.

Skinner, B.F. (1981) Selection by consequences. *Science*, **213**, 501–504.

Staddon, J.E.R. and Simmelhag, V. (1971) The 'superstition' experiment: a re-examination of its implications for the principles of adaptive behaviour. *Psychological Review*, **78**, 3–43.

Young, J.Z. (1979) Learning as a process of selection and amplification. *Journal of the Royal Society of Medicine*,72, 801–814.

On Piaget's genetic epistemology

Gilliéron, C. (1987) Is Piaget's 'genetic epistemology' evolutionary? In: Callebaut, W. and Pinxten, R., eds. *Evolutionary Epistemology: A Multiparadigm Program,* pp. 247–266. Reidel, Dordrecht.

Lewontin, R.C. (1982) Organism and environment. In: Plotkin, H., ed. *Learning, Development and Culture: Essays in Evolutionary Epistemology,* pp. 151–170. Wiley, Chichester.

Modgil, S. and Modgil, C. eds. (1982) *Jean Piaget: Consensus and Controversy.* Holt, Rinehart and Winston, London.

Piaget, J. (1968) *Structuralism.* Routledge and Kegan Paul, London.

Piaget, J. (1971) *Biology and Knowledge: An Essay on the Relations between Organic Regulations and Cognitive Processes.* Edinburgh University Press, Edinburgh.

Piaget, J. (1974) *Adaptation and Intelligence: Organic Selection and Phenocopy.* University of Chicago Press, Chicago.

Piaget, J. (1979) *Behaviour and Evolution.* Routledge and Kegan Paul, London.

Campbell's evolutionary epistemology

Ashby, W.R. (1952) *Design for a Brain.* Wiley, New York.

Baldwin, J.M. (1909) *Darwin and the Humanities.* Review Publishing, Baltimore.

Bradie, M. (1986) Assessing evolutionary epistemology. *Biology and Philosophy*, **1**, 401–460.

Campbell, D.T. (1956) Perceptions as substitute trial and error. *Psychological Review*, **63**, 330–342.

Campbell, D.T. (1959) Methodological suggestions from a comparative psychology of knowledge processes. *Inquiry*, **2**, 152–182.

Campbell, D.T. (1960) Blind variation and selective retention in creative thought as in other knowledge processes. *Psychological Review*, **67**, 380–400.

Campbell, D.T. (1974) *Evolutionary epistemology.* (Reference given above in section "On Evolutionary Epistemology in General").

Hull, D.L., Langman, R.E., and Glenn, S.S. (2001) *A general account of selection: biology, immunology, and behaviour.* (Reference given in chapter 3 in section "On the Essence of Selection Theory").

Lewontin, R.C. (1982) *Organism and environment.* (Reference given above in section "On Piaget's Genetic Epistemology").

Pringle, J.W.S. (1951) On the parallel between learning and evolution. *Behaviour*, **3**, 174–215.

Quine, W.V.O. (1969) Epistemology naturalized. (Reference given above in section "On Evolutionary Epistemology in General").

Riedl, R. (1984) *Biology of Knowledge: The Evolutionary Basis of Reason.* Wiley, New York. (Translation by P. Foulkes of Reidl's 1980 Biologie der Erkenntnis).

Thagard, P. (1980) Against evolutionary epistemology. *Philosophy of Science Association*, **1**, 187–196.

Wilson, D.S. (1990) Species of thought: a comment on evolutionary epistemology. *Biology and Philosophy*, **5**, 37–62.

Wuketits, F.M., ed. (1984) *Concepts* and Approaches in Evolutionary Epistemology. Reidel, Dordrecht.

Chapter 5

Basic misconceptions about biology and culture

Lorenz, K. (1969) *Innate bases of learning* (Reference given in chapter 4 in section "On learning as an adaptation").

Plotkin, H. (2004) *Evolutionary Thought in Psychology.* Blackwell, Oxford.

Plotkin, H. (2007) The power of culture. In: Dunbar, R.I.M. and Barrett, L., eds. *Oxford Handbook of Evolutionary Psychology*, pp. 11-19. Oxford University Press, Oxford.

On culture in non-humans

Boesch, C. (1996) The emergence of culture among wild chimpanzees. *Proceedings of the British Academy*, **88**, 251–268.

Emery, N. and Clayton, N. (2004) The mentality of crows: convergent evolution of intelligence in corvids and apes. *Science*, **306**, 1903–1907.

Fitch, W.T., Hauser, M.D., and Chomsky, N. (2005) The evolution of the language faculty: clarifications and implications. *Cognition*, **97**, 179–210.

Gentner, T.Q., Fenn, K.M., Margoliash, D., and Nusbaum, H.C. (2006) Recursive syntactic pattern learning by songbirds. *Nature*, **440**, 1204–1207.

Hauser, M.D., Chomsky, N., and Fitch, W.T. (2002) The faculty of language: what it is, who has it, and how did it evolve. *Science*, **298**, 1569–1579.

Lynch, A., Plunket, G.M., Baker, A.J., and Jenkins, P.F. (1989) A model of cultural evolution of chaffinch song derived from the meme concept. *The American Naturalist*, **133**, 634–653.

Rendell, L. and Whitehead, H. (2001) Culture in whales and dolphins. *Behavioural and Brain Sciences*, **24**, 309–382.

Van Shalk, C.P., Ancrenaz, M., Borgen, G., Galdikas, B., Knott, C.B., Singleton, I., Suzuki, A., Utami, S.S. and Merrill, M. (2003) Orangutan cultures and the evolution of material culture. *Science*, **299**, 102–105.

Whiten, A., Goodall, J., McGrew, W.G., Nishida, T., Reynolds, V., Sugiyama, Y., Tutin, C.E.G., Wrangham, R.W., and Boesch, C. (1999) Cultures in chimpanzees. *Nature*, **399**, 682–685.

Whiten, A., Goodall, J., McGrew, W.G., Nishida, T., Renolds, V., Sugiyama, Y., Tutin, C.E.G., Wrangham, R.W., and Boesch, C. (2001) Charting cultural variation in chimpanzees. *Behaviour*, **138**, 1481–1516.

Whiten, A., Horner, V., and de Waal, F.B.M. (2005) Conformity to cultural norms of tool use in chimpanzees. *Nature* on line 1038/04047.

On higher-order knowledge structures and their possible mechanisms

Arendt, H. (1963) *Eichmann in Jerusalem: A Report on the Banality of Evil.* Viking Press, New York.

Asch, J.E. (1951) Effects of group pressure upon the modification and distortion of judgement. In: Guetzkow, H. ed. *Groups, Leadership, and Men*, pp. 85–112. Carnegie Press, Pittsburgh.

Baron-Cohen, S., Tager-Flusberg, H., and Cohen, D.J. (2000) eds. *Understanding Other Minds: Perspectives from Developmental Cognitive Neuroscience.* Oxford University Press, Oxford.

Bartlett, F.C. (1932) *Remembering.* Cambridge University Press, Cambridge.

Browning, C.R. (1992) *Ordinary Men: Reserve Police Battalion 101 and the Final Solution in Poland.* Harper Collins, New York.

Christiansen, M.H. and Chater, N. (2008) Language as shaped by the brain. *Behavioural and Brain Sciences*, **31**, 489–558.

Goodenough, W.H. (1957) Cultural anthropology and linguistics. In: Garvin, P. ed. *Report of the 7th Annual Roundtable Meeting on Linguistics and Language Study*, Georgetown University Monograph Series on Language and Linguistics, Vol. 9, pp. 162–184. Georgetown University Press, Washington D.C.

Gopnick, A. (1993) How we know our minds: the illusion of first-person knowledge of intentionality. *The Behavioural and Brain Sciences*, **16**, 1–14.

Jacobs, R.C. and Campbell, D.T. (1961) The perpetuation of an arbitrary tradition through several generations of a laboratory microculture. *Journal of Abnormal and Social Psychology*, **62**, 649–658.

Kroeber, A.L. and Kluckholm, C. (1952) *Culture: A Critical Review of Concepts and Definitions.* Harvard University Press, Cambridge Mass.

Kuper, A. *Culture: The Anthropologists' Account.* Harvard University Press, Cambridge Mass.

Milgram, S. (1974) *Obedience to Authority: An Experimental View.* Harper Collins, New York.

Minsky, M.L. (1975) A framework for representing knowledge. In: Winston, P.H., ed. *The Psychology of Computer Vision*, pp. 211-277. McGraw-Hill, New York.

Plotkin, H. (2002) *The Imagined World Made Real.* The Penguin Press, London.

Premack, D. and Woodruff, G. (1978) Does the chimpanzee have a theory of mind? *The Behavioural and Brain Sciences*, **1**, 515–526.

Rubin, D.L. (1995) *Memory in Oral Traditions: The Cognitive Psychology of Epic Ballads and Counting-Out Rhymes.* Oxford University Press, Oxford.

Rumelhart, D.E. (1975) Notes on a schema for stories. In: Bobrow, D.G. and Collins, A., eds. *Representations and Understanding*, pp. 211–236. Academic Press, New York.

Schank, R.C. (1982) *Dynamic Memory.* Cambridge University Press, Cambridge.

Schanks, R.C. and Abelson, R. *Scripts, Plans, Goals and Understanding.* Erlbaum Associates, Hillsdale N.J.

Sherif, M. (1936) *The Psychology of Social Norms*. Harper and Row, New York.

Tobias, Ph. V. (1995) *The Communications of the Dead: Earliest Vestiges of the Origin of Articulate Language*. Zeventiende Kroon-Voordracht Gehouden voor de Stichting Nederlands Museum voor Anthropologie en Prehistorie, Amsterdam.

On social constructions

Bratman, M.E. (1992) Shared cooperative activity. *The Philosophical Review*, **101**, 323–341.

Plotkin, H. (2002) *The Imagined World Made Real*. The Penguin Press, London.

Searle, J.R. (1995) *The Construction of Social Reality*. The Penguin Press, London.

Tuomala, R. and Miller, K. (1992) We intentions. *Philosophical Studies*, **53**, 367–389.

On Memetics

Aunger, R.A. (2002) *The Electric Meme: A New Theory of How We Think*. The Free Press, New York.

Blackmore, S. (1999) *The Meme Machine*. Oxford University Press, Oxford.

Dawkins, R. (1976) (Reference given in Chapter 3 in section on "post-synthesis").

Hull, D. (1982) The naked meme. In: Plotkin, H. ed. *Learning, Development and Culture: Essays in Evolutionary Epistemology*, pp. 273–327. Wiley, Chichester.

Hull, D. (2000) Taking memetics seriously: memetics will be what we make it. In: Aunger, R., ed. *Darwinizing Culture: The Status of Memetics as a Science*, pp. 43–67. Oxford University Press, Oxford.

Kroeber, A.L. (1953) Concluding review. In: Tax, S., Eisely, L.C., Rousse, I., and Voegellin, C.F., eds. *An Appraisal of Anthropology Today*, pp. 357–376. Chicago University Press, Chicago.

Murdock, G.P. How culture changes. In: Shapiro, H.L., ed. *Man, Culture and Society*, pp 274–260. Oxford University Press, Oxford.

Williams, G.C. (1966) (Reference given in Chapter 3 in section on "post-synthesis").

A more inclusive approach to culture

Basalla, G. (1988) *The Evolution of Technology*. Cambridge University Press, Cambridge.

Boyd, R. and Richersen, P.J. (1985) *Culture and the Evolutionary Process*. University of Chicago Press, Chicago.

Cavalli-Sforza, L.L., Feldman, M.W., Chen, K., and Dornbusch, S.M. (1982) Theory and observation in cultural transmission. *Science*, **218**, 19–27.

Dunbar, K. (1995) How scientists really reason: scientific reasoning in real-world laboratories. In: Sternberg, R.J. and Davidson, J., eds. *Mechanisms of Insight*, pp. 365–395. MIT Press, Cambridge Mass.

Mesoudi, A., Whiten, A., and Laland, K.N. (2004) Is human cultural evolution Darwinian? Evidence reviewed from the perspective of *The Origin of Species*. *Evolution*, **58**, 1–11.

Mesoudi, A., Whiten, A., and Laland, K.N. (2006) Towards a unified science of cultural evolution. *Behavioural and Brain Sciences*, **29**, 329–383.

Plotkin, H. (2007) (Reference given in chapter 2, section on "Change and Constancy")

Wuchty S., Jones, B.F., and Uzzi, B. (2007) The increasing dominance of teams in in production of knowledge. *Science*, **316**, 1036–1039.

On problems with adaptations

Calvin, W.H. and Bickerton, D. (2000) *Lingua ex Machina: Reconciling Darwin and Chomsky with the Human Brain*. MIT Press, Cambridge Mass.

Corballis, M.C. (1999) The gestural orgins of language. *American Scientist*, **87**, 138–145.

Darden, L. and Cain, J.A. (1989) (Reference given in chapter 3, section "On the essence of Selection Theory").

Dennett, D.C. (1995) (Reference given in chapter 3, section on "Post Synthesis").

Godfrey-Smith, P. (1999) Adaptationism and the power of selection. *Biology and Philosophy*, **14**, 181–194.

Gould, S.J. (1991) Exaptation: a crucial tool for an evolutionary psychology. *Journal of Social Issues*, **47**, 43–65.

Gould, S.J. and Lewontin, R.C. (1978) The spandrels of San Marco and the Panglossian paradigm: a critique of the adaptationist programme. *Proceedings of the Royal Society B: Biological Science*, **205**, 501–598.

Gould, S.J. and Vrba, E.S. (1982) Exaptation: a missing term in the science of form. *Palaeobiology*, **8**, 4–15.

Laland, K.N., Odling-Smee, J., and Feldman, M.W. (2000) Niche construction, biological evolution, and cultural change. *Behavioural and Biological Sciences*, **23**, 131–175.

Lewontin, R.C. (1982) (Reference given in chapter 4, section on "*Piaget's Genetic Epistemology*").

Williams, G.C. (1966) (Reference given in chapter 3, on "*Post Synthesis*").

Wilson, F.R. (1998) *The Hand: How its Use Shapes the Brain, Language, and Human Culture*. Pantheon, New York.

Chapter 6

On game theory

Gale, J., Binmore, K.G., and Samuelson, L. (1995) Learning to be imperfect: the ultimatum game. *Games and Economic Behaviour*, **8**, 56–90.

Gintis, H. (2007) A framework for the unification of the behavioural sciences. *Behavioural and Brain Sciences*, **30**, 1–61.

Guth, W., Schmittberger, R., and Schwarze, B. (1982) An experimental analysis of ultimatum bargaining. *Journal of Economic Behaviour and Organization*, **3**, 367–388.

Heinrich, J., Boyd, R., Bowles, S., Camerer, C., Fehr, H., Gintis, H., McElreath, R., Alvard, M., Barr, A., Ensminger, J., Henrich, N.S., Hill, K., Gil-White, F., Gurven, M., Marlowe, F.W., Patton, J.Q., and Tracer, D. (2005) "Economic man" in cross-cultural perspective: behavioural experiments in 15 small-scale societies, *Behavioural and Brain Sciences*, **28**, 795–855.

Simon, H.A. (1982) *The Sciences of the Artificial*. Economic rationality, pp. 31-61. MIT Press, Cambridge Mass.

Skyrms, B. (1996) *The Evolution of the Social Contract*. Cambridge University Press, Cambridge.

On economic change as Lamarckian or Darwinian

Coriat, B. and Dosi, G. (2002) The institutional embedddedness of economic change: an appraisal of the "evolutionary" and "regulationist" research programmes. In: Hodgson, G.M., ed.

A Modern Reader in Institutional and Evolutionary Economics, pp. 95–123. Edward Elgar, Cheltenham UK.

Hodgson, G.M. and Knudsen, T. (2006a) Dismantling Lamarckism: why descriptions of socio-economic evolution as Lamarckian are misleading. *Journal of Evolutionary Economics*, **16**, 343–366.

Hodgson, G.M. and Knudsen, T. (2006b) Why we need a generalized Darwinism, and why generalized Darwinism is not enough. *Journal of Economic Behaviour and Organization*, **61**, 1–19.

Hull, D.L. (1982) *The naked meme*. (Reference given in chapter 4, section on "memetics").

Mayr, E. (1982) *The Growth of Biological Thought*. (Reference given in chapter 2 in section on "preDarwinian theories").

Nelson, R.R. (2007) *Universal Darwinism and evolutionary social science*. (Reference given in chapter 2 in section on "change and constancy").

Richards, R.J. (1987) *Darwin and the Emergence of Evolutionary Theories of Mind and Behaviour*. (Reference given in chapter 2 in section on "Darwin and his immediate successors").

Simon, H.A. (1981) *The Sciences of the Artficial*. (Reference given in chapter 4 in section on "learning as a process").

On the evolution of technology

Basalla, G. (1988) *The Evolution of Technology*. (Reference given in chapter 5 in "a more inclusive approach to culture").

Butler, S. (1872) *Erewhon*. Longmans, London.

Dyson, G. (1997) *Darwin Among the Machines*. Penguin Press, London.

Kroeber, A. (1948) *Anthropology*. Harcourt, Brace, and Jovonavich, New York.

Loasby, B.J. (2002) The evolution of technological knowledge: reflections on technological innovation as an evolutionary process. In: Wheeler, M., Zimon, J., and Boden, M.B., eds. *The Evolution of Cultural Entities*, pp. 145–159. Oxford University Press, Oxford.

Plotkin, H. (2002) *The Imagined World Made Real*. Penguin Press, London.

Ziman, J. (2000) *Technological Innovation as an Evolutionary Process*. Cambridge University Press, Cambridge.

Gene-culture coevolution

Boyd, R. and Richerson, P.K. (1985) *Culture and the Evolutionary Process*. Chicago University Press, Chicago.

Cavalli-Sforza, L.L. and Feldman, M. W. (1981) *Cultural Transmission and Evolution: a Quantitative Approach*. Princeton University Press, Princeton.

Durham, W.H. (1991) *Coevolution: Genes, Culture and Human Diversity*. Stanford University Press, Stanford.

Laland, K.N. (2008) Exploring gene-culture interactions: insights from handedness, sexual selection and niche-construction case studies. *Philosophical Transactions of the Royal Society, Series B*. **363**, 3577–3589.

Laland, K.N., Kumm, J., and Feldman, M.W. (1995) Gene-culture coevolutionary theory: a test case. *Current Anthropology*, **36**, 433–445.

Laland, K.N. and Brown, G.R. (2002) *Sense and Nonsense: Evolutionary Perspectives on Human Behaviour*. Oxford University Press, Oxford.

Lumsden, C.J. and Wilson, E.O. (1981) *Genes, Mind and Culture: The Coevolutionary Process.* Harvard University Press, Cambridge Mass.

Morgan, M.J. and Corballis, M.C. (1978) The inheritance of laterality. *The Behavioural and Brain Sciences*, **2**, 270–287.

Richerson, P.J. and Boyd, R. (2005) *Not by Genes Alone: How Culture Transformed Human Evolution.* University of Chicago Press, Chicago

Other forms of coevolution?

Beller, S. and Bender, A. (2008) The limits of counting: numerical cognition between evolution and culture. *Science*, **319**, 213–215.

Clark, A. (2008) *Supersizing the Mind: Embodiment, Action, and Cognitive Extension.* Oxford University Press, Oxford.

Clark, A. and Chalmers, D.J. (1998) The extended mind. *Analysis*, **58**, 10–23.

Cole, M. (2006) *Culture and cognitive development in phylogenetic, historical and ontogenetic perspective.* In: Damon, W. and Kuhn, D., eds. *Handbook of Child Psychology, Vol. 2: Cognition, Perception and Language.* Wiley, Chichester.

Lillard, A. (1998) Ethnopsychologies: cultural variations in Theories of Mind. *Psychological Bulletin*, **123**, 3–32.

Medin, D.L. and Atran, S. (2004) The native mind: biological categorization and reasoning in development and across cultures. *Psychological Review*, **111**, 960–983.

Nisbett, R.E., Peng, K., Choi, I., and Norenzayan, A. (2001) Culture and systems of thought. *Psychological Review*, **108**, 291–310.

Nisbett, R.E. and Miyamoto, Y. (2005) The influence of culture: holistic versus analytic perception. *Trends in Cognitive Science*, **9**, 467–473.

Putnam, H. (1975) *Mind, Language and Reality.* Cambridge University Press, Cambridge.

Simon, H.A. (1982) *The Sciences of the Artificial.* (Reference given in chapter 4 in section on "learning as a process").

Siok, W.T., Perfetti, C.H., Jin, Z., and Tan, L.H. (2004) Biological abnormality of impaired reading is constrained by culture. *Nature*, **431**, 71–76.

Chapter 7

On fire and human evolution

Aiello L.C. and Wheeler, P. (1995) The expensive-tissue hypothesis: the brain and the digestive in human and primate evolution. *Current Anthropology*, **36**, 199–221.

Dart, R.A. (1948) The Makapansgat proto-human *Australopithecus Prometheus. The American Journal of Physical Anthropology*, **6**, 259–284.

Goudsblom, J. (1992) *Fire and Civilization.* Allen Lane, London.

Hladik, C.M., Chivers, D.J. and Pasquet, P. (1999) On diet and gut size in non-human primates and humans: is there a relationship to brain size? *Current Anthropology*, **40**, 1–6.

Levi-Strauss, C. (1969) *The Raw and the Cooked: Introduction to a Science of Mythology.* Harper and Row, New York.

Wrangham, R.W., Holland Jones, J., Laden, G., Pilbeam, D., and Conklin-Brittain, N. (1999) The raw and the stolen: cooking and the ecology of human origins. *Current Anthropology*, **40**, 52–103.

Other examples of complexity

Bickerton, D. (1995) *Language and Human Beaviour*. University of Washington Press, Washington.

Donaldson, Z.R. and Young, L.J. (2008) Oxytocin, vasopressin, and the neurogenetics of sociality. *Science*, **322**, 900–905.

Fehér, O., Wang, H., Saar, S., Mitra, P.P., and Tchernichovski, O. (2009) De novo establishment of wild-type song culture in the zebra finch. *Nature*, **459**, 564–569.

Goldin-Meadow, S. and Mylander, C. (1998) Spontaneous sign systems created by deaf children in two cultures. *Nature*, **391**, 279–281.

Robinson, G.E., Fernald, R.D., and Clayton, D.F. (2008) Genes and social behaviour. *Science*, **322**, 896–900.

Senghas, A., Kita, S., and Ozyureck, A. (2004) Children creating core properties of language: evidence from an emerging sign language in Nicaragua. *Science*, **305**, 1779–1782.

On levels and group selection

Hauser, M.D. (2009) The possibility of impossible cultures. *Nature*, **460**, 190–196.

Lewontin, R.C. (1970) *The units of* selection. (Reference given in chapter 3 in section on "the essence of selection theory").

Margulis, L. (1970) *Origins of Eukaryotic Cells*. Yale University Press, New Haven.

Michod, R.E. (1999) *Darwinian Dynamics: Evolutionary Transitions in Fitness and Individuality*. Princeton University Press, Princeton N.J.

Okasha, S. (2006) *Evolution and the Levels of Selection*. Oxford University Press, Oxford.

Seeley, T.D. (1985) *Honey Bee Ecology*. Princeton University Press, Princeton N.J.

Seeley, T.D. (1989) The honeybee colony as a superorganism. *American Scientist*, **77**, 546–553.

Sober, E. and Wilson, D.S. (1998) *Unto Others: The Evolution and Psychology of Unselfish Behaviour*. Harvard University Press, Cambridge Mass.

Szathmary, E. and Maynard Smith, J. (1995) *The major evolutionary transitions*. (Reference given in chapter 1 in section "on general theory in biology").

Wade, M.J. (1978) A critical review of the models of group selection. *Quarterly Review of Biology*, **53**, 101–114.

Wheeler, W.M. (1911) The ant colony as an organism. *Journal of Morphology*, **22**, 307–325.

Wild, G., Gardner, A., and West, S.A. (2009) Adaptation and the evolution of parasitic virulence in a connected world. *Nature*, **459**, 983–986.

Williams, G.C. (1985) A defence of reductionism in evolutionary biology. *Oxford Surveys in Evolutionary Biology*, **2**, 1–27.

Wilson, D.S. (1975) A general theory of group selection. *Proceedings of the National Academy of Sciences*, **72**, 143–146.

Wilson, D.S. and Sober, E. (1994) Reintroducing group selection to the human behavioural sciences. *Behavioural and Brain Sciences*, **17**, 585–654.

Wilson, D.S. and Wilson, E.O. (2007) Rethinking the theoretical foundation of sociobiology. *Quarterly Review of Biology*, **82**, 327–348.

On hierarchy

Campbell, D.T. (1974) "Doanward causation" in hierarchically organized biological systems. In: Ayala, F.J. and Dobjansky, T., eds. *Studies in the Philosophy of Biology*, pp.179–186. Macmillan, London.

Dawkins, R. (1976) Hierarchical organization: a candidate principle for ethology. In: Bateson, P.P.G. and Hinde, R.A., eds. *Growing Points in Ethology*, pp.7–54. Cambridge University Press, Cambridge.

Gould, S.J. (1982) *The meaning of punctuated equilibrium and its role in validating a hierarchical approach to macroevolution.* (Reference given in chapter 3 in section on "post synthesis").

Gould, S.J. (2002) *The Structure of Evolutionary Theory.* Harvard University Press, Cambridge Mass.

Grene, M. (1987) Hierarchies in biology. *American Scientist*, **75**, 504–510.

Imai, T., Yamazaki, T., Kobayakawa, R., Kobayakawa, K., Abe, T., Suzuki, M., and Sokano, H. (2009) Pretarget axon sorting establishing the neural map topography. *Science*, **325**, 585–590.

Jablonski, D. (2007) A multilevel exploration. *Science*, **316**, 1428–1429.

Mayr, E. (1982) *The Growth of Biological Thought.* Harvard University Press, Cambridge Mass.

Odling-Smee, F.J. (1988) Niche-constructing phenotypes. In: Plotkin, H., ed. *The Role of Behaviour in Evolution*, pp. 73–132. MIT Press, Cambridge Mass.

Odling-Smee, F.J., Laland, K.N., and Feldman, M.W. (2003) *Niche Construction: The Neglected Process in Evolution.* (Reference given in chapter 1 in section "on niche construction").

Pattee, H.H. (1970) The problem of biological hierarchy. In: Waddington, C.H., ed. *Towards a Theoretical Biology, Vol. 3: Drafts*, pp. 117–136. Edinburgh University Press, Edinburgh.

Pattee, H.H. (1973) The physical basis and origin of hierarchical control. In: Pattee, H.H. ed. *Hierarchy Theory: The Challenge of Complex Systems*, pp. 72–108. George Brazziler, New York.

Simon, H.A. (1962) The architecture of complexity. *Proceedings of the American Philosophical Society*, **106**, 467–482.

Index